D0801551

the Heart of the Parashah

MOSAICA PRESS

דברים היוצאים מן הלב

the
Heart of the
Parashah

Short Ideas on the Parashah—and Life

RABBI JEREMY FINN

Published by Mosaica Press, Inc.
www.mosaicapress.com
info@mosaicapress.com

In loving memory
of our dear mother

Mrs. Sheila Finn, ע״ה

Who is deeply missed

לע״נ
שבע שיינדל בת יעקב וריזא
נולדה יום הכיפורים תרצ״ט
נלב״ע א׳ דראש השנה תשע״ט

NAOMI AND BENJY

DAVID AND ELISSA

JONATHAN AND AYALA

JEREMY AND RUTHIE

SIMON AND LISA

בס״ד

קהילת מנורת המאור
Kehillat Menorat HaMaor

It has been a great זכות for me to know Rabbi Jeremy Finn for almost 20 years. He has been a very active member of our community, as a מתפלל, a בעל תפילה, a מגיד שיעור and so much more. He has built מוסדות של תורה in Bait Shemesh, and has been a great force in הרבצת תורה in the community. His weekly Parsha Shiurim are an inspiration to all, and have become the highlight of the week for so many! Rabbi Finn's Pirkai Avoth series that he gave over the years has raised the bar regarding the concept of מידות טובות. His yearly Hagaddah Shiur has become the essential preparation for the Saider night for our community. His wisdom, love of Torah & Klal Yisrael have literally lit up our קהילה! His Shiurim are riveting, exciting, very well- prepared, and always inspiring.

Rabbi Finn has taught us all what it means to be a בעל חסד; he does not simply teach us what Chessed is, he lives and breathes it!

I have read-and often quote from-Rabbi Finn's incredible works, and I am very excited that they will be published-what a great זכות for Klal Yisrael!
What a meaningful commemoration for his mother Z"L, a true embodiment of the quintessential אשת חיל!

Rabbi Danny Myers
Rav Kehilat Menorat Hamaor

Table of Contents

Preface and Acknowledgments

Dear Reader,

Firstly, many thanks for buying this *sefer*—I hope you enjoy it! If you enjoy the ideas contained inside, please share them with others.

My mother, Mrs. Shelia Finn, *a"h*, passed away on the first day of Rosh Hashanah 5779 (2018). The loss of a parent leaves a void that is impossible to fill, and her passing was grievously felt by her family and friends.

It was during the following year of *aveilus* that I began sending a weekly *d'var Torah* to my siblings and extended family. These *divrei Torah* comprise the bulk of the *sefer* that you have in your hands.

I hope that in the same way that I found a measure of comfort being able to share Torah thoughts in her memory, so may my mother's *neshamah* "*shep nachas*" as she too enjoys the ideas contained within this *sefer*.

For the past fifteen years, I have had the privilege of giving a weekly *shiur* at the Menorat Hamaor community in Ramat Bet Shemesh, Israel. I am grateful to all those who regularly attend and encourage me to continue finding new ideas and insights into the week's *parashah*.

I am indebted to the community's Rav, Rav Daniel Myers, *shlita*, who is for me the fulfillment of the instruction in *Pirkei Avos* of "עשה לך רב וקנה לך חבר." My life is enhanced by his knowledge, advice, and friendship.

I would like to thank everyone at Mosaica Press, especially Rav Yaacov Haber and Rabbi Doron Kornbluth, for agreeing to take on this project and for editing, copyediting, proofreading, designing, and producing this volume.

A special mention to Jeremy Staiman of Staiman Design for all his help and advice.

Thank you to my parents-in-law, Mr. Bernard and Mrs. Faye Faber, for showering me with their love, advice, and support since I turned them into parents-in-law almost thirty years ago! They have been particularly encouraging about this *sefer*, and I appreciate it.

My father, Mr. Leonard Finn, has always been my guiding light in everything I do. He leads by example, and I owe him everything. Father, you are the rock of our family and may Hakadosh Baruch Hu grant you many more years of health with *nachas* from your children, grandchildren, and great-grandchildren.

To my siblings and siblings-in-law, nephews and nieces, aunts and uncles, thank you for your encouragement and feedback on the weekly *divrei Torah*.

To my children and grandchildren—my life is blessed because of you.

Finally, to my wife, Ruthie. In the immortal words of Rabbi Akiva, "שלי ושלכם שלה הוא"—I could not, nor would I want to, do anything without you.

With overwhelming thanks to Hakadosh Baruch Hu, I end with the prayer:

יהי רצון שתשרה שכינה במעשה ידינו.

Yours,
Jeremy
Ramat Bet Shemesh, Shevat 5781

ספר
בראשית

בראשית

Parents, Thank You!

Rashi begins his commentary on *Bereishis*, really his commentary on the entire Chumash, with a quote from Rabbi Yitzchak, who asks why the Torah begins with the words בראשית ברא אלוקים. He answers regarding the centrality of Eretz Yisrael in Judaism and the importance of understanding our connection to the Land when challenged by the nations of the world.

The *Sifsei Chachamim* notes that many of *Rashi's* comments, particularly those where he is citing others, are sourced in the Midrash or Gemara. Yet, there appears to be no such statement of Rabbi Yitzchak anywhere in Chazal, so where is *Rashi's* source?

The *Sifsei Chachamim* answers that the Rabbi Yitzchak who *Rashi* is quoting is not a Tanna or an Amora by that name but rather *Rashi's* own father. *Rashi* wished to give honor to his father at the very beginning of his commentary on Chumash, and thus he challenged his father to pose a question on any part of Chumash. The question *Rashi's* father asked him was why the Torah begins with the words בראשית ברא אלוקים.

Why was it so important to *Rashi* to mention his father by name at the beginning of his commentary on Chumash? *Rashi* understood that everything we are, and everything we achieve, is only due to the effort and love that our parents invested in our upbringing. *Rashi* knew that his commentary on Chumash was made possible only by his father.

Rabbi Yehoshua of Apta once embarked on a journey to visit several communities to share Torah with them, and wherever he went, he was greeted by large and enthusiastic crowds of admirers. Rabbi Yehoshua was disturbed and asked his son why the people were showering him with so much honor.

To placate his father, his son, Rabbi Yitzchak Meir of Tzinkov, answered that the crowds had not turned out to see his father but rather to see him!

The next day, Rabbi Yehoshua asked his son, "And why do they turn out to see you?"

"That's easy to answer," said Rabbi Yitzchak Meir to his father. "They come to see me because I am the son of Rabbi Yehoshua of Apta!"[1]

The requirement to show gratitude to our parents is obvious, but *Rashi* went out of his way to mention it because all too often it goes unmentioned.

Too often we become so busy with life that we miss the opportunity to turn to our parents and say thank you, and by the time we remember to do so, it is too late and our thank you instead becomes part of our eulogy!

Let us learn from *Rashi* and show our parents the appreciation they deserve with a simple "thank you" telling them that we appreciate all that they do for us.

If at First You Don't Succeed

Looking at the beginning of *Sefer Bereishis*, it seems to read like a catalog of mistakes or opportunities lost.

Hashem commanded the earth to grow trees that taste like fruit, and it instead grew trees that sprout fruit but not trees that themselves taste like fruit.[2]

---

1   *Mivchar HaSippur HaYehudi*, p. 173.
2   *Rashi, Bereishis* 1:11.

Adam and Chavah are instructed not to eat from the *Eitz Hadaas*, but they transgress their instruction and eat from it, and Hashem expels them from the Garden of Eden.

Kayin and Hevel are involved in a dispute that ends in murder.

Such a series of events hardly reflects the description of טוב מאוד[3] given to the creation.

How do we understand this rapid deterioration?

Rabbi Shalom Rosner quotes Rav Pam, who says that we learn from here that life doesn't always go according to plan, and when it doesn't go the way that we thought it would, we need to be flexible enough to embark on Plan B![4]

Even in a world described as טוב מאוד, not everything develops in the way that we think it will. We will find success if we have sufficient resourcefulness to adapt and embark on a new plan.

The idea that things do not always work out the way we expect them to is also found at the birth of our people as a nation.

In the Pesach Haggadah, at the end of עבדים היינו, we proclaim:

ואילו לא הוציא הקב״ה את אבותינו ממצרים, הרי אנו ובנינו ובני בנינו משועבדים היינו לפרעה במצרים.

And had Hakadosh Baruch Hu not taken us out of Egypt, then we and our children and grandchildren would still be enslaved to Pharaoh in Egypt!

History would seem to disprove this proclamation.

Over time, every nation that has become enslaved has eventually gone free.

Slaves have gone free as a result of a new benevolent ruler, others as a result of revolution, and others as a result of a change in societal norms.

---

3   *Bereishis* 1:31.
4   Rabbi Shalom Rosner, *Shalom Rav*, p. 3.

Why do we assume that had Hashem not come to our rescue 3,000 years ago in Egypt we would still be slaves? Would history not have inevitably followed its usual pattern?

The *Be'er Yosef* answers with a simple message: Life does not always follow the script that we expect it to![5]

If we analyze history with cold, scientific parameters and apply strict logic, then we can become disappointed when things do not turn out in the way that we expected. We will be unable to change our approach in light of unexpected disappointment.

The creation of individuals and the birth of our people as a nation teach us that we need to be aware that we may need to alter our path. Either individually or collectively, we may need to adopt a second plan because life is unpredictable. The better prepared we are and the more flexibility we show, the happier we will be.

---

5   *Be'er Yosef*, p. 403.

נח

The Good Old Days!

ויחל נח איש האדמה ויטע כרם.

And Noach began to be a man of the earth, and he planted a vineyard.[1]

Chazal criticize Noach and say that he should have planted wheat instead of grapes.[2] Rabbi Isaac Bernstein asks: What was wrong with grapes, and in what way is wheat better?

Rabbi Simchah Wasserman also asks: What, in fact, was Noach's motivation for choosing to plant grapes first? Why did Noach choose that particular plant as his first foray into agricultural endeavors in the new world?

Rav Simchah answers that when Noach stepped out from the ark, he wanted to sit down and to reminisce—to think back to how life was before the flood—the good old days—and therefore, he wanted wine to act as an *aide memoir*. After all, whenever we are instructed to recall or to remember something, it is over a glass of wine—זכרהו על היין!‎[3]

---

1   *Bereishis* 9:20.
2   *Rashi*, ibid.
3   *Pesachim* 106.

Therefore, the criticism of Noach is that rather than wallow in the past, and rather than drink wine, he should have looked to the future, and he should have planted wheat! Wheat has none of the negative effects that can be found in wine. Wheat is a necessity, and when rebuilding the world and looking to the future, necessities should come first.

On a similar theme, Rabbi Avraham Twersky suggests that Noach's mistake was that he assumed that the world after the flood was exactly the same as the world prior to the flood. What Noach failed to realize was that he lived in a new reality in which the potency of grapes had changed, and consequently, he became drunk on an amount of wine that before the flood would not have affected him adversely.

Noach's error lay in his inability to recognize a new existence and to move with it; he remained in the past and did not adapt to the new present.

As Rabbi Bernstein put it so beautifully, time travels in only one direction, and we cannot bring back that which was in the past. Our duty, while remembering the past, is to build for the future.[4]

It's All about the Future

ותבא אליו היונה...והנה עלה זית טרף בפיה.

And the dove came back to him...and behold! An olive leaf it had plucked with its beak![5]

Why was it specifically an olive branch that the dove brought back to Noach? What is the message contained in the fact that this particular tree was a sign that the waters had subsided?

---

4   Rabbi Isaac Bernstein, *Noach* series 1.
5   *Bereishis* 8:11.

The *Techeiles Mordechai* quotes the Midrash that says that Noach was only saved due to the future generations that would be born to him.

This, he says, is what is meant by juxtaposing the last verse in *Parashas Bereishis* that says, ונח מצא חן בעיני ה' with the beginning of our *parashah* that says, ואלה תולדות נח.

Why did Noach find favor in the eyes of Hashem? Because of ואלה תולדות נח, i.e., his future generations.

The *Ramban* adds that the Mishnah in *Tamid* says that "כל העצים כשרים למערכה חוץ מהזית והגפן—it is permitted to use any wood [on the pyre on the Altar in the Temple] except for olive wood or wood of the vine."[6]

The reason why these two types of wood are forbidden is that these woods represent olive oil and wine, namely, they have a future and therefore cannot be burned. They are saved on account of their future fruit. The fruit of a tree does not usually last long, but fruit that can be turned into oil or wine has a long-lasting future.

This is the message of the olive branch with which the dove returned: just as the olive wood cannot be burnt on the *Mizbei'ach* and is saved on account of its future products, so too, you Noach are being saved on account of your future generations.

Therefore, the first thing Noach did when he exits the ark is to plant a vine—the second of the woods that are not permitted on the *Mizbei'ach* because they have future potential as wine.[7]

By planting the vine, Noach showed that he had internalized the message that he was only saved on account of his future generations.

The future belongs to our children and grandchildren. Let us invest in the world's future by investing in them!

---

6   *Tamid* 2:3.
7   See previous chapter for a different approach.

Punishing to Improve

ויהי המבול ארבעים יום על הארץ.

And the flood was on the earth for forty days.[8]

The Torah uses two different words to describe the waters of the flood.

A few verses earlier, the waters of the flood are described as גשם—rain,[9] whereas in our verse they are called מבול—flood. Why is there a change in expression?

Rashi explains that when Hashem first brought the rain, it was with רחמים—mercy; it was a gentle rain as a warning of what was about to take place. The hope was that even at the last minute, the wicked people would realize that their actions were about to cause devastation, and they would repent. When Hashem saw that they were not changing their ways, He intensified the rain and brought a flood. This is a clear demonstration of Hashem's endless and boundless love for humanity.

It took Noach 120 years to build the ark, and he was instructed to construct it in public so that people would see and ask him what he was doing. He would tell them that there is going to be a flood.

They would ask him why.

He would tell them because of their depraved behavior.

They would ask him what they could do to avoid the impending disaster.

He would tell them to do *teshuvah*.

They would say no thanks!

And this continued for 120 years! They got to the point of no return. There was no hope for them.

However, Hashem never gives up on people, and maybe, just maybe, there is a chance that even at the last moment they will come back![10]

---

8   *Bereishis* 7:17.
9   Ibid., v. 12.
10   *L'titecha Elyon*, p. 80.

So, at first, He brought a light rain, hoping that the people will have a last-minute change of heart. Only when it was too late did Hashem change the rain into a flood.

The Lubavitcher Rebbe, *zt"l*, writes that this mixture of רחמים and דין is a message found in the flood in general.

The rain came down for forty days and destroyed the earth, the land. It wiped out civilization, and the world needed to start again from Noach, his family, and the animals in the ark. It was unprecedented destruction and מדת הדין—Hashem's manifestation of strict justice.

On the other hand, the rain of forty days is akin to the forty *se'ah* of rainwater needed to fill a *mikvah*. In the same way a *mikvah* purifies, so too, the rain cleansed and purified the earth that had become contaminated through the evil deeds of the people who inhabited it.

Hashem in His Mercy didn't just destroy the world and mankind but cleansed it and prepared it for a new beginning of purity and purpose.

Thus, the entire flood was a mixture of דין and רחמים, which teaches us the essential lesson that Hashem is not interested in punishment for punishment's sake. Hashem punishes as a way of preparing for a brighter future.

If I Am I

וימח את כל היקום...וישאר אך נח.

And He blotted out all existence…only Noach remained.[11]

Before the flood, Noach is described as "איש צדיק תמים היה בדורותיו—a righteous man, perfect in his generation."[12]

However, once his generation has been wiped out, Noach is described as "וישאר אך נח—and Noach remained," without any of the previous honorable titles.

---

11   *Bereishis* 7:23.
12   Ibid. 6:9.

The *tzaddik*, Rabbi Yaakov Yosef of Polonne, asks, why the change? He concludes that once Noach's generation had been destroyed, all we are left with is just Noach—a plain man, who, when there is no one to compare with, is no longer a *tzaddik* but, "אך נח—just Noach!"[13]

The Gaon, Rabbi Meir Shapiro of Lublin, adds that Noach is no longer referred to as a *tzaddik* but only as Noach because we do not find any evidence that Noach attempted to intercede with Hashem on behalf of humanity and to try and convince Him to save them.

If someone is faced with the destruction of humanity and does nothing else but save himself, he can no longer be considered a *tzaddik*![14] To earn the title of *tzaddik*, one has to be concerned with the welfare of others and not concentrate only on himself.

Middos Maketh the Man

ויפץ ה' אתם משם על פני כל הארץ.

And Hashem dispersed them from there over the face of the whole earth.[15]

The *Mikdash Mordechai* asks why the punishment of the the generation of the flood was destruction, while the punishment for the generation that built the Tower of Bavel was more lenient and was just dispersion. After all, *Rashi* tells us that the sin of the Tower of Bavel was nothing less than a rebellion against Hashem Himself! If so, why are they given a lighter punishment than those of the flood, whose transgressions did not extend to direct conflict with Hashem?

The *Mikdash Mordechai* answers that the problem with the generation of the flood was one of *middos*—character traits; it was an era of

---

13   *Parpera'os La'Torah*, p. 38.
14   *Maayanah shel Torah*, p. 45.
15   *Bereishis* 11:8.

wanton theft and extortion. When people have problems with their character traits, their bad ways can transfer down to the next generation. To avoid this, the first generation with such issues needs to be destroyed.

However, the problem with those involved in building the Tower of Bavel was not their character but their *deios*—their opinions and beliefs.

Such a problem might not get handed down to the next generation, for the next generation may be able to work out for themselves that such opinions are wrong. The punishment for misguided opinion is dispersion, which gives the next generation time and space for introspection.

Middos become part of one's DNA and are quickly passed down in the genes, and thus they are difficult to change. Views, outlooks, and beliefs are more personal and do not necessarily follow on from one generation to another.

This is why Avraham Avinu instructed Eliezer not to take a wife for Yitzchak from the daughters of Canaan but instead to find him a wife from "ארצי ומולדתי—my land and my family."

What was the difference between the two places? The inhabitants of Aram, where Avraham Avinu sent Eliezer, were also idol worshippers! Why was he so insistent that Yitzchak not marry someone from Canaan?

The answer is that while the people from Aram displayed misguided beliefs and an incorrect outlook, the people in Canaan had problematic *middos*. While opinion can be changed, it is much harder to perfect bad *middos*, and Avraham Avinu did not want these to be handed down to his descendants.

Thus, the incorrect practices and *deios* of the generation of the Tower are punished with dispersion, while the bad *middos* of the generation of the flood need to be eradicated to avoid them being handed down to the next generation.[16]

---

16   *Derashos HaRan, Talelei Oros*, p. 95.

Preparing for Salvation

וישלח את הערב...וישלח את היונה.

And Noach sent out the raven...and he sent out the dove.[17]

Noach had to be told when to enter and exit the ark. It seems that he saw his role as being a follower rather than taking initiative. But the Lubavitcher Rebbe notes that we find that Noach prepared for his exit by sending the raven and the dove. Why the switch?

After he entered the ark, Noach realized that he had to take charge and was now responsible for ensuring the continuity of life after the flood. Whereas before he may have been playing a passive part in the unfolding drama, now he has an active role and is the star of the show.

Therefore, when Noach thinks that the waters have subsided, he was active and sends out the birds.

While, indeed, he can only leave the ark when Hashem tells him, he can prepare himself now so that he is ready when that moment comes.

The Rebbe says that the same is true of the *galus*—the exile, that has enveloped the world for so long, in the same way that the flood covered the earth.

The waters of the *galus* seem to be receding, and although the end of the *galus* will only be when Hashem brings it, we must not be passive. We must actively prepare so that we are ready for the moment when the Mashiach arrives.[18]

- We must actively prepare by committing to fulfill the mitzvos in the best way we can.
- We must actively prepare by behaving in a way that will attract others toward a life of Torah and mitzvos.
- We must actively prepare by sincerely desiring an end to this painful exile and by asking Hashem to bring it.

---

17   *Bereishis* 8:7–8.
18   *Le'hachayos es Hayom*, p. 29.

לֶךְ לְךָ

An Heir, Not a Clone

ויאמר אברם ה׳ א׳ מה תתן לי ואנכי הולך ערירי ובן משק ביתי הוא דמשק
אליעזר.

*And Avram said, "My Lord, G-d, what can You give me, seeing
that I go childless, and the steward of my house is Damascene
Eliezer?"*

Rashi offers a few explanations as to why Eliezer is referred to
as "דמשק אליעזר—Damascene Eliezer," and one of the reasons
is that he is so-called because "דולה ומשקה מתורת רבו לאחרים—he
would draw water and give to drink from the Torah of his rabbi," i.e.,
he would learn and teach the Torah of his master to others. Avraham
is explaining why Eliezer is not suited to act as an heir because of his
דמשק אליעזר, his learning and teaching the Torah of Avraham Avinu
to the world. What could be wrong with that? Eliezer was, in effect,
Avraham's PR man, who ensured that his Torah was disseminated and
introduced to new audiences. What more would Avraham Avinu want
from an heir?

The answer is that precisely in the fact that Eliezer was דולה ומשקה
מתורת רבו לאחרים; Eliezer only had the ability to repeat, verbatim, that
which he heard from his teacher Avraham.

15

Eliezer could not inject any insight of his own into those teachings. He could not add to those teachings, adapt them to meet the needs of new situations, or lace them with any *chiddushim* of his own.

Avraham was not looking for a clone but an heir, and therefore Eliezer was unsuitable!

In the first of the *berachos* of the *Amidah*, we say: אלוקי אברהם, אלוקי יצחק, ואלוקי יעקב. Why do we need to repeat אלוקי each time, and not just say אלוקי אברהם יצחק ויעקב? The relationship that each one of the forefathers had with Hashem was different from that of his father. They each took what they had received from their father and injected their own personality into that relationship. They built on what they had received and forged something of their own. Thus, the word אלוקי is mentioned with each one individually to reflect this individual and unique relationship.

If we wish to be true heirs and continue the legacy of previous generations, we need to accept and preserve all that we received from them and then add our own unique flavor and carry that legacy forward.[1]

Growth through Resistance

אני ה' אשר הוצאתיך מאור כשדים.

I am G-d who brought you out from Ur Kasdim.[2]

The word אור—light, can be used to describe the burning light of a fire, and therefore אור כשדים is so-called in reference to the fiery furnace into which Avraham Avinu was thrown by Nimrod, which he miraculously survived unscathed.

---

1   *Maayanah shel Torah*, p. 66.
2   *Bereishis* 15:7.

Why is this great miracle not mentioned explicitly in the text? According to *Rashi*, this was one of Avraham's ten tests!

If we were to compare this test to that of the *Akeidah*, which is hailed as the most difficult of Avraham's tests, we would be entitled to ask that while the *Akeidah* posed no direct threat to Avraham, the furnace was a life-or-death decision.

Also, the *Akeidah* took place at the end of Avraham's life, when his relationship with Hashem was well-cemented and he had already been the recipient of miracles from Hashem.

By contrast, allowing himself to be thrown into a furnace for a G-d Whom he had only just discovered would seem to be a much higher act, and yet it goes almost unnoticed. Why?

The Chassid Yaavetz says that the difference between the two is that the *Akeidah* was the result of a direct command from Hashem, who told Avraham to take his son והעלהו לעולה, and offer him up.

אור כשדים was not commanded by Hashem but was a case of Avraham willing to sacrifice his own life for his beliefs.

Therefore, when Avraham was willing to give up his own life, it was due to what **he** thought to be correct, what **he** had worked out to be true and **his** religious beliefs. History is full of people who are willing to sacrifice themselves for what they believe to be true, and therefore the Torah does not make specific reference to this act.

However, when you go against everything you believe in, and when you go against your logic because G-d has told you to do so, it shows that you are a servant of G-d, and that deserves to be highlighted.

When what you believe in dovetails with what Hashem wants from you, it is easy to be a G-d-fearing person. The question is what happens when there is a clash. That is when the truth of your convictions is tested, and when we can truly demonstrate our commitment.[3]

---

3   *Talelei Oros*, p. 149.

Joining the Halves Together

וַיְבַתֵּר אוֹתָם בַּתָּוֶךְ.

He cut them up in the center.[4]

As part of the *bris bein ha'besarim*, Avraham Avinu divided the animals in two and set the parts opposite each other. What is the idea behind this action?

When two sides enter into a covenant, the aim is to cement the relationship and bond between them to such a level that they feel as one body and as one person.

Since they are one, they will feel the joy and the pain of the other person in the same way that every part of their own body shares in the pleasure and the pain of every other part.

Therefore, when the two parties walk between the two halves of an animal, it is to symbolize that just as the two parts of the animal were joined as one, and each half shared the experiences of the other and were only separated by death, so too those entering the covenant do so to be joined together—to share the ups and the downs, to be confidants, allies, and generally look out for each other to be separated only by death!

This is the meaning behind וְאָהַבְתָּ לְרֵעֲךָ כָּמוֹךָ; we should be as concerned about the welfare of others as we are about ourselves, because others are not to be seen as *apart* from us but as *a part* of us—כָּמוֹךָ.

It is for this reason that the *gematria*, numerical value, of the words אַהֲבָה and אֶחָד are the same; they both equal thirteen because love means not thinking of the other as someone else but as part of you. You are not two distinct entities but are one.

This, therefore, explains why, during the covenant that was being forged between them, Hashem tells Avraham the worrying news that גֵר יִהְיֶה זַרְעֲךָ וכו'—his descendants will be slaves.

Why would Hashem want to dampen the celebratory mood of the covenant by telling Avraham such bad news? Could it not wait? It wasn't going to take place for a few hundred years, what was the urgency to inform him now?

The answer is that a covenant means that what I know, you know. There can't be secrets, because secrets differentiate people. No one has secrets from themselves! Therefore, if a covenant means that the two parties are now to be seen as one, there can be no secrets, and the fact that Hashem told Avraham this news is a sign that they had entered into a covenant in earnest.[5]

Divide a Jew in Half and What Do You Find?

ויבתר אותם בתוך.

He cut them up in the center.[6]

The *Aruch Hashulchan* says that if the idea of the animals was to symbolize the covenant between Hashem and Avraham Avinu, then it should have been sufficient to have just one animal, divide it into two, and walk between its parts.

What is the symbolism of the range of animals that were used in the *bris bein ha'besarim*?

The *Aruch Hashulchan* explains that Avraham understood that the Land was being promised to him as a reward for following Hashem and for him being a *tzaddik*.

Therefore, he cries out, "במה אדע כי אירשנה—How do I know that [my children] will inherit the Land," even if they are not all *tzaddikim*?

The answer came in the fashion that the covenant was forged.

5   *Yalkut Yosef Lekach*, p. 105.
6   *Bereishis* 15:10.

Avraham was told to take "עגלה משולשת ועז משולשת ואיל משולש ותור וגוזל—three heifers, three goats, three rams, a turtledove, and a young dove."

These animals allude to the nations of the world:

- Egypt is referred to as a heifer.[7]
- Persia is referred to as a ram.[8]
- Greece is referred to as a goat.[9]
- The Jewish People are compared to a dove.[10]

The verse then says that "ויבתר אתם בתוך—he (Avraham) cut them in the center." Those animals that referred to the nations of the world were split in two.

Then "ויתן איש בתרו לקראת רעהו—and placed each opposite its partner," i.e., he put half of the heifer opposite the half of the goat, and the other half of the goat opposite the half of the ram. The second half of the ram he placed opposite the second part of the heifer.

"ואת הציפור לא בתר—and he did not cut up the birds." By instructing him not to cut up the birds, Hashem showed Avraham the answer to his question.

When one nation conquers another and rules over it, it does not take long for the conquered nation to become absorbed and assimilated into the victorious nation. After a few hundred years, the two countries become one.

Not so the Jews. They have been conquered, exiled, and scattered, but they have survived with their own identity.

If you cut any nation into two, you will see that it is a composite of two or more nations. It will be half-heifer, representing Egypt, and half-goat, representing Greece. It can be half-goat, i.e., Greece, and half-ram, i.e., Persia. However, the Jews will never be cut in two because there would be no point. After all, both sides would just be Jewish!

The birds were not cut up because the birds represent Am Yisrael.

---

7   *Yirmiyahu* 46:20.
8   *Daniel* 8:20.
9   Ibid., v. 21.
10 *Shir Hashirim* 2:14.

This was Hashem's answer to Avraham: your children will never die out. Your children may experience ups and downs in their relationship with the Almighty, but there will never be complete assimilation, as if the entire Jewish bird were comprised of two identities![11]

To Be Happy or Not to Be Happy— That Is the Question

ויפל אברהם על פניו ויצחק.

And Avraham fell on his face and laughed.[12]

In *Koheles*, there seems to be a contradiction in its approach to *simchah*. In one verse, it says, "ולשמחה מה זו עושה—And joy, what does it accomplish?"[13] meaning that there is no productivity attached to *simchah*, while in another verse, it says, "ושבחתי אני את השמחה—I praised enjoyment,"[14] implying that *simchah* is a good thing!

The Gemara resolves the contradiction by explaining that there are two types of *simchah*—שמחה של מצוה, which is positive, and the other, less positive is שמחה that is not associated with a mitzvah.[15]

Rashi states that an example of a שמחה של מצוה would be הכנסת כלה—helping bring a bride to her wedding.

Why does *Rashi* bring that example in particular? Out of all the מצות that we perform with joy, why is the mitzvah of הכנסת כלה singled out?

Rabbi Aviel Kotler suggests that the reason הכנסת כלה is chosen is because it is an example of a mitzvah who's purpose is to bring happiness to someone else.[16]

---

11   *V'Shalal Lo Yechsar*, p. 176.
12   *Bereishis* 17:17.
13   *Koheles* 2:2.
14   Ibid. 8:15.
15   *Shabbos* 30b.
16   *HaKeriyah L'simchah*, p. 22.

When we perform mitzvos that benefit other people, the *simchah* is magnified.

This is reflected in the *Midrash Rabbah* that says that rainfall is more significant than *Matan Torah* because while *Matan Torah* brought *simchah* to Klal Yisrael, rain brings joy to all of humanity.[17]

Therefore, the greatest *simchah* is that which is shared with others. Any joy that is kept to ourselves and not shared is not a שמחה של מצוה and is described by *Koheles* as "ולשמחה מה זו עושה—what does it accomplish?" It is here today and gone tomorrow!

If we share our *simchah*, if we cause others to experience joy and happiness, then it is a *simchah* that *Koheles* praises.

When Avraham Avinu laughs after being told that at the age of one hundred he will have a son, he is not rebuked. However, when Sarah does the same, Hashem reprimands her and says, "למה זה צחקה שרה—Why did Sarah laugh?"[18] What's the difference?

There was a big difference in the way that Avraham laughed and the way that Sarah laughed.

When Avraham laughed, the verse says, "ויפל אברהם על פניו ויצחק—And Avraham fell on his face and laughed." His laugh was an outward expression of his inner joy. Everyone could see him laughing. He shared his happiness with others.

When Sarah receives the news that she will give birth to a son, the verse says, "ותצחק שרה בקרבה—And Sarah laughed **inwardly**,"[19] i.e., to herself, without sharing her joy with others.

The charge against Sarah is that after having received such fantastic news, how was it possible not to share the *simchah* with others? How can it remain בקרבה—inwardly?

Whereas Avraham is involved in the שמחה של מצוה that is shared with others and brings joy to others, Sarah keeps it to herself. The latter is thus best described as מה זו עושה!

---

17   *Midrash Tehillim* 117.
18   *Bereishis* 18:13.
19   Ibid., v. 12.

We can now understand why Hashem instructs that the child be named Yitzchak, which means laughter.[20] If Sarah's laughter was negative, why does Hashem wish the child to have such a name?

The answer is that Yitzchak is not so-called after the laughter of his mother, but after the positive laughter of his father—a laughter that is shared and that brings joy to others.

This should be our approach to *simchah*. It is less profound if it isn't shared and doesn't benefit others, but when it is shared with others, it can light up the world!

---

20   *Bereishis* 17:19.

וירא

Just Being

וירא אליו ה׳.

And Hashem appeared to him.[1]

At the beginning of the *parashah*, *Rashi* tells us that Hashem appeared to Avraham three days after his *bris milah* in order to visit him and to perform *bikur cholim*.

The *Rosh* notes that if Hashem came to visit Avraham and to find out how he is feeling, why is that conversation not reported in the text? Why does the Torah make no mention of Hashem asking Avraham how he felt or how the operation went? Why is there no mention of all the usual questions that one would ask when visiting someone who was unwell?

The *Rosh* learns from here that the Torah is teaching us that when we visit the sick, sometimes there is no need to speak! Just being there and letting the person know that you care is sufficient and is a fulfillment of the mitzvah of *bikur cholim*.

Many people are afraid that they will not know what to say in such a situation, or they are shy and uncomfortable. The *Rosh* is instructing

---

1   Ibid. 18:1.

us that the essence of *bikur cholim*, or for that matter being *menachem avel*, is to let them know that you care, are thinking of them, and are available to help if needed. This doesn't necessarily have to involve talking. Sometimes your presence itself is sufficient to let people know that you care.

Therefore, the conversation between Hashem and Avraham Avinu is not recorded because there may not have been any conversation. After all, Hashem's presence itself was, in fact, the *bikur cholim*.[2]

I Am Everything I Am Because You Loved Me

ויאמר קח נא את בנך את יחידך אשר אהבת את יצחק...

Please take your son, your only one, whom you love, Yitzchak…[3]

Rabbi Y.Y. Jacobson notes that the first time that the word אהבה—love, is used in the Torah is in this *pasuk* when Hashem instructs Avraham Avinu to take his son Yitzchak and offer him up as a sacrifice: "קח נא את בנך את יחידך אשר אהבת את יצחק—Please take your son, your only one, whom **you love**, Yitzchak." The second time the word אהבה is used in the Torah is in connection to Yitzchak's love for Rivkah: "ויבאה האהלה שרה אמו ויקח את רבקה ותהי לו לאשה ויאהבה—And Yitzchak brought her into the tent of Sarah, his mother, he married Rivkah, she became his wife, and **he loved her**."[4]

As Yitzchak had been the recipient of love, he knew how to love others. Since Avraham had shown love to Yitzchak, he was able to show love to Rivkah.

It therefore comes as no surprise that the third time the word אהבה is used in the Torah involves both Yitzchak **and** Rivkah! In connection to

2   *Otzar Pela'os HaTorah*, p. 233.
3   *Bereishis* 22:2.
4   Ibid. 24:67.

their children, Yaakov and Eisav, the verse says: "ויאהב יצחק את עשו כי ציד בפיו ורבקה אהבת את יעקב—And Yitzchak **loved** Eisav for game was in his mouth, but Rivkah **loved** Yaakov."[5]

The lesson being taught so clearly is that if we wish for our children to grow up as loving, productive, and well-balanced members of society, we need to show them love.[6]

Our children will not know how to love others unless they have experienced being loved properly.

It was because Yitzchak had experienced his father's love that he was able to love Rivkah, and it was because Rivkah received her husband's love that she, in turn, was able to love her son Yaakov.

Wool, Linen, Yishmael, and Yitzchak

ותאמר שרה לאברהם גרש האמה הזאת ואת בנה.

And Sarah said to Avraham, "Drive out this maidservant with her son."[7]

The *Yalkut Shimoni*, in connection with the episode of the banishment of Hagar and Yishmael by Avraham, quotes the *pasuk* in אשת חיל and says,

- "דרשה צמר ופשתים—She seeks out wool and linen." This refers to the choice between Yitzchak and Yishmael, as it says, "ותאמר שרה לאברהם גרש האמה הזאת ואת בנה—And Sarah said to Avraham, 'Send out this maidservant and her son.'"

- "ותקם בעוד לילה—She arises while it is still night," refers to Avraham, as it says, "וישכם אברהם בבוקר—Avraham arose early in the morning."

What does this very cryptic Midrash mean?

5   Ibid. 25:28.
6   Rabbi Y.Y. Jacobson, *Emet* Outreach Couples Gala (7:32).
7   *Bereishis* 21:10.

Rav Chaim Brisker explains that when Sarah approached Avraham and demanded that he send away Yishmael, Avraham was faced with a dilemma. There is an explicit prohibition against favoring the child of a loved wife over one who is despised, as the verse states: "לֹא יוּכַל לְבַכֵּר אֶת בֶּן הָאֲהוּבָה עַל פְּנֵי בֶן הַשְּׂנוּאָה הַבְּכֹר—He cannot give the right of the firstborn to the son of the beloved one ahead of the son of the hated one, the firstborn."[8]

So even though Avraham loves Sarah more than Hagar, he cannot deny Yishmael what is rightfully his, and by banishing him, Avraham would be doing precisely that.

On the other hand, Hashem had told Avraham: "כֹּל אֲשֶׁר תֹּאמַר אֵלֶיךָ שָׂרָה שְׁמַע בְּקֹלָהּ—Listen to whatever Sarah tells you."[9]

So, on the one hand, he had a negative commandment not to banish Yishmael, and on the other hand a positive command to listen to Sarah!

If a person has contradicting negative and positive commands, the law is, "עֲשֵׂה דּוֹחֶה לֹא תַעֲשֶׂה—The positive command pushes away the negative." Therefore, the positive command to listen to Sarah outweighed the negative command of not being able to deny Yishmael that which was rightfully his.

How is this connected to the verse in אֵשֶׁת חַיִל?

The source for the law that עֲשֵׂה דּוֹחֶה לֹא תַעֲשֶׂה is from the positioning of the words גְּדִלִים תַּעֲשֶׂה לָּךְ, which instructs us to make צִיצִת, next to the verse of לֹא תִלְבַּשׁ שַׁעַטְנֵז צֶמֶר וּפִשְׁתִּים יַחְדָּו, which is the prohibition of shaatnez.[10] Rashi comments that the two are placed together to teach us that the positive mitzvah of צִיצִת outweighs the negative commandment of שַׁעַטְנֵז, and thus you are permitted to have שַׁעַטְנֵז in צִיצִת because of עֲשֵׂה דּוֹחֶה לֹא תַעֲשֶׂה.

Now we can understand the Midrash.

דָּרְשָׁה צֶמֶר וּפִשְׁתִּים—Since we have the exposition from the verse concerning wool and linen, which teaches us that עֲשֵׂה דּוֹחֶה לֹא תַעֲשֶׂה, therefore Avraham knew that the positive commandment to listen to Sarah

8   Devarim 21:16.
9   Bereishis 21:12.
10   Devarim 22:12.

trumped the negative commandment not to deny Yishmael what was rightfully his. As a result, וישכם אברהם בבקר, and he sent Yishmael away![11]

Don't Ruin a Good Story with the Facts

ותאמר מי מלל לאברהם הניקה בנים שרה כי ילדתי בן לזקוניו.

And she said, "Who is the One who said to Avraham, 'Sarah would nurse children'? For I have borne a son in his old age."[12]

Rashi notes that the word בנים is in the plural form because of an interesting occurrence that happened on the day that they made a feast to celebrate the weaning of Yitzchak. All the nobles brought their babies with them and gave them to Sarah to be nursed. They did not believe that she had returned to being fertile and accused Avraham and Sarah of bringing home a lost baby and claiming it as their own.

When Sarah fed all the children, they all accepted that a miracle had indeed taken place and that Yitzchak was, in fact, their baby.

If they all brought their babies to see whether or not Sarah could nurse them, this must have meant that they left their nurses at home![13]

This would seem to be counter-intuitive, for if they were claiming that a miracle had not taken place and that Yitzchak was not Avraham and Sarah's son, they were also claiming that Sarah could not nurse. If Sarah could not nurse and they didn't bring their wet nurses with them, who would feed the children?

This is an example of what happens so often when we become so fixed in our ways and opinions that we are unwilling to change, even if the facts seem to contradict us. People did not believe that a miracle took place, and they brought their babies to Sarah in an attempt to ridicule

---

11   *Talelei Oros*, p. 194.
12   *Bereishis* 21:7.
13   *Chiddushei HaMaharsha al HaTorah*, p. 14.

her and disprove her story. They were so caught up in their theory that they did not entertain the possibility that they were wrong, even though their very actions would seem to contradict what they believed.

We need to be intellectually honest enough to be open to change when our opinion is proved to be wrong. We cannot continue with old beliefs and ideas just because this is the way we have always thought. If we are shown to be incorrect, we need to be open to change; otherwise, our relationships with other people and our relationship with Hashem cannot flourish.

The whole concept of *teshuvah*—repentance, depends on our realization that we were wrong and our commitment to change.

We cannot leave our nurses at home and take our babies to be nursed by someone we do not believe can nurse! We need to be honest and open to change.[14]

---

14   *Minchas Chayeinu*, vol. 1, p. 29.

חיי שרה

Chessed Takes Effort!

וַתְּמַהֵר וַתֹּרֶד כַּדָּהּ עַל יָדָהּ וַתַּשְׁקֵהוּ.

And quickly she lowered her jug to her hand and gave him drink.[1]

Rabbi Avraham Rivlin notes that in its description of Rivkah's actions, the Torah uses phrases such as, "וַתְּמַהֵר וַתֹּרֶד, וַתְּמַהֵר וַתְּעַר, וַתָּרָץ עוֹד—She quickly lowered, she hurried and emptied, she kept running." What message is being imparted with the use of these words? What was the rush?

In order to understand the enormity of Rivkah's actions, we need to really picture the scene at the well. When we visualize the scene in our mind, we tend to picture Eliezer, his men, and the camels standing by a well of water, and the kind Rivkah saves them the bother of having to place their buckets in the water by instead drawing the water for them to drink.

The reality was somewhat different. The water source was deep down beneath the surface, and to draw water one needed to descend many stairs to fill up a bucket. Then, when you reached the top, there was

---

1   *Bereishis* 24:18.

a system that determined how close your camel could be parked to the well! The more senior, influential, and respected you were, the nearer you parked to the well. A stranger could find himself at some distance from the well.

Therefore, not only did Rivkah have to contend with going up and down many stairs to fetch the water, but once she reached the top of the stairs, she also had to carry the water some further distance to where Eliezer, being a stranger, would be parked!

Therefore, the Torah tells us that despite these difficulties, Rivkah performed her *chessed* with zeal and alacrity—ותמהר ותרץ—and in this way, Eliezer knew that she was a perfect match for Yitzchak.

There is one more point that highlights the level of *chessed* performed by Rivkah.

The Torah tells us that when we see someone's donkey crouching under its burden, עָזֹב תַּעֲזֹב עִמּוֹ,[2] on which Chazal say that one is only obligated to help if the owner is also involved in trying to help the animal.[3] Should the owner sit back and refuse to help, then one is not obligated to help.

Neither Eliezer nor his men offered to help Rivkah give the camels to drink. It may have been, therefore, that Rivkah was exempt from helping them, and yet the Torah tells us that not only did she help them, but she did so with purpose and speed.[4]

There are many occasions when *chessed* opportunities present themselves when it is inconvenient, when they do not fit in with our personality, or when they are just plain difficult! The test of a true *baal chessed* is if, like Rivkah, he rises to the occasion and not only embraces these opportunities but does so with zeal, zest, and enthusiasm.

2   *Shemos* 23:5.
3   *Bava Metzia* 32b.
4   *Iyunei Parashah*, p. 123.

Seeing Things for What They Are (I)

ותפל מעל הגמל...ותקח הצעיף תתכס.

She let herself down from her camel...she then took the veil and covered herself.[5]

One of the most moving parts of any wedding ceremony is the "*bedekin*" when the groom approaches his bride and places a veil over her face in preparation for the *chuppah*.

This seems to be a strange practice. Why, if he loves her so much, does the groom cover the bride's face?

Rabbi Aharoni Bernstein traces the roots of this ceremony to when Rivkah encounters Yitzchak for the first time. Accompanied by her entourage, as Rivkah notices Yitzchak approaching, she lowers herself from her camel and covers her face. At this first emotional moment of meeting his new wife, Yitzchak is unable to see her! Why?

A healthy tree has very deep roots that are of the same volume underneath the surface as the volume of the tree above it.

While the branches and leaves or the fruit may catch the eye, without firm roots, all of these would wither and die. The uninspiring roots below are the life source of all the beauty above. When the seasons change and the leaves fall from the tree, it is the roots that will cause the new life to grow.

Likewise, with people, it is essential to remember what their roots are and what is external; what merely looks beautiful and what causes them to grow. Without deep roots, the externals are just a façade.

Rivkah, and all brides who follow her, cover their faces before the *chuppah*. At the moment of covenant between the *chassan* and the *kallah*, they announce that their love for each other is more than surface deep. The face (פָּנִים) is covered to reveal and to emphasize the interior (פְּנִים).[6]

5   *Bereishis* 24:65.
6   *Paam B'Shabbos*, p. 38.

The Palindrome of Bolton Is Notlob!

ויהיו חיי שרה מאה שנה ועשרים שנה ושבע שנים שני חיי שרה.

Sarah's lifetime was one hundred years, twenty years, and seven years; the years of Sarah's life.

Rashi explains that the seemingly redundant words at the end of the *pasuk* of שני חיי שרה come to tell us that כולן שוים לטובה, every year of Sarah's life was filled with goodness—from her very first until her last, from her youth until her old age.

Youth and old age both have advantages. The advantage of old age is that with it comes a level of experience and wisdom, a certain calmness and level-headedness.

The advantage of youth is an energy and excitement that is missing later in life. There is a determination and idealism in youth that unfortunately tends to wane and die out with the advancement of age.

But for Sarah, כולן שוים לטובה. At every stage of Sarah's life, she was blessed with the advantages of both youth and old age. On the one hand, even though she was young, she had the benefit of the wisdom usually born of experience, while at the other end, she had the energy and excitement that comes with youth even in her old age.[7]

This is also indicated in the fact that the word ויהיו, as in ויהיו חיי שרה, is a palindrome, a word that reads the same backward as forward. The beginning and end of Sarah's life were equal.

The *Baal Shem Tov* notes the existence of a palindrome in connection with the mitzvah of *tzedakah*. The *pasuk* dealing with donating a half-*shekel* for the building of the *Mishkan* says, ונתנו איש כפר נפשו,[8] where the word ונתנו—to give, is a palindrome. This teaches us that **when you give, you receive; it goes both ways.**[9]

---

7   *Maayanah shel Torah*, p. 94.
8   *Shemos* 30:12.
9   *Otzar Chaim*, p. 81.

Rabbi Moshe Midner explains *Rashi's* words of כולן שוים לטובה slightly differently. Whatever Sarah experienced in her life, she always looked on the bright side—in the spirit of גם זו לטובה.

This was no simple feat. Sarah experienced real challenges; she was unable to have children, Pharaoh and Avimelech abducted her, she experienced famine, Hagar and Yishmael, the *Akeidah*, and more.

Each one of these on its own was a formidable challenge, and yet כולן שוים לטובה—to her, everything was equally טוב.[10]

Every Moment Counts

ויהיו חיי שרה מאה שנה ועשרים שנה ושבע שנים שני חיי שרה.

Sarah's lifetime was one hundred years, twenty years, and seven years; the years of Sarah's life.[11]

The great Rabbi Akiva was once giving a shiur, and the participants began to dose off. To wake them up, he asked them: "Why did Queen Esther merit reigning over 127 countries? Because she was a descendant of Sarah, who lived to the age of 127. Esther therefore reigned over 127 countries."[12]

What is the connection between Esther and the students falling asleep? How was this piece of information supposed to wake them up?

If Queen Esther was rewarded with 127 countries as a result of the 127 years of Sarah's life, then she received one country for every year of Sarah's life.

If so, said Rabbi Akiva, for each month of Sarah's life, Queen Esther was rewarded with a city, and for each week of Sarah's life, Queen Esther reigned over a town, and for each day, she ruled over a street, etc.

What we see is the value of time and the cost of wasting it.

---

10 Ibid. p. 83.
11 *Bereishis* 23:1.
12 *Midrash Rabbah* 58:3.

Every single moment of Sarah's life was used correctly and as a result, for every moment Queen Esther ruled over an area. Sarah used her time correctly, and it had long-lasting effects, even many years afterwards.

Rabbi Akiva was telling his students to wake up and not to waste time, for each moment lost can cost them dearly.

Rabbeinu Avraham, son of the Vilna Gaon, writes that the reason why Sarah insisted that Yishmael be banished and distanced from Yitzchak was that she saw that Yishmael was a typical teenager who wasted time and was not occupying himself with a drive to attain perfection.

Rabbi Moshe Shmuel Shapiro asks that in light of what *Rashi* says—that Yishmael was engaged in the three cardinal sins[13]—influencing Yitzchak to waste time seems a little trivial. What is Rabbeinu Avraham driving at?

The conclusion that we must draw is that Sarah was not as worried about the three cardinal sins, because as grave as they are, it is possible to repent and receive atonement for them.

However, once you have wasted even a single moment, there is no way of retrieving it. It has been lost forever, and it damages your long-term goal of achieving perfection.

If Yitzchak was going to be included as one of the forefathers, this was a risk that Sarah could not afford to take. The primary vehicle to achieving greatness is knowing how to make the best use out of every minute.

Rav Elchonon Wasserman once returned from a visit to Warsaw, and when asked what the most memorable part of his visit was, he answered that he saw that the Rebbe of Gur had *sedarim*—learning sessions of five minutes in length! Every moment was precious, and even a five-minute interlude between appointments or meetings could be used productively.[14]

13 *Bereishis* 21:9.
14 *Yalkut Yosef Lekach*, p. 130.

Seeing This for What They Are (2)

ויקם השדה והמערה אשר בו לאברהם לאחזת קבר.

Thus, the field with its cave confirmed as Avraham's as an estate for a burial site.[15]

Rabbi Akiva Kashtiel notes that the very first acquisition of the Land of Israel is a burial plot. Why is it that the first time that Avraham Avinu connects to the Land, and consequently our very first connection with it, is for a burial plot? Could it not have been something a little more majestic like the site of the future בית המקדש or a space on which to build an altar to offer sacrifices?

The first answer is that, unfortunately, a burial is permanent (until *techiyas ha'meisim*). Therefore, the symbolism of this being our first purchase is that our attachment to the Land is permanent.

Secondly, and more fundamentally, the purchase of a burial plot is a purchase from which no future benefit can be derived. I cannot develop the land and make profits; I cannot even build a hospital or some other useful institution on that land. I cannot plant it and will not receive any fruits from it. The land is bought for the land's sake and not because I will gain any future benefit from it.

This idea is made more evident if we consider that *Rashi* tells us that Chevron is the rockiest of all the land of Eretz Yisrael and is unsuitable for any agricultural endeavor, making it only suited for burial.[16]

That is why it was the first act of purchase recorded in the Torah—to teach us that our attachment to the Land is not due to what we can derive from it. Instead, our attachment is due to the land itself, literally the rocks and the dirt. This is our place, and our connection is permanent.

---

15   *Bereishis* 23:20.
16   *Bamidbar* 13:22.

This is reflected in the Gemara that tells that when Rabbi Abba made *aliyah*, he kissed "כיפי דעכו—the stones of Akko."[17] Why did he kiss the stones?

Rav Kook explains that Rabbi Abba wished to express his love for Eretz Yisrael that was not connected to any benefit or profit that the land would provide for him. It was love, pure and simple, and therefore to show his love, he kissed the hard rocks that would never produce anything.

His inspiration was the first purchase of Avraham Avinu in Eretz Yisrael of a rocky burial place in Chevron. Avraham Avinu showed us that our attachment to Eretz Yisrael is permanent, and the attachment is with the ground itself—literally—and not because of any benefit that may accrue from that land.[18]

---

17   *Kesubos* 112a.
18   *Taaroch Lefanai Shulchan*, p. 56.

תולדות

I Remember When I Was Young

ויהי כי זקן יצחק ותכהין עיניו מראות.

And it came to pass, when Yitzchak had become old, and his eyes dimmed from seeing.[1]

Rashi offers an explanation as to why Yitzchak's eyes dimmed, namely, that it was a result of the smoke from the incense that Eisav's wives offered to their idols.

However, Rivkah lived in the same house as Yitzchak, and she too would have seen the smoke, so why were her eyes not affected?

Tosafos suggests that since Rivkah had grown up in a house that was full of idol worship, she was used to such smoke, and therefore her eyes remained unaffected by the incense offered up by Eisav's wives.

Let us analyze this for a minute: How old was Rivkah when Eisav married these wives? She was sixty-three years old. How old was Rivkah when she married Yitzchak and left home? According to many commentaries, she was three years old. This means that Rivkah had had no contact with idols for over sixty years! For sixty years, she had not seen, heard, or encountered idol worship, and nevertheless, because

---

1   *Bereishis* 27:1.

she was exposed to the negativity of idol worship as a small child, she is less sensitive to its negative influences over sixty years later!

We see from here the importance of protecting our children from being exposed to any kind of negativity, for it is still significant, even many years later.

If this is true in the negative, it is undoubtedly true in the positive. We need to expose our children to positivity—to light, warmth, music, color, and most importantly, love. In this way, many years later, they will look back warmly at their childhood, and that warmth, happiness, and positivity will carry them through any challenge they may confront, and it will enable them to be productive, stable, and happy members of society.[2]

Feelings Are Reflective

וישבת עמו ימים אחדים עד אשר תשוב חמת אחיך...עד שוב אף אחיך ממך.

And remain with him a short while until your brother's wrath subsides…Until your brother's anger against you subsides.[3]

These two expressions uttered by Rivkah would seem to be saying the same thing, namely, that Yaakov should escape until his brother is no longer angry with him. Why do we need two expressions that mean the same thing?

HaGaon Rabbi Pinchas Horowitz, the *Baal Haflaah*, explains that Rivkah was not repeating herself, she was giving Yaakov the following advice: Escape to somewhere far away and remain there until your brother has calmed down and decided that he is not going to kill you.

How will you know that he has calmed down, no longer wishes to kill you, and therefore it is safe to return home? עד שוב אף אחיך ממך—

---

2   *L'titecha Elyon*, p. 224.
3   *Bereishis* 27:44–45.

When the day comes that you cease to feel any anger toward him! When you no longer feel anger toward him, it is a sign that he feels the same, because love generates love, and hate breeds hate.

If we feel negatively toward others, it is a sign that they feel the same. The only way to create an atmosphere of love and harmony is if we feel that love. If we have no ill will toward others, then none will be felt toward us.

Even though Eisav hated his brother and had sworn to kill him, the minute that Eisav forgives Yaakov, Yaakov will no longer have any negative thoughts toward Eisav![4]

What is interesting is that Yaakov must have had negative thoughts against Eisav, because Eisav had become a *rasha*. This is reflected in the use of two different words for "anger" by Rivkah.

When it comes to Eisav calming down, she says: עד אשר תשוב חמת אחיך, and regarding Yaakov not harboring negative thoughts about Eisav, the words used are: עד שוב אף אחיך ממך.

The *Alshich* says that אף is a more definite form of anger than חמה. This means that not only is Yaakov angry with Eisav, but that he has more anger toward Eisav than Eisav has toward him!

The importance of Rivkah's advice to Yaakov now becomes more evident. If Yaakov wishes to return home, he first needs to expunge the anger that he has toward his brother Eisav. Eisav's anger toward him is not the problem, as that anger can be overcome. Only if Yaakov acts to remove the anger that he has toward Eisav will it be safe for Yaakov to return.

With this idea, Rabbi Horowitz, in *Panim Yafos*, explains the rather strange behavior of Yosef in *Parashas Vayeishev*.

At the beginning of the *parashah*, Yosef informs his brothers of his dreams, which foretold that he was going to rule over them. The brothers are none too impressed with these proclamations, as the verse says, "ויוסיפו עוד שנא אתו על חלומותיו ועל דבריו"—And the brothers hated him even more because of his dreams and because of his talk."[5]

---

4   *Parperaʼos LaTorah*, p. 115.

5   *Bereishis* 37:8.

Yosef was aware of his brothers' dislike for him, and yet when his father sends him to "ראה את שלום אחיך—Look into the welfare of your brothers," and he doesn't find them in Shechem, instead of protecting himself and returning home, he actively seeks them out.

He meets a man and asks him if he knows where they are. In reply to the man's inquiry as to why he wants to see them, Yosef replies, "את אחי אנכי מבקש—I am looking for my brothers."

What is Yosef trying to do? Has he become a Kamikaze pilot, leading himself into certain danger?

The *Panim Yafos* suggests that Yosef was saying that if he approached his brothers with love in his heart, and they saw that he bore them no malice and the dreams were not an effort to dominate them, then they, likewise, would be unable to feel anything other than love for him.

The same principle would apply as it does in our *parashah* with Yaakov's feelings toward Eisav.

So why didn't it work for Yosef? How was it that the brothers ended up placing him in a pit and selling him as a slave down to Egypt?

The answer is "ויראו אותו מרחק וטרם יקרב אליהם ויתנכלו אתו להמיתו—They saw him from afar, and when he had not yet approached them, they conspired against him to kill him."[6]

The brothers saw Yosef **from a distance** and never allowed him to approach. They never allowed him to show that he had no anger toward them.

The brothers knew that were Yosef to approach, and were they to see that he loved them, they would love him back. So, they hatched a plan to kill him **before** he approached and while they still had hate for him in their hearts!

The way we feel toward others is a barometer as to how they feel toward us. If we want to be loved, we must start by only having positive feelings toward others.[7]

---

6   Ibid., v. 18.
7   *Meorah shel Torah*, p. 86.

Connecting through Receiving

ויתן לך האלוקים מטל השמים.

And may G-d give you of the dew of the heavens.[8]

The word ויתן seems to have a superfluous letter ו at the beginning; why is it needed?

Rashi suggests that the ו comes to tell us that Yitzchak was blessing his son that Hashem should give him the dew, etc., and then renew the blessing and bring the dew and give again and again.

Harav Shmuel Rozovsky asks that surely Hashem can give His goodness all in one go. He knows how much we need and how much we will need, so why is it a blessing that He will repeatedly provide? Why not all at once?

Rav Rozovsky answers that the actual act of giving establishes a bond between the giver and the recipient, and therefore, contained in the *berachah* of ויתן לך is another blessing—that through the giving and receiving, we will have a close connection with Hashem.[9]

The same idea, but in the negative, can be seen in the punishment that Hashem gives the snake after it enticed Adam and Eve to sin and eat from the Tree of Knowledge.

The punishment given to the snake was that it would eat the dust of the earth.

Rav Shimshon Raphael Hirsch asks what kind of punishment this is. The snake will always have food, as there is never a shortage of dust. Where is the punishment?

The answer is that in providing for all that the snake needs, Hashem is giving it the message that He is not interested in having a relationship with it. There will be no continuous act of giving and receiving, but rather Hashem writes out a blank check to the snake. "Take whatever

---

8   *Bereishis* 27:28.
9   *Talelei Oros*, p. 292.

it is you need, just do not have contact with Me, and I do not want to hear from you!"

The message of Yitzchak to his son was that ויתן—Hashem should provide and provide again for you, because every time you receive from Him, every time we engage in prayer to Him to provide, and every time He does provide, it strengthens the relationship between us.

This idea is also used by HaGaon Rav Zeidel Epstein to explain the difference between the *berachah* that Yitzchak gives Yaakov (thinking that it is Eisav) and the one he later gives Eisav.

The wording of the *berachah* given to Yaakov is, ויתן לך האלוקים מטל השמים ומשמני הארץ,[10] and the *berachah* that Eisav received is, משמני הארץ יהיה מושבך ומטל השמים מעל.[11]

Aren't these essentially saying the same thing?

Rav Epstein suggests that the difference is in the way that Eisav and Yaakov will relate to these blessings.

With Eisav, there is no mention of Hashem as the bestower. Eisav feels that these blessings are his by right. He has worked hard for them, deserves them, and therefore has earned them. Yaakov, by contrast, is aware that all blessings are ויתן לך האלוקים—a gift from Hashem, and as such, each blessing enhances the relationship between Hashem and Yaakov.[12]

If we do not realize that all blessings are a gift from Hashem, then the blessing does not act to strengthen the relationship, and it may even serve to distance the receiver from the giver.

By acknowledging that all we have is a gift from Hashem, and every time we receive we recognize Him as the Provider, not only will we enjoy the benefits of the blessing, but we will also strengthen our relationship with the Almighty.

10 *Bereishis* 27:28.
11 Ibid., v. 39.
12 *L'titecha Elyon*, p. 229.

Tears vs. Tears

ויצעק צעקה גדולה ומרה עד מאד ויאמר לאביו ברכני גם אני אבי.

He cried out an exceedingly great and bitter cry, and said to his father, "Bless me too, Father!"[13]

The Midrash tells us that because of the tears that Eisav shed when he said, ברכני גם אני אבי, he merited all the good that he received and all the fortune that his descendants have had against us over the generations.[14]

Rav Shmelke of Nikolsburg asks that the Jewish People have shed an ocean of tears over the millennia of exile; why have those tears not drowned out the tears that Eisav shed all those years ago? The halachah is that any matter is בטל בשישים, and we have definitely shed more than sixty times the tears that he did, so why have our tears not been effective?

The Gemara says that the law of בטל בשישים does not apply to מין במינו—two things that are the same, just that one is permitted and one is prohibited.[15]

Therefore, if our tears have not drowned out the tears of Eisav, the reason must be that they are the same type of tears.

What does this mean?

When Eisav cries, it is because he wants the physical blessing, and he fears that he has missed out. He is not crying, however, because losing out on the spiritual elements of the blessings upsets him.

If our tears during the exile are the same as Eisav's, it means that we have been crying due to the physical and material hardship that the exile has brought, and not over the spiritual destruction.

---

13   *Bereishis* 27:34.
14   *Midrash Tanchuma, Kedoshim* 15.
15   *Avodah Zarah* 73a; this is not the halachah in practice.

If this is the case, then our tears are identical to Eisav's; they are tears over a loss of material pleasures and blessings. If they are alike, they cannot be מבטל, and Eisav still has the upper hand.

Only if we cry over the *chillul Hashem* that is a result of *galus*; only if we grieve over the fact that the Divine presence is in exile, and our spiritual existence is challenged, only then will our tears be different from Eisav's and be able to annul them![16]

---

16   *Otzar Chaim*, p. 122.

וַיֵּצֵא

The Making of
Extraordinary People

וַיִּזְכֹּר אֱלֹקִים אֶת רָחֵל וַיִּשְׁמַע אֵלֶיהָ וַיִּפְתַּח אֶת רַחְמָהּ.

*G-d remembered Rachel; He hearkened to her and He opened
her womb.*[1]

R*ashi* tells us that Hashem remembered that Rachel had given
the signs to Leah when Leah married Yaakov, and in that merit,
וַיִּפְתַּח אֶת רַחְמָהּ, she had children.

HaGaon Harav Moshe Chevroni asks why Hashem only remembered
Rachel's act of *chessed* and rewarded her for it now, so many years after
the *chessed* took place. Why did He not bless her with a child as a reward
for this act of *chessed* closer to when it was performed?

Rav Chevroni answers that revealing the signs was without a doubt
an act of supreme sacrifice.

Through this act, Rachel was willing to forgo marrying Yaakov and
with it the chance of being the mother of some of the *shivtei Kah*.
Moreover, even if somehow Yaakov now wanted to marry her in

---

1   *Bereishis* 30:22.

addition to Leah, it would not seem possible that he would be permitted to marry two sisters.

Nonetheless, everyone is capable of a single moment of heroism.

When we have a moment of inspiration, a rush of adrenaline, we are capable of raising ourselves and acting extraordinarily. Many in history have seized that one moment to perform a remarkable act on behalf of someone else.

Such behavior, however, does not make them exceptional people or worthy of being a matriarch of the Jewish People.

Many people have risen to the occasion only to be unable to rise to it again when called upon a second time. Some even regret rising to that occasion in the first place. What makes extraordinary people is that they perform the remarkable regularly.

Many years later, Leah challenges Rachel: "המעט קחתך את אישי ולקחת גם את דודאי בני—Was your taking my husband insignificant? And also you'll take my son's *dudaim*!"[2]

Rachel would have been entitled to say in amazement, "If it wasn't for me, you wouldn't be married to Yaakov in the first place!" or, "If that is your attitude, I wish I had never helped you!"

But Rachel's reaction is consistent with her first act of *chessed*. She remains silent, reinforcing that such was the behavior demanded then, and that she would repeat it if necessary.

Once Rachel showed that she consistently acted extraordinarily, Hashem blessed her with a child as a reward for that first act of *chessed*.

To rise to the occasion and act extraordinarily is within reach of every ordinary person. To do so regularly takes someone extraordinary.[3]

---

2   Ibid. 3:15.
3   *Yalkut Yosef Lekach*, p. 235.

Draw from the Well and Perfect the World

וירא והנה באר בשדה.

He looked and behold a well in the field![4]

R abbi Shlomo Yosef Zevin notes that there are three types of areas:

- בית—house
- שדה—field
- מדבר—desert

The בית offers protection, shelter, and warmth, whereas the מדבר leaves you exposed and vulnerable. They are opposites.

Then there is the שדה, which can either be an extension of the בית or an extension of the מדבר.

If the שדה is plowed, sown, and harvested, then it offers sustenance and is an extension of the בית. If, however, it is ignored and left to lie fallow and wild, it is an extension of the מדבר.

Rabbi Zevin suggests that these three correspond to three types of people:

- בית is the person interested solely in studying Torah and performing mitzvos with little or no interaction with the world.
- Then there is the מדבר, the person who is wild and devoid of any Torah or mitzvos.
- Finally, there is the שדה, the person who is involved and interacts with the world. The question such a person faces is: Is he going to be an extension of the בית, or is he going to be an extension of the מדבר?

In your interaction with the world, are you going to ensure that you are honest, trustworthy and fair? Are you going to base all your actions on Torah principles? If you do, you are an extension of the בית.

---

4   *Bereishis* 29:2.

If, however, the opposite is the case, and your life is devoid of Torah values and principles, then you are merely an extension of the מדבר.

We need to emulate the words of the *pasuk*, וירא והנה באר בשדה. When we look at the שדה, we need to see the באר of Torah. The Torah needs to be a well from which we draw our instruction and inspiration and on which we base our every decision and action. In that way, we will be an extension of the בית and bring protection, shelter, and warmth to the world.[5]

Where Have All the Spaces Gone?

I f we look at a *Sefer Torah*, we notice that usually there are paragraph breaks between the sentences that delineate the end of a subject or *parashah*.

Parashas Vayeitzei is unique in that from the beginning of the *parashah* until the end, there are no gaps. It is one long, continuous series of *pesukim*.

What can we learn from this unique aspect of the *parashah*?

The *Sefas Emes* writes that Yaakov Avinu's main challenge during the long years that he was away from his parents' home was to stay focused on his mission.[6]

When Yaakov left home, he knew exactly where he needed to go and why he needed to go there. He needed to go build a family and then return to continue the legacy of his grandfather and father, Avraham and Yitzchak.

However, the reality of the situation was a little more complicated.

He met Lavan, a cruel and cunning swindler, who would do whatever it took to ensure that Yaakov became so preoccupied with his current activities that he would never return home and complete his mission.

5 La'Torah U'Le'moadim, p. 57.
6 Al Sefas Emes, p. 45.

Many people in such circumstances would settle into the new reality, forget what had been planned in the past, and begin a new and different path, swapping the good intentions of the past for the new reality of the present.

However, Yaakov Avinu never forgot his mission. He was accompanied by the mantra that his years away from his parents were ימים אחדים—days united by a central theme, and that theme was that he was on a mission, and nothing was going to derail that mission.

Every day, Yaakov arose and asked himself how he was going to use that day to further his mission of building a family and then returning home.

The lack of breaks in this *parashah* indicate that for Yaakov Avinu, there were no pauses or breaks. His life was one long continuum of working toward that mission and fulfilling it.

Each of us needs to realize that we have a unique mission to perform in our lives. Without this unique mission, we would not have been born.

We must not allow life to interfere with living; we must remain focused and set about our mission without breaks and pauses and, in that way, give ourselves the best chance of being successful.

Don't You Remember the Time I...?

המעט קחתך את אישי ולקחת גם את דודאי בני.

Was your taking my husband insignificant? And also you'll take my son's dudaim!

How could Leah accuse Rachel of "taking" her husband when, if it weren't for Rachel's intervention in giving her the signs, Leah would not be married to Yaakov in the first place? Where was Leah's gratitude toward her sister?

Rabbi David Dunner explains that there are many people who perform *chessed* and will forever remind you about the *chessed* that you received from them. Sometimes, they drive you mad reminding you to such an extent that you end up wishing that they had not helped you in the first place!

Rachel practiced true *chessed*, which meant that she performed *chessed* in such a way that the recipient did not even realize that they were the recipients of an act of *chessed*!

When Rachel gave the signs to Leah, Rachel did so in such a way as to ensure that Leah never realized that Rachel was saving her! Leah just thought that this must be the standard way an older sister marries—with her younger one giving her some signals to share with her husband!

As a result of this pure act of *chessed*, Leah was able to charge המעט קחתך את אישי in all innocence, as she was blissfully unaware of the *chessed* performed by Rachel.

Rachel is teaching us an invaluable lesson about *chessed*. The highest level of *chessed* is for it to be accompanied with no fanfare, loud noises, or anyone knowing of it—not even the recipient!

וישלח

I Can't Wait!

כה אמר עבדך יעקב עם לבן גרתי ואחר עד עתה.

So said your servant Yaakov: "I have sojourned with Lavan and have lingered until now."[1]

O

n this *pasuk*, *Rashi* makes his famous comment of עם לבן גרתי
ותרי"ג מצוות שמרתי, Yaakov was telling Eisav that he had kept
Torah and mitzvos even while living with a *rasha* like Lavan.
But how could Yaakov Avinu claim to have kept all of the 613 mitzvos?
He was outside of Eretz Yisrael and therefore not able to fulfill מצות ישוב
ארץ ישראל; he was away from his parents, so he was unable to fulfill מצות
כיבוד אב ואם; and so on?

The *Chasam Sofer* instructs us to read *Rashi* more carefully.

Rashi does not say ותרי"ג מצוות קיימתי—I observed/fulfilled all the
commandments, but rather that "תרי"ג מצוות שמרתי." What, then does
שמרתי mean?

In *Parashas Vayeishev*, when Yosef tells his dreams to his family, the
pasuk says, ויקנאו בו אחיו ואביו שמר את הדבר,[2] on which *Rashi* comments

---

1   *Bereishis* 32:5.

2   Ibid. 37:11.

that שמר means: היה ממתין ומצפה מתי יבוא, Yaakov, his father, waited in anticipation for the moment when the dreams would come to fruition.

When *Rashi* says regarding Yaakov Avinu that תרי"ג מצות שמרתי, it does not mean that Yaakov Avinu fulfilled all 613 mitzvos. Rather, it means that he anticipated and longed for the day that all the impediments preventing him from fulfilling all the mitzvos would be removed, thus enabling him to keep them all.

The Gemara tells us that if someone genuinely wants to fulfill a mitzvah but is unable to do so due to an *ones*, something that is outside of his control, he is credited as if he nonetheless fulfilled that mitzvah.[3]

Therefore, Yaakov Avinu is telling Eisav that while it may have been impossible, for reasons beyond his control, to have kept all the 613 mitzvos while he was in the house of Lavan, nevertheless, תרי"ג מצות שמרתי, he keenly anticipated the moment when he would be able to observe them all, and therefore it is considered as if he did, in fact, fulfill all of the mitzvos.

In our observance of mitzvos are we keen to observe as many as possible, or are we pleased for the reprieve when circumstances arise that make it impossible for us to perform a particular mitzvah? Do we actively seek opportunities to perform, or are we happy to avoid?

Rashi is teaching us that the path to תרי"ג מצות קיימתי starts with תרי"ג מצוות שמרתי, a keen anticipation and desire for mitzvah observance opportunities.[4]

---

3   *Kiddushin* 40a.
4   *L'hisaden B'ahavasecha*, p. 399.

Stop, Wait, Think!

ויצו את הראשון לאמר כי יפגשך עשו אחי ושאלך לאמר למי אתה ואנה
תלך ולמי אלה לפניך.

He instructed the first one, saying, "When my brother Eisav meets you and asks you saying, 'Whose are you, where are you going, and whose are these that are before you?'"[5]

As part of his preparations for the showdown, Yaakov sent gifts through messengers to Eisav. Yaakov told the messengers that when they meet Eisav, he will ask three questions:

1. Who are you?
2. Where are you going?
3. To whom do these (gifts) in front of you belong?

Is there a message in the three questions that Yaakov said Eisav would ask?

Harav Avinoam Maimon suggests that these three questions describe how a person should lead their life.

- The first question was "למי אתה—To whom do you belong?" Which community do you identify with? Who influences your opinions and your beliefs? How important are those beliefs in your day-to-day life?
- Second, "ואנה תלך—Where are you going?" What goals and aspirations drive you forward?
- Finally, "למי אלה לפניך—To whom are these in front of you?" Will your children, who go before you, continue in your path? Will your grandchildren continue the legacy of their past?

These are the questions that each one of us needs to consider regularly to ensure that we set our compass in the direction that will ensure that we know who we are, where we are going, and that our children will continue on the same path.

---

5   *Bereishis* 32:18.

The story is told of an elderly Rav in Soviet Russia who one morning was on his way to shul. Suddenly, an armed police officer approached him, drew his gun, and asked the elderly rabbi, "Who are you? What are you doing here? Where are you going?"

The rabbi smiled and quietly asked the officer, "Tell me, officer, how much do you earn as a policeman?"

The officer replied that he earned twenty kopeks a day.

"I would like to ask a favor from you," said the rabbi. "I will pay you twenty kopeks a day if you promise me that every day on my way to shul, you will wait for me here, stop me, and ask me those three questions:

- Who are you?
- What are you doing here?
- Where are you going?!"[6]

Accepting Gifts Can Ruin Your Day!

ויאמר עשו יש לי רב אחי יהי לך אשר לך.

Eisav said, "I have plenty. My brother, let what you have remain yours."[7]

Why did Eisav not want to accept Yaakov's gifts? The question is strengthened by the *Kli Yakar*, who says that by using the expression יש לי רב, and not יש לי כל as used later by Yaakov,[8] we see that Eisav was not satisfied with the wealth that he had and wanted more. If so, why did he reject Yaakov's gifts?

The *Panim Meiros* explains the *pasuk* by referencing the laws of *chazakah*.

When a person occupies a field for three years without anyone challenging his claim to that field, we assume that the property is his, and

---

6   *Bein Adam LaParashah*, p. 129.
7   *Bereishis* 33:9.
8   Ibid., v. 11.

we cannot question his ownership without producing proper evidence to back up our claim.

There is a discussion in the Gemara as to what constitutes a challenge. One thing is for sure: If the person on the land sends a gift to the "challenger" of fruits from the field in dispute, and the "challenger" accepts this gift, then instantly the "challenger" loses any rights, and we award title to the person on the field.

The assumption is that if the challenger truly felt that the land belonged to him, he would be insulted to accept a gift of fruit from that land, as he would think that the fruit legally belonged to him! By taking the present, the challenger shows that he isn't convinced that the property is his.

The blessing that Yitzchak gave Yaakov had to do with material wealth, מטל השמים ומשמני הארץ, and therefore, had Eisav accepted material gifts from Yaakov, he would have been admitting that the *berachah* belonged to Yaakov. Consequently, he had no choice other than to reject it.

The *Chida*, in the name of *Maharam Chaviv*, writes that this is part of the reasoning behind the mitzvah of *bikkurim*—the first fruits.

Hashem instructs us to take our first fruits up to Yerushalayim and to give them to the Kohanim, who are His representatives.

Since Hashem, Master of the Universe, accepts our first fruits, brought from the Land of Israel, it is a sign that He agrees that Eretz Yisrael belongs to Am Yisrael.

If Hashem agrees that the Land of Israel belongs to the Jews, then any challenges to that fact are invalid![9]

---

9   *Shenayim Mikra*, p. 384.

Look Right, Not Left

כִּי חַנַּנִי אֱלוֹקִים וְיֵשׁ לִי כֹל.

As G-d has been gracious to me and I have everything.[10]

Rashi draws a comparison between Eisav, who says, יֵשׁ לִי רַב, and Yaakov Avinu, who says, יֵשׁ לִי כֹל.

Eisav speaks haughtily, saying, "I have plenty," implying that he would like much more. Yaakov, on the other hand, says that he has everything that he needs and is satisfied with what he has. The *sefer Bas Ayin* notes that we find the same idea in the *pasuk*, "לֵב חָכָם לִימִינוֹ וְלֵב כְּסִיל לִשְׂמֹאלוֹ—A wise man's mind tends to the right, while a fool's mind tends to the left."[11]

If we look at the letters that immediately precede the word לב (the 'א precedes the 'ב, and the 'כ precedes the 'ל), we find the letters that spell out אָךְ.

אָךְ comes to limit. It is the same as רק—only.

The Gemara notes that אכין ורקין מיעוטים הם—wherever we find the word אך or רק, it acts as a limitation.[12]

A wise person lives his life content with what he has, not in constant pursuit of more and more, and is happy to live within limits—לֵב חָכָם לִימִינוֹ.

The fool, on the other hand, looks at the letters that follow the word לב as we look from the left. What follows לב is the word גם, which means "also." I am not satisfied with what I have; I want what I have and also what I don't have. I want more and more. Such a person is a fool—לֵב כְּסִיל לִשְׂמֹאלוֹ.[13]

---

10   *Bereishis* 33:11.
11   *Koheles* 10:2.
12   *Rosh Hashanah* 17b, and other places.
13   *Bas Ayin*, by Ha'Admor Avraham Dov of Avritch (1760–1841).

וישב

It's Not What You Say
but How You Say It!

וַיֵּט אֵלֶיהָ אֶל הַדֶּרֶךְ וַיֹּאמֶר.

So he detoured to her by the road and said.[1]

abbi Yosef Zvi Dunner points out that in the exchange between Yehudah and Tamar found in the *parashah*, the word ויאמר appears three times in connection with Yehudah speaking, and the word ותאמר appears three times in connection with Tamar speaking.

If we look at the cantillation (*trop*) above these words, we see that every note above the ויאמר of Yehudah is the same as the note above the ותאמר of Tamar.[2]

The Torah is subtly teaching us that people will react to and interact with us according to the way that we speak to them. A soft, kindly spoken word will usually be greeted with the same, whereas an angry word usually degenerates into an ugly exchange.[3]

---

1   *Bereishis* 38:16.
2   In *pasuk* טז, they both have a פשטא; in *pasuk* יז, they both have a זקף קטן; and in *pasuk* יח, they both have a רביעי.
3   *Mikdash Halevi*, p. 146.

When describing the pit into which the brothers threw Yosef, the *pasuk* says, וְהַבּוֹר רֵק אֵין בּוֹ מָיִם,[4] on which *Rashi* makes his famous comment that "מַיִם אֵין בּוֹ, אֲבָל נְחָשִׁים וְעַקְרַבִּים יֵשׁ בּוֹ—the pit was empty of water, but it did have scorpions and snakes."[5]

The *Oznayim La'Torah* notes that the pit had something positive and something negative. It was positive for Yosef that it did not have any water, and negative that it had scorpions and snakes. Yet, the *pasuk* only makes direct reference to the positive aspect of the pit: that it didn't have any water, while the negative is only inferred: it had snakes and scorpions.

This teaches us, says the *Oznayim La'Torah*, that if this is the way the Torah speaks about an inanimate object such as a pit—highlighting only its positives—how much more so is it necessary when talking about human beings. We must highlight only that which is positive about them, and if need be to bring attention to something negative, it should only be done through subtle means.

Our speech needs to be positive and uplifting, our focus on that which is constructive and encouraging, and our relationships on hope and optimism.

Our responsibility is to attract people to the observance of Torah and mitzvos, something that is only possible if we talk in a positive and uplifting manner.

Yosef's Dreams

Yosef dreamed two dreams. In the first dream, his brothers' sheaves bow down to his.

The second dream would seem to mirror the message of the first, but in a slightly different way. Instead of sheaves, Yosef dreamed that the sun and the moon and eleven stars bow down to him.

---

4   *Bereishis* 37:24.
5   As per *Shabbos* 22a.

While the dreams have the same message—Yosef in a leadership role over the rest of the family—analysis of the differences between the two reveals a valuable lesson.

The first difference is that in the first dream, the sheaves do not bow down to Yosef but rather to his sheaf, whereas in the second, the luminaries bow down to Yosef himself.

A second difference is the reaction of the brothers to the dreams.

After the first dream, the *pasuk* writes that "ויוסיפו עוד שנא אתו"—They **hated** him even more,"[6] whereas the Torah records the response after the second as "ויקנאו בו אחיו"—His brothers were **jealous** of him."[7]

What can we learn from these differences?

The *Beis Halevi* suggests that the first dream dealt with material matters, and the second dream dealt with spiritual ideas.

The props in the first dream are the sheaves. Sheaves represent wealth and material success. That the other sheaves bowed down to Yosef's sheaf suggests that one day, the brothers will be financially dependent on Yosef.

The performers in the second dream were the sun, moon, and stars.

These represent heavenly and spiritual attainment. The bowing down of these luminaries to Yosef alludes to the possibility that Yosef will achieve a level of spiritual success that is greater than the rest of his family.

When the sheaves bow down in the first dream, they do not bow down to Yosef, because wealth and economic success are not a measure of the person himself.

A wealthy person is no more moral or just than a poor one, and vice versa.

The advantage of wealth is not an internal attribute but an external one, and it is certainly not a reflection of a person's character. Therefore, in the first dream, the brothers do not bow down to Yosef but to his sheaf. The Torah teaches us to respect and value a person for what they are, rather than for what they have.[8]

---

6   *Bereishis* 37:5.
7   Ibid., v. 11.
8   Moshe Sheinfeld, *L'shulchan Shabbos*, p. 128.

The second dream is the exact opposite. The sun, moon and stars represent spiritual achievement and refinement, and so the brothers bow down to Yosef himself because such a person is to be valued.

Now we can understand the different reactions to the dreams.

The reaction to the first dream is שנאה—hatred, not קנאה—jealousy, because although the brothers did not want Yosef to rule over them, they did not see material success as something to be envied.

The reaction to the second dream, which talked of spiritual attainment, is one of jealousy, as the Gemara tells us, "קנאת סופרים תרבה חכמה—The jealously between scholars increases wisdom."[9] The brothers wanted to achieve those spiritual heights alluded to in the dream, and they were, therefore, jealous of Yosef. They certainly did not hate him for attaining spiritual perfection; on the contrary, they wanted to emulate him.

The differences in the dreams and the reaction to them shows us that we value and want to emulate a person's spiritual achievements over any material success with which Hashem may have blessed them.

Try, Try, Try Again!

ויהי כדברה אל יוסף יום יום לא שמע אליה לשכב אצלה להיות עמה.

And so it was, she coaxed Yosef day after day, and he didn't listen to her to lie with her to be with her.[10]

The *Alshich* asks why is it that when the *yetzer hatov* wishes to encourage someone to do something positive, it tries once or maybe twice, and if the person is not interested, then the *yetzer hatov* leaves him alone and does not try again to encourage them.

The *yetzer hara*, on the other hand, will try and try to entice someone and will not give up until he has them ensnared in his trap.

9   *Bava Basra* 21a.
10   *Bereishis* 39:10.

The *Alshich* answers with an insight from the world of commerce:

If someone has an excellent product to sell, he does not need to try and convince people to buy. If he does not manage to trade in one place, he will be confident of finding a buyer in another, because the merchandise is high quality.

If, however, the products are of inferior quality, the merchant will have to try and convince people to buy them, and if he sees that he is not successfully convincing people to buy, he will have to keep trying.

The *yetzer hatov* knows that it has the most beautiful commodity to offer. It has the truth, the good, that which will bring happiness. The *yetzer hatov* does not need to convince people to "buy its goods." If these people don't listen to him, others will.

The *yetzer hara*, however, is peddling lies and falsehood. No one will be interested unless the *yetzer hara* batters them into submission. So, the *yetzer hara* will try and try again to entice a victim, not relenting until he is successful.

The *sefer Shaar Bas Rabim* writes that Chazal tell us Potiphar's wife had good intentions, as she saw, using astrology, that great people were going to be born to her from Yosef. If so, why did Yosef not see it as well? Why did he resist?

The answer is that ויהי כדברה אל יוסף יום יום—Potiphar's wife consistently pestered Yosef, and Yosef realized that if this were a positive thing, there would be no need for her to try so hard to convince him, and therefore, he realized that it must only be the work of the *yetzer hara*.

Often, the way to decide whether an act is positive or not is to look at how much convincing you need before you do it. If you find that you need to tell yourself again and again to perform it, then it may be the work of the *yetzer hara*, because if it were the truth, you would need very little convincing.[11]

---

11   *Otzeros HaTorah*, p. 243.

How Do I Know That God Loves Me?

וְאֵיךְ אֶעֱשֶׂה הָרָעָה הַגְּדֹלָה הַזֹּאת וְחָטָאתִי לֵאלֹקִים.

How then can I perpetrate this great evil and have sinned against G-d![12]

Hakadosh Harav Yankele Gutman notes that Yosef begins the *pasuk* by talking about sinning against his master, Potiphar, who had trusted him etc., and then he finishes by talking about G-d. Why?

The Midrash tells us that Potiphar's wife told Yosef that she had seen in her astrology that she was to have children with Yosef, and that therefore legitimized their actions together. (She was correct in the fact that Yosef would have children related to her, but they were born to her adopted daughter Osnas, who would marry Yosef.)

Yosef replied to her that to betray his master, who had placed his trust in him, was against human decency, and furthermore that Hashem would never sanction such actions.

If it is a "רָעָה גְדֹלָה—great evil" against his master and a betrayal of trust, then without a shadow of a doubt, it is a case of "וְחָטָאתִי לֵאלֹקִים—sinning against G-d."

Sometimes, we try to find religious justifications for actions about which we have serious misgivings.

The rule of thumb needs to be that if it is unacceptable to society, it is intolerable to Hashem.

Hashem wants us to behave in a way that is acceptable to society. Unless we have a direct mitzvah to the contrary, we must follow the dictum in *Pirkei Avos* that says: "כל שרוח הבריות נוחה הימנו רוח המקום נוחה הימנו—If the spirit of one's fellow is pleased with him, the spirit of the Omnipresent is happy with him."[13]

---

12   *Bereishis* 39:9.
13   *Avos* 3:13, quoted in *Maayanah shel Torah*, p. 172.

מקץ \ חנוכה

The Power of Deeds,
the Power of Words

ויאמרו איש אל אחיו אבל אשמים אנחנו.

They said to one another, "Indeed we are guilty."[1]

The story of Chanukah rests on the Chashmona'im finding one jar of oil that was still intact with the seal of the Kohen Gadol. They lit from the oil in this flask, and instead of lasting for one night, it shone for eight nights.

This famous flask with the seal has gone down in history. Every year, we retell its story. The question we need to ask is why the flask was sealed with the seal of the Kohen Gadol in the first place. Where in the Mishnah or the Gemara does it say that the oil in the Beis Hamikdash must be sealed with the seal of the Kohen Gadol?

The *Shabbos shel Mi* suggests that the reason the miracle occurred was because a certain Kohen Gadol performed his personal service in a manner that was above and beyond that which was required.

A Kohen Gadol is required to bring a personal *Korban Minchah* daily, which included oil as one of its ingredients. Although this only requires

---

1   *Bereishis* 42:21.

regular-grade oil, out of his love for this mitzvah, this particular Kohen Gadol used only extra-pure olive oil, and to differentiate his special oil from the regular oil, he placed it in unique jars to which he affixed his personal seal.

This is the jar that was found by the Chashmona'im and became famous in perpetuity.

This shows the importance of small acts and the effect that they can have. This Kohen Gadol performed an innocent act; the seal was merely a way of identifying his oil and differentiating it from the others, and yet it changed Jewish history and led to Chanukah.

We can never be aware of the full impact of our actions. Simple, trivial acts can have ramifications for generations. We have to be sure to act positively so that, as far as possible, we can ensure that our actions help perfect and bring optimism to the world and make a positive impact for generations to come.[2]

The Chafetz Chaim has a similar insight on *Parashas Mikeitz* regarding the power of words and their ramifications.

Not knowing that his beloved Rachel had stolen her father's idols, Yaakov Avinu says: "עם אשר תמצא את אלהיך לא יחיה—With whomever you find your gods, he shall not live,"[3] the consequence of which is Rachel's death. His words had come back to haunt him.

Therefore, when faced with a seemingly cruel and cunning adversary in Egypt, Yaakov Avinu does not fall into the same trap again. He does not curse this viceroy, but instead blesses his sons that they should be granted mercy by Hashem: "וא-ל ש-די יתן לכם רחמים לפני האיש—And [Hashem] will give you mercy before the man."[4]

The benefits of such an approach are obvious: Had he cursed the viceroy with death, it would have led to the death of his own son, Yosef![5]

---

2   *Inside Chanukah*, p. 177.
3   *Bereishis* 31:32.
4   Ibid. 43:14.
5   *Talelei Oros*, p. 304.

From the story of the flask of oil on Chanukah, we see the effect of positive acts, and from the way that Yaakov Avinu speaks regarding the viceroy in Egypt, we learn the power of and need for positive words.

Change? Yes I Can!

ואת אחיכם הקטן תביאו אלי ויאמנו דבריכם ולא תמותו ויעשו כן.

"Then bring your youngest brother to me so your words will be verified, and you will not die. And they did so."[6]

After accusing the brothers of being spies, Yosef insists that they bring Binyamin down to Egypt to corroborate their pleas of innocence.

Rav Shimon Schwab asks why it is necessary for the *pasuk* to end by saying, "ויעשו כן—And they did so." A few *pesukim* later, the Torah tells us that the brothers returned home to bring Binyamin, so why does the Torah need to say ויעשו כן; we know that they did it?

Rav Schwab suggests that at this stage, even though Yosef had accused them of being spies, when faced with their protests of innocence, he was willing to re-examine his position and to entertain the notion that he was wrong. Therefore, he sent them to bring Binyamin.

ויעשו כן tells us that the brothers were so impressed that the viceroy of Egypt could entertain the notion that perhaps he was wrong that ויעשו כן; they too began to entertain such thoughts.

Perhaps, despite all the years of justifying their actions against Yosef, they also had made a mistake.

The brothers had one opinion for twenty-two years, namely, that their actions toward Yosef were justified and that they were blameless. After twenty-two years, they begin to re-evaluate and arrived at a different conclusion.

---

6 *Bereishis* 42:20.

The lesson is that we need to continually evaluate and reassess our long-held positions and attitudes on so many topics. We need to ensure that what we hold to be true and correct and the way that we behave and conduct ourselves is in fact true and correct.[7]

On the theme of changing attitudes, Rabbi Isaac Bernstein highlights a meaningful change that we witness in connection with Yosef's behavior.

At the beginning of *Parashas Vayeishev*, Yosef is busy with dreams, as a result of which he ends up at the bottom of a pit.

At the beginning of this *parashah*, Yosef is once again dealing with dreams.

This time, as a result of those dreams, Yosef is elevated to viceroy over all of Egypt.

What is the difference between these two events involving dreams that caused such radically different results?

Rabbi Bernstein answers that at the beginning of *Parashas Vayeishev*, Yosef is busy telling everyone about what **his** dreams meant for the future. If you go around just talking about your dreams, then the inevitable result is that others will dislike you—to the point that they would throw you into a pit.

Parashas Mikeitz begins with Yosef interpreting Pharaoh's dreams. So, if you no longer focus on **your** dreams, but instead help other people and assist them in realizing **their** dreams, then instead of languishing at the bottom of a pit, it will elevate you to enjoy spiritual summits.

---

7   *L'titecha Elyon*, p. 347.

ויגש

Yes, We Can!

ואלה שמות בני ישראל הבאים מצרימה יעקב ובניו.

Now these are the names of the children of Israel who were coming to Egypt—Yaakov and his children.

P arashas *Vayigash* contains the first mini-census of the children of Yaakov who were in Egypt. The poll reveals that Binyamin had ten children, Gad had seven, Shimon had five, etc. Dan had only one child—Chushim—who, according to Chazal, could neither hear nor speak.

We can imagine the conversation in Dan's home, where he and his wife fear for the future as all their hopes rest solely on Chushim, and Chushim himself seems to face an uncertain and challenging future. On the other hand, Binyamin would feel quite confident that the future looks rosy with his large family of ten healthy sons.

Many years later, in *Parashas Bamidbar*, we find a counting of the nation of Am Yisrael after they left Egypt.

We would expect to see that Binyamin is a vast tribe, whereas Dan should be one of the smallest. Yet, Binyamin had only 35,400 men in its tribe, whereas Dan was the second-largest tribe with a total of 62,700.

The lesson is that it doesn't matter what cards life deals you; it's what you do with them that matters. Even if the odds seemed stacked against you, you can still be a success and live a fruitful and constructive life. A family of one disadvantaged child can grow into a tribe numbering in the thousands!

Rabbi Michoel Fletcher asks why it was that Binyamin, who started as the largest member of Yaakov's family with ten children, ended up as one of the smallest tribes? Does the Torah give us a clue that would perhaps help us to understand?

Rabbi Fletcher draws our attention to a comment of *Rashi* that Binyamin named each of his ten sons after their uncle Yosef and the *tzaros* that befell him. One was called Bela (בלע) to remind everyone that Yosef had been "swallowed up" (נבלע) somewhere amongst the nations. Another was called Becher (בכר) as a reminder that Yosef was the firstborn (בכור) of his mother, and so on.[1]

If your kids grow up in an environment with an unhealthy attachment to the past and its woes, it will affect them negatively. If their names, i.e., their very essence, are a continual reminder of troubles gone by, they will find it challenging to face the future with anything other than pessimism and negativity.

Under such circumstances, it is not too difficult to predict that a family of ten may not grow at the rate we would expect and would remain small.

We need to surround children with joy and happiness, laughter and fun, warmth and love. If we are successful in doing so, then our children have the foundation to face the future with optimism and to grow with confidence. Then, even if they seem to be disadvantaged and face challenges, they will be able to develop and grow to become great people capable of exceptional success.[2]

1   *Rashi, Bereishis* 43:30.
2   *Do You Know Parashas Hashavua?*, p. 90.

Where Did Prayer Take Me?

ויגש אליו יהודה ויאמר בי אדוני.

And Yehudah drew near to him and said, "If you please, my lord."[3]

The *Rokeach* writes that before we begin the *Amidah*, we take three steps forward, based on the three places in the Torah where it says ויגש.[4]

Hagaon Harav Shteinman wonders about this parallel. When Yehudah drew near to Yosef, it was because that is the way people behave when they want to speak privately to another person; they get as close as they can.

However, when we stand in front of Hashem, how are three small steps going to bring us closer to Him? They seem to be irrelevant.

The answer is that before we pray, we need to do some act, some movement, to make us feel that we can't stay in the same place and remain the same person as we were before prayer. Although the three steps are irrelevant in bringing the person physically closer to Hashem, they represent the realization that prayer is supposed to "move" us, and we can't remain in the same place.[5]

---

3   *Bereishis* 44:18.
4   Ibid. 18:23, 44:18; *Melachim I* 18:21.
5   *Talelei Oros*, p. 300.

One Kind Act Today, Many Effects Tomorrow

כִּי עַבְדְּךָ עָרַב אֶת הַנַּעַר מֵעִם אָבִי לֵאמֹר אִם לֹא אֲבִיאֶנּוּ אֵלֶיךָ וְחָטָאתִי לְאָבִי כָּל הַיָּמִים.

For your servant guaranteed the youth from my father, saying, "If I do not bring him back to you, then I will be sinning to my father for all time."[6]

There is a powerful Midrash that highlights the reverberations of Yehudah's undertaking to protect Binyamin.

The Midrash says that the guarantee Yehudah gave Yaakov to bring back Binyamin never needed to be activated, because Yosef revealed his identity and everyone lived happily ever after.

When was the *arvus*—guarantee, implemented? The Midrash says that it was the days of Goliath.

Goliath was terrorizing the Jews during the reign of Shaul HaMelech, a descendant of Binyamin. A proclamation went around that anyone who could defeat Goliath would be given Michal, Shaul's daughter, as a wife.

Yishai said to his son, David, "We are the descendants of Yehudah, and now is our chance to fulfill the *arvus* that our grandfather Yehudah gave to Yaakov regarding Binyamin. If we save Shaul from Goliath, we will have helped a descendant of Binyamin."

When David defeated Goliath, he did so mainly to fulfill the guarantee of his grandfather Yehudah.

The story did not end with the death of Goliath. On a few occasions, as Shaul was chasing David to kill him, David had the chance to kill Shaul but never touched him. David, a member of the tribe of Yehudah, had a responsibility to protect those from the tribe of Binyamin.

The Midrash concludes that Hashem said to David HaMelech, "Because you protected Shaul of the tribe of Binyamin in the same way Yehudah

---

6   *Bereishis* 44:32.

guaranteed the safety of his brother Binyamin, the Beis Hamikdash will be built in the portion of Yehudah and the portion of Binyamin."[7]

The Midrash is a beautiful example of the far-reaching effects of our actions.

Yehudah stands up and places himself in possible danger to guarantee the safety of Binyamin. This act had implications in the battle of David and Goliath.

This act was instrumental in the way that David treated Shaul, and this act was responsible for the positioning of the Beis Hamikdash.

We must never underestimate the far-reaching effects of our positive acts.

We must never fall into the trap of saying, "What difference does it make?"

Everything we do makes a difference, even if the effects are only felt generations later.[8]

With Malice toward None

ויגש אליו יהודה ויאמר בי אדני.

And Yehudah drew near to him and said, "If you please, my lord."[9]

T he Kotzker Rebbe suggests that the word אליו means אל עצמו—that Yehudah rehearsed what he was going to say to Yosef by repeating it to himself—אליו. His words would be deep in his heart so that they would be דברים היוצאים מהלב—words that emanate from the heart, and thus would be נכנסים אל הלב—enter the heart of the one who hears them.[10]

7   Midrash Tanchuma, Vayigash.
8   L'shulchan Shabbos, p. 159.
9   Bereishis 44:18.
10 Otzar Chaim, p. 314.

In a similar vein, the Ohr Hachaim Hakadsoh suggests that the meaning of ויגש אליו is that Yehudah knew that to ensure that his petition stood a chance of succeeding, he had to harbor no negative thoughts about Yosef.

In *Mishlei* it says, "כמים הפנים לפנים כן לב האדם לאדם—As water reflects back to a face, so one's heart is reflected back to him by another."[11] Had Yehudah approached Yosef with malice in his heart, he would stand no chance of success. Yehudah had to put love for Yosef in his heart, which would hopefully engender a similar response in Yosef. But this needed effort, and therefore, ויגש אליו, Yehudah had to make an effort, אליו, in order to draw Yosef near to him in his heart so that Yosef would feel the same way toward him!

The Brisker Rav says that it would seem that Yehudah's pleas of אב זקן, ילד זקונים קטן, ואחיו מת וכו׳ are not connected to the actual act of Binyamin stealing the goblet but are requests for clemency, over and above the letter of the law.

Clemency is usually only granted by the king, and that is why Yehudah says to Yosef, כי כמוך כפרעה, which *Rashi* understands to mean, "חשוב אתה בעיני כמלך—In my eyes you are like a king" and therefore you can grant a pardon and clemency.

This is why the *pasuk* says, ידבר נא עבדך דבר באזני אדני, i.e., without the interpreter between us, because amnesty is better asked personally, not through another party.

The problem is that Yosef had pretended not to understand their language and therefore placed an interpreter between them, so what did Yehudah hope to achieve by removing the interpreter? Yosef would not understand him!

The Brisker Rav says that we see from here the power of a heartfelt plea. דברים היוצאים מהלב נכנסים אל הלב—sometimes language is secondary to the sincerity of the intent!

Since Yehudah had worked hard to place love for this viceroy into his heart, it was not necessary for there to be a common language.[12]

---

11   *Mishlei* 27:19.
12   *Talelei Oros*, p. 302.

ויחי

Say "No" to Sibling Rivalry!

ויברכם ביום ההוא לאמור בך יברך ישראל לאמר ישמך א׳ כאפרים
וכמנשה.

*And he blessed them on that day, saying, "With you shall Israel
bless, saying, 'May G-d bless you like Ephraim and Menasheh.'"*[1]

The custom is to bless our sons on Friday night with the blessing:
ישמך אלוקים כאפרים וכמנשה. Why do we specifically want our children to be like Ephraim and Menasheh as opposed to Avraham,
Yitzchak, and Yaakov, or Moshe, Aharon, and David?

One answer suggested by Rabbi Shlomo Riskin is that when Yaakov
Avinu placed his right hand on Ephraim, clearly indicating that although he was younger than Menasheh it was he who was to have the
main *berachah*, what was Menasheh's reaction? Does the Torah record
that he was upset with his grandfather? Did he bear a grudge against his
younger brother from that moment on?

The Torah makes no mention of Menasheh's reaction because there
was no reaction. Menasheh did not allow the situation to cause any rift
between him and his younger brother. He did not use it as an excuse for

---

1   *Bereishis* 48:20.

sibling rivalry. Therefore, we bless our sons with the blessing of ישמך אלוקים כאפרים וכמנשה—that in the same way that they did not suffer from sibling rivalry or jealousy, we wish for our sons to likewise grow up in harmony and love without the pettiness of jealousy and rivalry![2]

The Dubno Maggid says that Menasheh learned this lesson from Yaakov Avinu himself. When Yaakov Avinu wanted to give the blessing to Ephraim, the younger grandchild, he could have just placed Ephraim on his right and avoided the necessity to cross his hands. Why did he keep Menasheh on his right and Ephraim on his left and cross his hands? It was to teach an important lesson: that not every child needs to get the same from their parents, but every child needs to get what they need.

By keeping Menasheh on the right, Yaakov Avinu was informing him that, "you are still the older grandchild, and you will always receive what it is that you need as the older grandchild. It is just that at this particular time, I need to place my right hand on Ephraim and not on you."

Menasheh was thereby reassured that he would receive what he needed and that his brother would likewise receive what he needed, and therefore any ill-feeling was avoided, and the incident passed without adverse effects.[3]

What Generation Gap?

ישמך אלוקים כאפרים וכמנשה.

May G-d bless you like Ephraim and Menasheh.[4]

It is a tradition that every Friday night, we bless our sons with the words ישימך אלוקים כאפרים וכמנשה.

Why specifically Ephraim and Menasheh as opposed to any of the other great men in Jewish history? Why not Avraham, Yitzchak, and

---

2   *Torah Lights*, p. 317.
3   *Otzar Chaim*, p. 238.
4   *Bereishis* 48:20.

Yaakov to parallel the blessing of Sarah, Rivka, Rachel, and Leah that we give our daughters?

Rabbi Yisroel Moshe Fried infers an answer from a previous *pasuk* where Yaakov says, "אפרים ומנשה כראובן ושמעון יהיו לי—Ephraim and Menasheh shall be mine like Reuven and Shimon."[5]

We know that every generation is said to experience a spiritual decline from the previous generation, a phenomenon called *yeridas ha'doros*.

Yaakov saw that this was not the case with Ephraim and Menasheh. They had not experienced a drop in their spirituality and were כראובן ושמעון, on the same level as their uncles, one generation before them.

The Gemara tells us that "בכל אדם מתקנא חוץ מבנו ותלמידו"—A person is jealous of everyone other than his son and his pupil."[6] A father is never jealous of a son, and therefore he hopes that his son will one day grow to be spiritually higher than he is.

Therefore, every Friday night, the father blesses his son that he should outshine his father. The father hopes that there will be no *yeridas ha'doros* and that the son will reach up to and even exceed all that the father has accomplished. The father's wish is that his son should emulate Ephraim and Menasheh, two Jews who did not experience spiritual decline but were instead כראובן ושמעון יהיו לי[7]!

Therefore, the blessing is ישימך אלוקים כאפרים וכמנשה.

---

5   Ibid. v. 5.
6   *Sanhedrin* 105.
7   *Shalom Rav*, p. 254.

We Can and Must Bring Mashiach! Now!

ויקרא יעקב אל בניו ויאמר האספו ואגידה לכם את אשר יקרא אתכם באחרית הימים.

Then Yaakov called for his sons and said, "Assemble yourselves, and I will tell you what will befall you in the End of Days."[8]

Rashi says that Yaakov Avinu wished to reveal the date of the arrival of the Mashiach, but Hashem did not wish him to do so, so Hashem removed the *Shechinah* from Yaakov Avinu, and he moved on to a different topic.

Why did Hashem not wish that Yaakov Avinu reveal the date of the "end of days"?

The *Shnei HaMeoros* quotes the Midrash that says that when Yaakov Avinu wanted to reveal this information, Hashem said to him that since He had changed his name from Yaakov to Yisrael, he was not permitted to disclose the date!

What is the connection between his name change and the inability to reveal when Mashiach will arrive?

The Gemara tells us that there are two possibilities as to when Mashiach will arrive. It will either be בעתה—in its designated time, or, if we all do *teshuvah*, then אחישנה—it will be hastened and will arrive before its predetermined time.[9]

The Jewish People have two names: Yaakov and Yisrael.

Yisrael appears after Yaakov Avinu had defeated the angel of Eisav and represents the Jewish People when they fulfill the will of Hashem.

The name Yaakov represents the opposite. It appears at Yaakov's birth and relates to him holding on to Eisav's heel. It represents an attachment to physicality and is used when we are not behaving as we should.

---

8   *Bereishis* 49:1.
9   *Sanhedrin* 98, interpreting *Yeshayahu* 60:22: בעתה אחישנה. הקטן יהיה לאלף והצעיר לגוי עצום אני ה' בעתה אחישנה.

With this understanding, we can now approach the Midrash and answer our question.

The reason Yaakov was not allowed to reveal the *acharis ha'yamim* is because his name has changed to Yisrael, and as Yisrael, we can hasten Mashiach's arrival. As Yisrael, we do not have to wait for the predetermined date of Mashiach's arrival but through *teshuvah* we can bring him earlier than expected.

Therefore, says Hashem, do not reveal the date of *acharis ha'yamim*, because you can now ensure that the time is earlier, and to disclose the predetermined date is to negate the power you and your children have to bring Mashiach.

The message is that **we** have the ability to hasten the arrival of Mashiach.

Not only do we have the ability, but we have the duty as well. Hashem did not want Yaakov Avinu to reveal the predetermined date, because Hashem expects us to do all that we can to hasten Mashiach's arrival.[10]

> *Rabbi Shlomo Riskin tells the story of the time that he was in Meah Shearim in Jerusalem and went to visit a bookseller by the name of Reb Shmuel.*
>
> *Reb Shmuel was a mystic who used to abstain from talking and frequently entered into taanis dibbur.*
>
> *On this particular occasion, when Reb Shmuel saw Rabbi Riskin, he greeted him warmly and even exchanged a few words with him!*
>
> *Surprised, Rabbi Riskin inquired as to the reason for his unusual behavior, and Reb Shmuel informed him that "Mashiach has arrived in Yerushalayim."*
>
> *Although not totally convinced, when Rabbi Riskin prayed later at the Kosel, he did so with more enthusiasm than usual.*

---

10   *Maayanah shel Torah*, p. 220.

Later that evening, Rabbi Riskin listened to the news, half expecting there to be a special announcement regarding the sighting of Mashiach in Yerushalayim.

The newscaster made no such announcement!

When he returned to the bookstore, Rabbi Riskin challenged Reb Shmuel and said that he had waited for the Mashiach in vain.

Reb Shmuel corrected him and said, "You are gravely mistaken. We do not wait for Mashiach; he is waiting for us!"[11]

---

11   Rabbi Shlomo Riskin, *Listening to G-d*, p. 300.

ספר
שמות

שמות

Challenge the Status Quo, Wake the Yetzer Hara

The pattern that repeats itself throughout the *parashah* seems to be that after a ray of positivity and a glimmer of hope that the dream of salvation is about to be realized, comes a crushing blow of increased servitude and a worsening of the situation.

- Moshe Rabbeinu is born, and the house fills with light,[1] and later he is placed in a basket in the river to escape from Pharaoh's murderous decree.
- Moshe is brought up in the palace, but later Pharaoh wants to have him killed.
- Moshe turns up with cries of "Let my people go," and not only are they not released but their position becomes worse.

From here we learn a valuable lesson that applies to our private lives as well as to understanding the process of our national rebirth.

Pharaoh epitomizes the *yetzer hara*. The *yetzer hara* loves nothing more than inactivity. It craves the status quo. It does not want us to wake up and start engaging in new projects, ideas, or endeavors. Its *modus operandi* is as Pharaoh said, תכבד העבודה על האנשים...ואל ישעו בדברי שקר—

---

1   *Rashi, Shemos* 2:2.

83

let's keep the people so busy earning a living, dealing with the family, taking care of the house, following sports, etc., that they will not have time to engage in *divrei sheker*, literally, false words—what the *yetzer hara* thinks of the Torah!

As long as we remain within that inactive mode, the *yetzer hara* is happy.

However, if we start to wake up and see that there is more to life than that presented by the *yetzer hara*, then it has to get busy doing all that it can to prevent us from straying from its path.

When Moshe begins the process of redemption, Pharaoh—the epitome of *yetzer hara*—is stirred into action.

The Jews want to leave.

They have a leader demanding their release.

They are challenging the status quo!

To combat this reawakening, Pharaoh increases the workload, placing barriers in the way of any progress.

It is an exact metaphor for how the *yetzer hara* reacts to any attempt a person makes to grow.

This being the case, we can approach life's challenges with an optimistic outlook.

If I am experiencing challenges, large or small, it is a sign that I have stirred the *yetzer hara* into action. If I have shaken the *yetzer hara* into action, and it is trying with all means available to stop me, I must be doing something positive.[2]

We find the same idea in connection with the *rasha* in the passage about the four sons in the Haggadah.

The reply we give the wicked son is "הקהה את שיניו—Knock out his teeth," which seems a little extreme. What is it teaching us?

Rabbi Shai Piron relates that his father was a dentist, and as a child, he was always fascinated by the various noises that he heard in his father's clinic. He was particularly interested in the fact that when his father would take a tool and blast some air against a tooth, the reaction of the patient would be to jump or to squeal.

---

2   *Taaroch Lefanai Shulchan*, p. 139.

He asked his father to explain, and his father told him that if the tooth is dead, the patient will not react when having air sprayed against it. If, however, the tooth was alive, then the patient would it feel and scream. We can now understand the meaning of הקהה את שיניו.

In the same way that a live tooth causes a reaction, if the *rasha* reacts and starts to shout and to defend his lifestyle, then the *rasha* is alive. If he is alive, then there can be dialogue, discussion, and connection.

If, however, he shows no reaction to הקהה את שיניו, then we may have lost him in the same way as we would a dead tooth!

The fact that the *yetzer hara* wishes to make things as hard as possible for us is because we are alive!

- Alive to the possibility of achieving our potential in life.
- Alive to the possibility of forging a relationship with the Almighty.
- Alive and unwilling to remain with the status quo of spiritual inertia and religious apathy.

If the *yetzer hara* is snapping at our heels, let us take that as a sign that we are moving in the right direction, and let us work to defeat the *yetzer hara* and continue to move forward.

Individual, Nation, and Humanity

ויקח משה את אשתו ובניו וירכבם על החמר וכו'.

And Moshe took his wife and children and mounted them on a donkey.[3]

Rashi quotes a Midrash and says that the donkey on which Moshe Rabbeinu placed his family was the same donkey that was used by Avraham Avinu on his way to perform the *Akeidah*, as it says,

---

3   *Shemos* 4:20.

וישכם אברהם בבקר ויחבש את חמורו.[4] It is the same donkey on which the Mashiach will arrive.

What is the connection between these three events?

The *Oznayim La'Torah* suggests that they each played a critical role in bringing the world toward its ultimate goal.

Man was put in this world with the mission of perfecting his animal side and elevating it in the service of Hashem. Adam HaRishon failed in the first test, allowing the physical to dominate him, and as a result he damaged the entire creation, and we have been trying to amend for his actions ever since.

Along came Avraham Avinu, and instead of allowing his animal to ride over him, ויחבש את חמורו, he rides over his animal and is able to suppress his natural desire and to follow only that which Hashem wishes. This enables him to perform the *Akeidah*. Thus, Avraham Avinu shows that an individual can control the *chamor* within him and elevate it to a higher calling. Avraham Avinu's task was to amend the failing of Adam and to show that *tikkun ha'middos* in an individual is possible.

Then we have Moshe Rabbeinu, who received the Torah and taught that it is possible not only for an **individual** to rule over his *chamor*, but that an **entire nation**, by adhering to the teachings of the Torah, can also elevate and perfect itself. That is why, when he is on his way to redeem the Jewish nation from Egypt, a redemption that will lead them to becoming a ממלכת כהנים וגוי קדוש, he places his family on the *chamor* to symbolize that the path to spiritual perfection begins with having control over the animal/physical. This is a graduation from Avraham, in that Avraham saddled his *chamor* for himself, while Moshe put others on the *chamor*, namely his family, showing that the control over the *chamor* was now a communal act.

Finally, it will be the turn of the Mashiach. If Avraham Avinu proves what is possible for an individual, and Moshe Rabbeinu teaches what is expected of a nation, the Mashiach will come riding on his *chamor* to teach what is possible for all of humanity. When Mashiach arrives, the

4   *Bereishis* 22:3.

entire world will be aware that the *chamor* of Avraham Avinu, the *chamor* of Moshe Rabbeinu, and the *chamor* of the Mashiach are all the same. They all teach us that spirituality begins and ends with the obligation and the ability to control our physical desires.

The Pursuit of Perfection

ויאמר יתרו למשה לך לשלום.

And Yisro said to Moshe, "Go to peace."[5]

Rabbi Shimshon Raphael Hirsch quotes the Gemara that says that when a person takes leave of his friend, he should not say, "לך בשלום—Go in peace," but rather, "לך לשלום—Go to peace," as this is the language used by Yisro to Moshe, whose subsequent mission to free the Jews was successful. As opposed to when David HaMelech said to Avshalom, לך בשלום, where things did not end well![6]

What is the reason for this?

One's life is a perpetual exercise in seeking *sheleimus*—perfection. We are continually working and striving **toward** it, but it is not attainable, hence, לך לשלום, "toward" peace and completion but not reaching it.

When life is over, we no longer can seek perfection; we have, to whatever degree, arrived. The level one has attained is the level at which he will stay. Hence, we say to the deceased, לך בשלום ותנוח על משכבך בשלום because the chase is over.[7]

We find the same idea in the language of the Mishnah. We say at the beginning of *Pirkei Avos*, כל ישראל יש להם חלק לעולם הבא, which we usually translate as "every Jew has a portion in the World to Come."

However, if that is correct, then it should have said, כל ישראל יש להם חלק בעולם הבא! What does it mean by saying לעולם הבא?

---

5 *Shemos* 4:19.
6 *Berachos* 64a.
7 *Otzar Mefarshei HaTorah*, p. 98.

One explanation is that while every Jew may have a portion in the World to Come because he is a Jew (כל ישראל), the size and quality of that portion depends on their actions while they are alive in this world. Therefore, every positive deed they perform impacts their עולם הבא; it counts **toward** their share, and hence the correct wording is לעולם הבא.

The message is that we must spend our lives seeking to achieve perfection with the knowledge that perfection does not exist. However, we must realize that the journey toward perfection and the effort made to attain it are the keys to the rewards that await us in the World to Come.

The Power of Belonging

ה׳ אלוקי אבתיכם נראה אלי אלוקי אברהם יצחק ויעקב לאמר פקד
פקדתי אתכם.

Hashem, the G-d of your forefathers, has appeared to me, the G-d of Avraham, Yitzchak, and Yaakov, saying, "I have surely remembered you."[8]

The Lubavitcher Rebbe notes that in addition to the incredible physical cost of the exile in Egypt, the Jews also paid a spiritual price.

When Hashem instructed the Yam Suf to split to permit the Jews safe passage through it, the sea asked, "What merit do the Jews have that the Egyptians do not? הללו עובדי עבודה זרה והללו עובדי עבודה זרה—Just as these (the Egyptians) are idol worshipers, so too these (the Jews) are idol worshipers!"[9]

We see that the spiritual level of Am Yisrael had indeed fallen.

Yet, when Hashem instructs Moshe to go down to Egypt and to begin the process of redemption, the first thing Hashem tells him to relay to the people is not a criticism about their spiritual shortcomings.

---

8   *Shemos* 3:16.
9   *Shemos Rabbah* 21.

The first message that the people receive from Hashem via Moshe is a reminder of their ancestry. Moshe reminds them from whom they descend, namely, Avraham, Yitzchak, and Yaakov.

Hashem charges Moshe to talk to the people about the beauty of their heritage, not to chastise them over their low level of spirituality.

Only later, before the command to bring the *Korban Pesach*, Moshe demands that they remove all their *avodah zarah*.

So too, in today's generation, the way to bring people closer to Judaism is not to lecture to them about the spiritual dangers of a non-observant life. The challenge is to inspire them about their heritage, their history, their ancestors and what they stood for. No one enjoys being lectured or rebuked!

When we find ourselves in positions of leadership—as parents, educators, or as friends—we need to inspire and be positive, and not to rebuke and to reprimand.

We need to connect people to their achievements and successes, and to assist in their growth and development.

וארא

But You Only Had Yourself in Mind!

Regarding the story of *yetzias Mitzrayim*, we find at least two occasions where the Torah teaches us the importance of *hakaras ha'tov*—having gratitude and showing appreciation for the good one has received.

In *Parashas Shemos*, when Moshe Rabbeinu was charged by Hashem with the mission of starting the process of the Exodus from Egypt, Moshe did not travel directly to Egypt from the desert where Hashem appeared to him at the burning bush, but instead took a detour and went first to visit his father-in-law, Yisro.

Why did Moshe Rabbeinu make this extra stop? Moshe said that when he arrived in Midyan, he was a refugee from Egypt, alone in a foreign land, and Yisro took him into his home, married him to one of his daughters, and sheltered him. He owed it to Yisro, as an act of *hakaras ha'tov*, to take leave of him properly.

So, even though the whole future of the B'nei Yisrael rested in Moshe's hands, and even though he had been given a direct commandment from Hashem to begin the process, *hakaras ha'tov*, showing gratitude and appreciation to Yisro, came first.

The problem is that before Moshe arrived in Midyan to begin with, Yisro had been ex-communicated by the people of Midyan for rejecting their *avodah zarah*, of which he had been the high priest. As a result, both he and his daughters were alone without any friends or support. So, when Moshe arrived in Midyan, a stranger who was unaware of their situation, it served Yisro's interests to invite Moshe in and to befriend him.

Perhaps this would be the opportunity to marry off one of his daughters. Hence, Yisro's kindness was not a noble act but one motivated by self-interest—and indeed, Moshe did marry Yisro's daughter Tzipporah!

We see from here that the obligation to show *hakaras ha'tov* is so significant that it applies even to someone who acted well to you only due to their self-interest! We need not ask what the motivation was; we just have to show gratitude for having been the beneficiary of someone's actions.

In another instance of *hakaras ha'tov*, *Rashi* tells us that Moshe could not bring the plague of lice because it entailed hitting the dirt, and it was that dirt that saved him when he buried the Egyptian who had been attacking the Jew.

The problem is that the dirt didn't save Moshe, because people informed Pharaoh as to what had happened, and Moshe needed to flee. The ground did not end up really saving him, so why did he owe the dirt a debt of gratitude?

We see from here to what degree one needs to have *hakaras ha'tov*. If someone tried to help but was unsuccessful, one still needs to have *hakaras ha'tov* toward him for his effort.

Even if someone acts in self-interest, or even if he tries to help but ends up being unsuccessful, we still have a duty to be grateful, to show appreciation, and to have *hakaras ha'tov*.[1]

1   *Yagdil Torah*, p. 103.

Correct Attitudes and Missing Letters

וְשַׂמְתִּי פְדֻת בֵּין עַמִּי וּבֵין עַמֶּךָ לְמָחָר יִהְיֶה הָאֹת הַזֶּה.

I shall make a distinction between My people and your people;
tomorrow this sign shall come about.[2]

When warning Pharaoh about the impending plague of
עָרוֹב —wild animals, Hashem says that He will bring about
a salvation that will set apart His people from Pharaoh's
Egyptians and that this miracle will occur tomorrow.

In other words, the wild beasts would only attack the Egyptians and
ignore the Jews.

The *Divrei Yisrael* quotes the Mishnah that says: "הָאוֹמֵר אֶחֱטָא וְאָשׁוּב
אֶחֱטָא וְאָשׁוּב אֵין מַסְפִּיקִין בְּיָדוֹ לַעֲשׂוֹת תְּשׁוּבָה —One who says, 'I will sin and
repent [tomorrow], I will sin and repent [tomorrow]' will not get the
opportunity to do *teshuvah*."[3]

A homiletical interpretation of this Mishnah is that the *tzaddik*
doesn't wait for tomorrow but repents immediately in case he doesn't
get the chance tomorrow. Whereas the *rasha* sins every day, thinking,
mistakenly, that he can always do *teshuvah* tomorrow.

It turns out, therefore, that the difference between a *tzaddik* and
a *rasha* is their approach to "putting things off until tomorrow."

Thus, we can now understand the *pasuk* as follows:

- וְשַׂמְתִּי פְדֻת —I will make a distinction between my people and
  your people
- לְמָחָר יִהְיֶה הָאֹת הַזֶּה —The sign of this distinction will be לְמָחָר, i.e.,
  what is their attitude toward tomorrow?

Is it that of the *rasha*, that we should sin today and put off *teshuvah*
until tomorrow, or is it that of the *tzaddik*, who does *teshuvah* now, for
who knows what tomorrow will bring?[4]

---

2   *Shemos* 8:19.
3   *Yoma* 8:9.
4   *Idis She'B'idis*, p. 79.

The approach of the *tzaddik* brings with it the rewards of a better tomorrow.

The *P'nei David* notes that the word אות can mean either a sign or a letter.

In our *pasuk*, the word פדת—distinction, is written חסר, missing the letter ו. Even though the plagues distinguished between the Jews and the Egyptians and brought a measure of salvation in that the Jews were unaffected by them, nonetheless, since the B'nei Yisrael were not free, the redemption was incomplete; it was חסר.

However, if we adopt the correct attitude toward מחר and do *teshuvah* now, rather than delaying it until tomorrow, then this will bring the final redemption. The פדות will be total and complete, and we will spell the word with all of its letters, including the ו.

Then, it will be a case of מחר יהיה האות הזה—that the redemption of tomorrow, the final redemption, will have all of its letters—האות הזה![5]

It is our responsibility to bring the complete redemption of tomorrow by embracing the *tzaddik's* attitude and not putting off the *teshuvah* of today until tomorrow.

Slowly, Slowly Wins the Race

ויאמרו החרטמים אל פרעה אצבע אלוקים הוא ויחזק לב פרעה ולא שמע אליהם כאשר דיבר ה'.

The sorcerers said to Pharaoh, "It is the finger of G-d!" However, Pharaoh's heart became hardened, and he did not listen to them, as G-d had said.[6]

Rabbi Yitzchak Meir Shapira asks why Hashem first brought two plagues that the sorcerers could imitate, i.e., blood and frogs, and only at the third plague of lice was it impossible for them to

---

5   *Ohr Chaim*, p. 47.
6   *Shemos* 8:16.

copy, so much so that they said, אצבע אלוקים הוא. Why not bring the lice first to forestall any misunderstanding of what was going on?

The answer is a clear insight into human nature, and that is that when confronted with a truth that contradicts our own opinion, it takes time for that truth to sink in, even if the evidence is indisputable!

Had the lice been the first plague, then the Egyptians would have found a way to dismiss it out of hand.

Hashem first brought blood and then frogs because even though the Egyptian sorcerers could replicate them, the truth was slowly seeping in. They were aware that there was a difference between the blood and frogs brought through witchcraft and those created by Hashem.

Slowly, slowly, the truth sank in, to the point that at the plague of lice, they were ready to proclaim, "אצבע אלוקים הוא—It is the finger of G-d."

It is the cumulative effect of little actions and thoughts that have a more significant and longer-lasting impact than a sudden major event of substantial proportions.[7]

Rabbi Yechiel Bruckner explains that the rule of תדיר ושאינו תדיר that something that is more frequent takes precedence, is one that governs all of our relationships:

- בין אדם למקום—Our relationship with Hashem needs to be based on a consistency of service—a תדיר.
- בין אדם לחבירו—Likewise, the ingredients of a good friendship or relationship are not the one-off acts of kindness that we may perform for other people. Instead, we evaluate relationships by the "constant" actions, the תדיר, that more often than not go unnoticed.

Having said all that, the תדיר itself presents its challenges.

How do I keep a relationship fresh, spontaneous, and exciting, and avoid it becoming stale?

If all I have are the constants, the תדיר, then, in essence, it is the same thing repeating itself over and over!

Once again, we turn to the rule of תדיר ושאינו תדיר and note that the

7   *L'titecha Elyon*, p. 127.

law ends by saying, תדיר קודם, which means that תדיר does not eradicate the שאינו תדיר but rather that it takes precedence over the שאינו תדיר.

In any relationship, between man and G-d, or between man and man, there must be a שאינו תדיר element. As the Gemara notes regarding *tefillah*, a stale prayer is called, כל שאינו יכול לחדש בה דבר[8]—one in which one cannot find anything new, exciting, or spontaneous to say.

In *Parashas Bechukosai*, referring to the blessings that will accrue if בחוקותי תלכו, it says: "ואכלתם ישן נושן וישן מפני חדש תוציאו—You will eat ancient grain and remove the old to make way for the new."[9]

We need to eat, consume, and remove the old attitudes that lead to stale and lifeless relationships, and make way for התחדשות—renewal, a renewing and refreshing of our relationship with Hashem and of finding new ways to connect with family and friends.[10]

In essence, therefore, every relationship needs to have at its core loyalty and consistency that is represented by the תדיר, which is קודם.

However, we need to ensure that at the same time, every relationship has spontaneity and freshness, as represented by the שאינו תדיר, which is not ignored completely but is just secondary to the תדיר.[11]

Your Troubles Are Hurting Me

ואלה שמות בני לוי לתלדתם, גרשון וקהת ומררי.

And these are the names of Levi's sons in order of their birth: Gershon, Kehas, and Merari.[12]

Our *parashah* lists the names of the families of Reuven, Shimon, and Levi. However, if we look at the *pesukim*, we find that the verse speaking about Levi adds the words: "And these are the names…"

8 *Berachos* 29b.
9 *Vayikra* 26:10.
10 *Otzar Chaim*, p. 195.
11 *Seridei Aish, Haggadah shel Pesach*, p. 10.
12 *Shemos* 6:16.

The *Shelah Hakadosh* asks why the words ואלה שמות are mentioned only in the context of the sons of Levi.

He suggests that the words ואלה שמות are an indicator that we should carefully examine the names of Levi's children and the reasons for them. They were all a reflection of the pain that Levi felt for his brothers who were suffering under the oppressive hand of Pharaoh and Egypt.

- גרשון is an allusion to the fact that B'nei Yisrael were strangers (גרים) in a foreign land.
- קהת is in testimony to Levi's teeth feeling blunt due to his brothers' suffering.
- מררי stands for the bitterness of slavery.

Although the tribe of Levi was not involved in the physical aspect of the slavery, Levi named his children with allusions to it so that during the dark days and nights, they would at least identify emotionally with their brothers' plight.

They may be powerless to change the situation, but that did not exempt them from feeling their brothers' pain.

Therefore, the Torah says, ואלה שמות—look at these names and take note.[13]

Hashem Himself acts in a similar fashion. The Torah tells us that before *Matan Torah*, Moshe, Aharon, the Elders, Nadav, and Avihu all approached the mountain and "ויראו את אלקי ישראל ותחת רגליו כמעשה לבנת הספיר—They saw the G-d of Israel, and under His feet was the likeness of sapphire brickwork."[14]

Rashi explains that the brickwork that Hashem kept under His feet was there at the time of the slavery in Egypt as a constant reminder of the trials that the Jews were experiencing.

The Egyptians forced the Jews to find the raw materials with which to build bricks and imposed on them an impossible daily quota. The bricks

---

13   This is not the same as Binyamin, who named his children after his personal suffering (see above, *Parashas Vayigash*, "Yes, We Can!"). Here, the B'nei Levi were acknowledging other people's pain.

14   *Shemos* 24:10.

symbolized the Jews' suffering, and therefore, Hashem kept a sapphire brick under His feet.

The time was not yet right for Hashem to bring the *geulah*; it was as if there was nothing He could do. However, that did not prevent him from identifying with their pain through the symbolism of the brick.

Through this action, Hashem teaches us a powerful lesson. Often, we face painful situations that we are powerless to change. We hear of someone's misfortune, illness, or tragedy. We read of a community's struggle or a country facing national disaster. We may be powerless to act, but that does not absolve us from feeling their pain.

No man should be an island, and at the very least, in the same way as Hashem always feels our pain, we should feel theirs as well.[15]

---

15   *L'shulchan Shabbos*, p. 199.

בא

The Challenge Not to Speak

ולכל בני ישראל לא יחרץ כלב לשונו.

But against all the Children of Israel, no dog shall whet its tongue.[1]

The Midrash says that as a reward for not barking on the night of makkas bechoros, dogs were rewarded forever after in that meat found to be treif is given to them, as the pasuk says: "ובשר בשדה טרפה לא תאכלו לכלב תשלכון אותו—You shall not eat the flesh of an animal that was torn in the field; to the dog you shall throw it."[2]

In Parashas Va'era, we find that when Moshe Rabbeinu brought the plague of frogs, the pasuk says:

"ובאו בביתך ובחדר משכבך ועל מיטתך ובבית עבדך ובעמך ובתנוריך ובמשארותך—The frogs will come into your palace and your bedroom and your bed and into the house of your servants…**and into your ovens and into your kneading bowls.**"[3]

---

1   *Shemos* 11:7.
2   Ibid. 22:30.
3   Ibid., v. 28.

Yet, when Moshe Rabbeinu ends the plague, the *pasuk* says: "וימתו הצפרדעים מן הבתים מן החצרת ומן השדות—And the frogs died from the houses, from the courtyards, and from the fields."[4]

What happened to those in the ovens and the kneading bowls? Why are they not mentioned at the conclusion of the plague?

The *Kli Yakar* answers that those frogs who were *moser nefesh al kiddush Hashem* by going into the difficult places, i.e., the kneading bowls and the ovens, were actually saved and did not die together with the other frogs! As a reward for jumping into the ovens and risking life and limb for Hashem, they were saved.

Hakadosh Reb David of Tolna asks that for just keeping quiet and not barking, the dogs are rewarded with a reward that is ongoing for generations, namely, that they will always receive the *treif* meat, and yet for risking their lives and jumping into the ovens, the frogs were rewarded with a one-off reward, that they would not die in Egypt with all the other frogs.

Wouldn't we expect the reward for risking one's life to be greater than for holding their tongues? What is the message here?

The message, says Reb David, would seem to be that controlling one's mouth and keeping quiet when you have something to say is more challenging than jumping into a boiling hot oven!

So strong is the temptation to share gossip or *lashon hara* that someone who controls his mouth and overcomes such a temptation is rewarded in a far greater way than someone who performs a one-off act of heroism![5]

4   Ibid. 8:9.
5   *Yagdil Torah*, p. 132.

What You Mean and What You Say

ולכל בני ישראל לא יחרץ כלב לשונו.

But against all the Children of Israel, no dog shall whet its tongue.[6]

The *Chasam Sofer* quotes the Gemara that says that when Eliyahu HaNavi is in town dogs play, and when the *malach ha'maves*—the Angel of death, is in town, the dogs bark.[7]

If so, we would have expected the dogs to be barking in full force during *makkas bechoros*, and yet the *pasuk* tells us that ולכל בני ישראל לא יחרץ כלב לשונו. How did this happen?

The *Chasam Sofer* explains that the dogs did not bark at *makkas bechoros* because there was no *malach ha'maves* at *makkas bechoros*. Hashem Himself performed the plague. Therefore, the dogs did not start barking.

We can infer this from the words of our *pasuk*: ולכל בני ישראל לא יחרץ כלב לשונו—and why not? Because, as the *pasuk* continues, "למען תדעון אשר יפלה ה' בין מצרים ובין ישראל—In order [that] you should know that I, Myself, differentiated between Egypt and Israel."

If you want a proof that it was Hashem Himself who brought *makkas bechoros*, it is found in the fact that the dogs did not bark.[8]

Another lesson that emerges from this *pasuk* is a warning to B'nei Yisrael not to think one thing in one's heart but say another with one's mouth.

When davening, concentrate on the words, their translation, and their meaning, and keep in mind to Whom we are praying so that our heart and our words are in sync.

Likewise, in business, don't say one thing but mean another. Be honest, speak clearly, and say what you mean.

6   *Shemos* 11:7.
7   *Sanhedrin* 60a.
8   *Talelei Oros*, p. 174.

In every relationship, be authentic and genuine.

- ולכל בני ישראל—all Jews
- לא יחרץ—don't be too clever
- כלב לשונו—*K-lev*, what they say should be what they mean (in their heart).[9]

The Moon and Humility

החדש הזה לכם ראש חדשים, ראשון הוא לכם לחדשי השנה.

This month shall be for you the beginning of the months; it shall be for you the first of the months of the year.[10]

The *Chida* explains why it is that the Jewish calendar is lunar and not solar-based.

The *pasuk* says:

"לא מרבכם מכל העמים חשק ה' בכם, ויבחר בכם כי אתם המעט מכל העמים"—Not because you are more numerous than all the peoples did Hashem desire you and choose you, for you are the fewest of all the peoples."[11]

The Gemara explains the *pasuk* to mean that what endears us to Hashem is the fact that even when He charges us with greatness, we do not make ourselves big or large but rather we act with humility.[12]

Although He gave greatness to Avraham Avinu and told him that he was to be "אב המון גוים—a father of many nations," Avraham Avinu nevertheless was able to say, "ואנכי עפר ואפר—I am but dust and ash!"

Although He gave greatness to Moshe and Aharon, they were able to say, "ואנחנו מה—And what are we?" David HaMelech said of himself, "ואנכי תולעת ולא איש—I am worm and not man."

---

9   *Idis She'B'idis*, p. 157.
10   *Shemos* 12:2.
11   *Devarim* 7:7.
12   *Chullin* 89a.

Therefore, *Rashi* explains the words לא מרבכם to mean: "you do not make yourselves large but little, and therefore Hashem desires you as His nation."

This lesson is also learnt from *kiddush ha'chodesh*—sanctifying the new month, which takes place when the moon is at its smallest.

The Gemara cites the famous complaint of the moon as to why Hashem created them equal in size.

The moon turned to Hashem and complained: "אי אפשר לשני מלכים שישתמשו בכתר אחד—Two kings cannot wear the same crown," and as a result Hashem shrunk the moon, making it smaller than the sun.[13]

Each month, when we proclaim the new month by seeing the moon in its smallest state, we are reminded of the consequences of *gaavah*—arrogance and pride, and are moved to live a life of humility.

Thus, when the *pasuk* says, החדש הזה לכם, it means that the fact that we count the months according to the moon should be a lesson for you (לכם) about humility.

Why So Many Plagues?

Why did Hashem impose ten plagues on the Egyptians? Couldn't He have extended one plague over a longer period and accomplished the same goal? Imagine if the plague of blood had extended for six months. The Egyptians would not have survived without any drinkable water for that length of time.

If locusts hovered over Egypt for six months, it would have been unbearable.

Yet, Hashem chose to afflict the Egyptians with a variety of plagues rather than to just focus on one specific plague. Why?

To answer this question, Rabbi Shalom Rosner quotes the Dubno Maggid, who offers a parable:

---

13   Ibid. 60b.

There is a difference in the way one prepares food for himself versus how he prepares it for others. If I am cooking for myself, I cook the one dish that I want at the time. However, if I am cooking for a large group of people, I have to offer a variety of dishes. A restaurant cannot offer just one main dish on its menu. Different people's palates are touched in different ways. There must be a choice so that one can select the item that is most attractive to him.

Based on this parable, Rabbi Rosner quotes the *sefer V'Karasa La'Shabbos Oneg*, which explains the purpose of the plagues.

The plagues were not just a tool to convince Pharaoh to free the Jews. Instead, they were an educational tool for the Egyptians and the Jews.

Different events inspire different people. Hashem implemented a spectrum of plagues because people related to each plague differently. Some felt that darkness was the worst, others were affected most when Hashem struck them personally with lice, etc. The purpose was to be able to connect with each and every individual Egyptian and Jew.

This applies concerning mitzvah observance as well. The last Mishnah in *Masechta Makkos* states: "רצה הקב״ה לזכות את ישראל לפיכך הרבה להם תורה ומצות—[Hashem] wanted to give merit to Yisrael, therefore He increased for them Torah and mitzvos." Why are they considered a merit?

Everyone is obligated to fulfill each mitzvah, but there are certain mitzvos that speak to us more than others.

There are *bikur Cholim* Jews, Talmud Torah Jews—all types. For people, it is easier to connect to a particular mitzvah and to excel in it.

The same is true of the *chagim*. Some connect to one more easily than another. Some are Purim Jews, while others identify most with Pesach, and yet others with Shavuos. We each must fulfill all of them, but we may connect to some more deeply than to others.

That is why it is a merit that Hashem blessed us with so many mitzvos, because it ensures that there is a favorite mitzvah for everyone.

Hashem inflicted a variety of plagues on the Egyptians to touch the hearts of each and every Egyptian and Jew. No two people experience or view things the same way. Ask those gathered around your Shabbos or Seder table to state which plague they believe was the worst, and there surely will be a variety of answers.

Thus, the Torah is providing us with a methodology: When we teach our children, we need to keep in mind the principle of חנוך לנער על פי דרכו.

Education is not a one-size-fits-all exercise; as each pupil experiences things differently, and different subjects will appeal to different students.

When transmitting Torah, we must find the proper approach so that we can motivate and excite each of our children to appreciate and internalize Torah in their own unique fashion.[14]

---

14   *Torah Tidbits* vol. 1358, p. 28.

בשלח

Challenges, Challenges

ויהי בשלח פרעה את העם.

And it was when Pharaoh sent out the people.[1]

Why does the Torah use the word ויהי when describing *yetzias Mitzrayim* if the word ויהי has negative connotations?[2]

The word ויהי has negative connotations because the word יהי is future tense, "it will be," and the letter ו, when used as a prefix, changes the tense from future to past; hence ויהי, "and it was." When the future looks so bleak that you want it to be in the past, that is something negative.

The opposite is the word והיה, "and it will be," where the word היה is past tense and the prefix ו changes it into the future; hence והיה, "and it will be." When the past was so good that you wish it to be repeated in the future, that is positive.

So, what negative aspect of ויהי בשלח פרעה את העם is being alluded to with the use of the word ויהי?

The Manchester Rosh Yeshiva, Rav Yehudah Zev Segal, explains that

---

1   *Shemos* 13:17.
2   *Megillah* 10b.

we see that Hashem took B'nei Yisrael on a circular route so that they should not become disheartened if they should have to fight a war. It is axiomatic that Hashem never gives us a challenge that we cannot overcome.[3] If the straight path would lead us to war, and Hashem didn't lead us on that path because it would be too difficult for us, it means that the circular path was one on which we could overcome any obstacle that would be placed in our way, and it would not be too difficult for us.

There would be challenges, but ones we would be able to overcome, because challenges by definition are conquerable.

So, if we went on the circular path, it meant that we could overcome any challenge we'd encounter, and yet we find that B'nei Yisrael nonetheless often complained to Hashem. Several times, they complained about the lack of water; they grumbled about the lack of meat, so Hashem sent the quail, etc. The B'nei Yisrael did not seem to overcome the challenges that were presented to them.

That is why the verse states, ויהי בשלח פרעה את העם. The Jews were led out of Egypt in a way that showed that Hashem is looking after them and does not challenge them with a challenge they cannot overcome. However, they did not understand this and complained, hence ויהי.[4]

Nature Is One Big Miracle

ובני ישראל הלכו ביבשה בתוך הים.

And the Children of Israel went on dry land in the midst of the sea.[5]

I n one verse, it says, "ויבאו בני ישראל בתוך הים ביבשה—B'nei Yisrael came into the sea on dry land,"[6] placing the sea first. Seven verses later, it says, ובני ישראל הלכו ביבשה בתוך הים, mentioning the dry land first. Why the change?

---

3   *Avodah Zarah* 3a.
4   *L'titecha Elyon*, p. 225.
5   *Shemos* 14:29.
6   Ibid., v. 22.

The *Chasam Sofer* explains that the change is to teach an essential lesson in our approach to nature. He uses an analogy to explain:

There was once a very talented artist who decided to paint a life-size painting of the king's horse. Using all his skill, he managed to produce a stunning replica of the horse.

Due to its size, the painting was too large to bring inside his gallery, so the artist left it outside by the door.

As he watched from inside the gallery, he noticed that people were walking by and not paying any attention to his master-piece—the horse. He was so troubled by this that he went outside for a closer look.

He realized that the reason why people were not stopping to marvel at his painting of the horse was because the depiction was so accurate and so lifelike that people thought it was just a horse standing at the door of an art gallery, and consequently, they paid it scant attention.

What did the artist do? He placed a frame around the paint-ing. People then instantly realized that it wasn't a horse but a picture, and they started to stop and inspect this marvel of a portrait outside the gallery.

Human nature is such that we are so used to "the dry land" that we pay it little attention and do not marvel at the wonder of Hashem's creation. Therefore, Hashem put a "frame" around it in the form of *k'rias Yam Suf* that forever reminds us of the glory of Hashem's world.

When we started walking, the ground turned from dry land, which we usually ignore, to dry land within the sea—בתוך הים ביבשה!

From that moment on, we could never look at the dry land as just dry land. It would always be part of the wonder of Hashem's creation; it became יבשה, dry land that was made special בים—because of what happened at the sea.[7]

---

7   *Raayonos U'Biurim*, p. 87.

All of nature is one big miracle that we tend to ignore. Hashem places a frame around it, and then we start to take notice.

Faith vs. Knowledge

ויאמינו בה׳ ובמשה עבדו.

And they believed in Hashem, and in Moshe His servant.[8]

If *emunah* means faith or belief, then its use seems to be out of place in this *pasuk.*

Rashi tells us that the words זה א-לי ואנוהו teach us that the manifestation of G-dliness at *k'rias Yam Suf* was so clear that every Jew who crossed the sea, even the humblest, could point with his finger and say, "This is my G-d."[9]

After the people had seen Hashem clearly enough to "point at Him," where is there room for faith? They know Hashem, they have experienced Hashem. They do not simply believe in Hashem, but rather know of Him clearly.

We see from here that the word אמונה does not mean "faith," but "faithful."[10]

Now that they knew Hashem, they undertook to be faithful to that knowledge—even at times when Hashem might seem distant from them, or if they did not see Hashem or hear from Him for the next 3,000 years.

Thus, when we talk about a Jew needing to have *emunah*, we do not mean faith or belief but rather faithfulness to the knowledge handed down over the generations.

---

8   *Shemos* 14:31.
9   Ibid. 15:2.
10   See *Daas Torah, Bereishis.*

This explanation is apparent in the *pasuk* that describes Moshe holding his hands up during the battle with Amalek, where it says, ויהי ידיו אמונה עד בא השמש.[11]

None of the classical translations of the word, such as faith or belief, make sense in this context. Moshe did not believe his hands were there; he knew his hands were there. What it means is that his hands were faithful to him and did the job he needed them to do.

Likewise, when we talk about the need to have *emunah*, it means being faithful to the job that we need to do in perfecting this world through *avodas Hashem*.

A Brief Glimpse of G-d, a Lifetime of Work

ויאמינו בה׳ ובמשה עבדו.

And they believed in Hashem, and in Moshe His servant.[12]

The *Kedushas Levi* writes that once the Jewish People had experienced such a spiritual elevation that they reached the level of ראתה שפחה על הים מה שלא ראה יחזקאל בן בוזי, they then began to realize that it was possible for a human being to reach the level of Moshe Rabbeinu. This is the meaning of the words ובמשה עבדו in this *pasuk*. It does not mean that until now the Jews had doubts over the leadership of Moshe Rabbeinu and now, due to the miracle of the splitting of the sea, those doubts had been allayed.

Instead, it means that having been shown what level of prophecy a person can rise to, they now believed that each one of them could reach the level of Moshe Rabbeinu.

11   *Shemos* 17:12.
12   Ibid. 14:31.

This was the point of giving people who didn't really deserve it a taste of what they could achieve. Now, no one doubted what could be attained if they put their minds to it, and the gap between who they were and the level they needed to be on to receive the Torah at Sinai became less daunting.

They were now able to accept the spiritual demands of receiving the Torah because they had tasted, albeit for a brief moment, achieving that level.

The same idea is echoed in the Gemara that tells us that a baby in the womb is taught the entire Torah and then forgets it as he exits the womb and enters the world.[13] If that is the case, what is the point of teaching it all to him?

The answer is so that he has tasted what could be achieved and can now work his way back to making it![14]

---

13   *Niddah* 30a.
14   *Maayanah shel Torah*, p. 69.

יתרו

It's Only One Word, Why All the Fuss?

לֹא תִשָּׂא אֶת שֵׁם ה' לַשָּׁוְא כִּי לֹא יְנַקֶּה אֶת אֲשֶׁר יִשָּׂא אֶת שְׁמוֹ לַשָּׁוְא.

You shall not take the name of the Lord, your G-d, in vain, for the Lord will not hold blameless anyone who takes His name in vain.[1]

T he *Ohr Hachaim Hakadosh* writes that included in this prohibition is to carry Hashem's name by pretending to be a religious person while engaging in activities that are anything but pious.

"Do not take Hashem's name in vain"—if you are going to present yourself as a G-d-fearing person, then behave like a G-d-fearing person should—in private and in public.[2]

However, the simple reading of the *pasuk* is that it is referring to taking Hashem's name in vain.

Why is taking Hashem's name in vain such a serious offense that the Torah says, לֹא יְנַקֶּה, Hashem will not absolve anyone who does it?

Rabbi Meir of Premishlan suggests, almost tongue-in-cheek, that when someone transgresses any other sin, it is recorded in his personal

---

1   *Shemos* 20:7.
2   *Maayanah shel Torah*, p. 91.

file. When that person repents, the record is erased from the file. However, if he takes Hashem's name in vain and then repents, when the file is taken out to erase the sin, there will be a problem.

It is forbidden to erase Hashem's name, so there is no way to remove it.[3]

Wit aside, a serious point is being made here. We are very quick to weigh which mitzvos or *aveiros* have more importance than others. But our calculations are likely to be wrong, and something such as taking Hashem's name in vain is seen as a severe violation, whereas something that we hold to be more extreme is not. Our task is just to do what is correct, leaving the calculations up to Hashem.

Mountains and Molehills

וירד ה׳ על הר סיני אל ראש ההר.

Hashem descended upon Mount Sinai, to the peak of the mountain.[4]

The Gemara relates that Hashem chose Mount Sinai as the mountain on which to give His Torah to the Jewish people because it was the humblest of all the mountains.[5]

We are familiar with the Midrash that describes how all the mountains assumed that the Torah would be given on them because they were the highest, most significant, most fertile, etc.

Only Mount Sinai was humble and thought that the Torah would not be given on it because it had no advantage over the others.

The Kotzker Rebbe asks that if the idea was to impart a lesson in humility, why give the Torah on a mountain in the first place? Why not give it in a low valley or in a crater? A lowly venue would demonstrate the importance of humility better than any mountain.

---

3   *Otzar Chaim*, p. 117.
4   *Shemos* 19:20.
5   *Sotah* 5a.

The Kotzker Rebbe learns from this that we can only find humility in great people.

A person is not being humble by not boasting about his achievements if he has not achieved anything. A person who has nothing to show off about also has nothing about which to be humble. The lesson of humility could only be taught on a mountain. Although it was an impressive mountain, it maintained its humility.

Hashem wants us to be achievers. He wants us to change and perfect the world and live a life that is full of achievements and contributions to our community and society.

However, at the same time, we should realize that as this is the reason why we are put on this earth in the first place, to boast about it is like bragging that you can breathe air.

Hashem wants us to be a mountain, but a humble one![6]

The Icing on the Cake

When Hashem offered the Torah to Am Yisrael, their unequivocal reply was נעשה ונשמע, where the נעשה represents the physical fulfillment of Torah and mitzvos, and נשמע relates to the learning of Torah. What is the relationship between the two? How much emphasis and importance in that relationship is to be placed on the נעשה, and how much on the נשמע?

The story is told of the great Reb Zusha, who once arrived in a city where there was a person steeped in Torah knowledge and who spent endless hours learning and studying the texts but had very little time for *gemilus chassadim*.

Reb Zusha approached this gentleman and requested his help in collecting funds for a particular worthwhile cause. The man refused, noting that he did not wish to waste valuable time from his learning. After all, he said, תלמוד תורה כנגד כולם!

---

6   *Talelei Oros*, p. 310.

Reb Zusha sat the man down and told him the following story:

In a particular village lived a very wealthy man who bought a very expensive, beautiful coat and wore it to shul. After davening, everyone approached the man to tell him how impressed they were with the coat, and the wealthy man went home with many compliments ringing in his ears.

Seeing how impressed people were with this coat, one of the town's poor people sold all his possessions and with the money went and bought the identical coat to the one that the rich man had worn to shul. However, when the poor man wore the coat to shul, instead of complimenting him, everyone laughed and ridiculed him.

The poor man was at a loss as to why everyone laughed. Wasn't his coat identical to the rich man's?

The people replied that under the rich man's coat is a perfectly tailored jacket that sits atop a custom-made shirt that is crisp and clean. The man's pants are made to measure and ironed to perfection, and his shoes sparkle in the sunlight. Therefore, the expensive overcoat perfectly complements all that is underneath it.

"You, however," they told him, "are still dressed in rags, and therefore, the coat is out of place, sitting in stark contrast to that which is underneath it."

So too, said Reb Zusha, when we are taught that תלמוד תורה כנגד כולם, it means that Torah learning needs to be the cherry on the top of the cake, i.e., that it complements all the other mitzvos that are beneath it. תלמוד תורה is the expensive coat that completes the look.

However, if all you have is *talmud Torah* and nothing else, it is akin to placing an expensive coat on top of rags; not only does it not compliment, but it is also out of place![7]

---

7   *Matamei Shulchan Shabbos*, p. 338.

Our נשמע—dedication to Torah study, must complement our נעשה—commitment to observing all of the mitzvos. They must work hand in hand so that our relationship with Hashem is total, for one without the other is incomplete.

The First, the Last, and the Summary

לא תחמד.

Do not covet.[8]

The *Rosh* writes that from the first letter of the Ten Commandments—the letter א' of אנכי—to the last letter—the ך' of לרעך—there are 613 letters, which correspond to the 613 mitzvos.[9]

The *Maadanei Melech* writes that it is no accident that the Ten Commandments finish with the word לרעך.

The halachah is that when one writes a document, one needs to summarize it at the end, just above where the witnesses sign.[10]

Now, when the non-Jew came to Hillel and asked him to teach the whole Torah while he was standing on one foot, Hillel's reply was, "Do not do to others what you would not want to be done to you. This is the whole Torah; the rest is commentary, now go and learn."

Apparently, ואהבת לרעך כמוך is the essence of the entire Torah. The word לרעך is the last word of the Ten Commandments because it summarizes all of the commandments—in the form of ואהבת לרעך כמוך.[11]

In relation to the prohibition to covet, the obvious question is that people are human. If we see something that is pleasing and it is

8 *Shemos* 20:14.
9 *Bein Adam LaParashah*, p. 275.
10 *Choshen Mishpat* §44.
11 *Idis She'B'idis*, p. 329.

something that we want, it is only natural that we will desire it. How can we observe לא תחמד?

The *Ibn Ezra* draws an analogy to a country lad who travels to the big city and catches a glimpse of the beautiful princess as she passes by in her parade.

The country lad will not covet the princess, as he knows that she is way above his station, and it is unthinkable that their lives would cross paths. So should be our attitude to anything that we desire that isn't ours. It is not ours in the same way that the princess is not for the country lad. It is above our station, we have no way of getting it, and thus there is no point in craving it. It is as futile as coveting a bird's wings because you want to be able to fly.

According to this approach, the first and last of the Ten Commandments are both matters of the heart.

אנכי ה' demands that we entrench knowledge of Hashem in our hearts, and the last commandment forbids desiring with our hearts that which isn't ours.

However, a more in-depth perspective is that by fulfilling the first commandment and being conscious of אנכי ה', it means that we appreciate that what we have is all that we're supposed to have. If we're supposed to have what our friend has, we would have it.

Therefore, the key to observing לא תחמד (and all of the other commandments) is to keep אנכי ה'.

In fact, for this reason, the *Beis Halevi* rejects the analogy of the *Ibn Ezra* and suggests that the way to overcome the desire that leads to לא תחמד is not to consider the item outside of your realm of possibility but to strengthen your relationship with the mitzvah of אנכי ה'.

I *do* want it, but I am not permitted to covet it because Hashem has instructed me not to.

The more יראת ה' a person has, the easier it is to fulfill לא תחמוד and all the other mitzvos.[12]

---

12   *Taam V'Daas*, p. 133.

משפטים

Hate Falsehood, Love People

מדבר שקר תרחק ונקי וצדיק אל תהרג כי לא אצדיק רשע.

Distance yourself from a false matter; and do not kill a truly innocent person or one who has been declared innocent, for I will not vindicate a guilty person.[1]

Two gentlemen were speaking, and one said to the other that they are very much alike except for one significant difference. "You love *emes*, and therefore, anything that contains a grain of *emes* is exciting for you. Although the majority may be *sheker*, since there is a grain of *emes*, you will concentrate and magnify that shred of *emes* and accept the whole situation. I am completely the opposite. I detest *sheker*, and therefore, a situation that is overwhelmingly *emes* but contains some *sheker*, I reject out of hand."

Which one of these is the correct approach?

The Torah tells us that the approach of hating *sheker* is the one to follow. מדבר שקר תרחק—anything that contains *sheker* needs to be distanced.

---

1   *Shemos* 23:7.

However, that only applies to situations, ideas, or philosophies, not to people.

In our quest to uproot *sheker*, we must not fall into the trap of demeaning people who are held in high regard because we feel that there must be some *sheker* contained within them; they can't be as good/holy/religious as everyone thinks.

When it comes to human relationships, we need not seek out any *sheker* that we think may be hiding beneath the surface, but we must treat people as we find them.

The *pasuk* tells us, ונקי וצדיק אל תהרוג[2]—if someone is a *tzaddik*, don't go looking for anything wrong in them. Why not? Because כי לא אצדיק רשע—we can leave it to Hashem. If someone who is thought of as a *tzaddik* really isn't, Hashem will see to it that the truth comes out.

Our hatred for *sheker* has to be complete, but not aimed toward righteous people.[3]

What a Wonderful World!

שלש פעמים בשנה יראה כל זכורך אל פני האדון ה'.

Three times during the year, all your males shall appear before the Master, Hashem.[4]

The Gemara states, regarding the mitzvah of *aliyah la'regel*, מה לראות בשתי עיניו אף ליראות בשתי עיניו[5]—that if someone is visually challenged in one eye, he is exempt from the mitzvah of *re'iyah*.

The *Noam Elimelech* says that we are born with two eyes: one to see the *gadlus ha'Borei*—the greatness, grandeur, and magnificence of

2   *Shemos* 23:7.
3   *Idis She'B'idis*, p. 369.
4   *Shemos* 23:17.
5   *Chagigah* 2a.

Hashem and His world—and the other to see *shiflus atzmo*—how, in comparison, we are nothing.

When a person only sees with one eye, he doesn't see *shiflus atzmo* and doesn't realize that life is a journey of continual hard work toward perfecting oneself. Even if he considers *gadlus ha'Borei* with the other eye, he is still exempt from turning up in front of Hashem on Yom Tov, because there is no place for such a person. Hashem does not need ego-driven individuals to visit His house three times a year!

And, perhaps, the reverse is also true. If someone is so preoccupied with his own self-perfection and working on his *middos* that he does not stop for a moment to acknowledge *gadlus ha'Borei*, the magnificence of the world and its Creator, he too is not welcome in Yerushalayim.[6]

We live in a world of glorious beauty that Hashem has given us to enjoy, and through that enjoyment to grow closer to Him. We must not miss this opportunity by declaring that we are not worthy.

Healthy self-esteem allows us to know who we are and what we can achieve.

What we are is the handiwork of the Almighty, and while we may be insignificant when compared to Him, He has told us that what we can achieve in this world is of significance.

True Tzaddikim and Bribes

ושחד לא תקח...ויסלף דברי צדיקים.

You shall not accept a bribe, for a bribe will blind the clear-sighted and corrupt words that are right.[7]

I n the rest of the Torah, whenever the word "*tzaddikim*" is written, it is written *chaser*, without the extra letter י. Only in our *pasuk* is it written *malei* with two. Why?

---

6   *Otzar Chaim*, p. 148.

7   *Shemos* 23:8.

Rav Chaim Kanievsky explains that the reason why the word is usually written *chaser* is to indicate that there is no such thing as a complete *tzaddik*, as the *pasuk* says, אֵין צַדִּיק בָּאָרֶץ אֲשֶׁר יַעֲשֶׂה טּוֹב וְלֹא יֶחֱטָא. Everyone is human, and everyone makes mistakes.[8]

However, here the word is written *malei* to tell us that even if the individual **is** a complete *tzaddik*, if he takes a bribe, then even such an individual will become corrupted.

What is even more important to bear in mind is that *Rashi* asks that later, the Torah warns the judges against taking bribes,[9] so what is the difference between these two warnings?

Rashi says that the latter verse is a warning against taking bribes to rule falsely, whereas the caution against bribes in our *pasuk* is not to take a bribe, even if it is to give the correct verdict. Even in such a scenario, there is a prohibition against accepting a bribe.

If so, our *pasuk* is talking about a complete *tzaddik* who may be tempted to take a bribe to ensure that the **correct** verdict is reached, and yet the Torah tells us that even this is a recipe for corruption and is forbidden.[10]

The *Oznayim La'Torah* writes that the prohibition regarding accepting bribes—in the form of gifts or favors—applies even **after** the case has been concluded, and this is what the *pasuk* means when it says:

- כִּי הַשֹּׁחַד יְעַוֵּר פִּקְחִים—The bribe blinds those who see
- וִיסַלֵּף דִּבְרֵי צַדִּיקִים—And corrupts the words of the one who has already found to be correct in this case.

Even after the case, the judge must not accept a gift.

When the Steipler Gaon was involved as an arbitrator between Rav Yaakov Halperin and the Eidah Chareidis, he was walking together with Rav Halperin in the street. Rav Halperin took out a cigarette and offered it to the Steipler as he would always do when they walked along. The Steipler refused to take it, as he was now an arbitrator in a case

---

8   *Koheles* 7:20.
9   *Devarim* 16:19.
10   *Talelei Oros*, p. 85.

that involved Rav Yaakov Halperin, and to accept would be akin to accepting a bribe.

Rav Yaakov Halperin used to add that not only while the dispute was ongoing was the Steipler careful not to accept anything that might be a bribe, even after the case had been settled, he could no longer bring the Steipler his esrog as he had been accustomed to doing. He constituted that as accepting a bribe, even after the case was closed.

A bribe need not be financial. Anything that may sway the judge's opinion is considered a bribe and disqualifies the judge from presiding over the case.

A widow once came in front of Hagaon Rebbe Yeshayaleh Kotner in tears, complaining about the cruel way that the townspeople were treating her.

Rebbe Kotner immediately disqualified himself from being involved in this case on the grounds that a bribe can also come in the form of tears. Who can fail to become emotionally involved when faced with the tears of a widow?[11]

---

11   *Maayanah shel Torah*, p. 104.

תרומה

No Jew Will Be Left Behind!

והיו הכרבים פרשי כנפים למעלה...ופניהם איש אל אחיו.

The keruvim shall have their wings spread upwards...with their faces toward one another.[1]

The *parashah* deals with the building of the *Mishkan* and its vessels. Perhaps the holiest of all the *keilim* was the *Aron*, on top of which stood the two *keruvim*. The *pasuk* specifies that the wings of the *keruvim* were spread upward, while the base formed a single unit with the cover of the *Aron*.

What is the symbolism of this formation?

Rabbi Shalom Rosner quotes the *Shem Tov*, who suggests that the spread wings symbolize that the goal of every Jew is to strive upward toward greatness.

The base signifies that our spiritual yearnings need to be grounded in the Torah, which lies inside the *Aron* from which the *keruvim* grow.

We must recognize that spiritual highs are only positive if they are grounded in the Torah.

---

1   *Shemos* 25:20.

Rabbi Rosner notes that there is another message in the *pasuk* that qualifies the first message: the *keruvim* must face each other. The Torah is teaching us that spiritual accomplishments must never come at the expense of others.

We must never step on someone else in order to improve our relationship with Hashem. We must bring others up with us, not push them down in order to raise ourselves.

We must spread our wings but still face our fellow human beings.[2]

Rabbi Y.Y. Jacobson quotes the Lubavitcher Rebbe, who says that Jewish exile began with Reuven. In the episode of Yosef and his brothers, it was Reuven's idea that the brothers should not kill Yosef but place him in a pit. Chazal tell us that Reuven intended to return and help Yosef escape from the pit. The *pasuk* tells us that after the brothers had placed Yosef in the pit, they sat down to have a meal. It was during this meal that a group of Yishmaelim came by, and Yehudah had the idea to sell Yosef to them, and the brothers agreed.[3]

Later, the *pasuk* tells us that Reuven returned to the pit to save Yosef, and to his horror, he found the pit empty.[4]

Rashi asks where Reuven had been, seeing as he was not present at the sale. Where is he returning from?

Rashi answers that he had been engaging in fasting and wearing sackcloth to atone for the sin of moving his father's bed after the death of Rachel. He was involved in the process of *teshuvah* and spiritual refinement. He was working on himself to grow in spirituality and get closer to Hashem.

The Rebbe says that this was Reuven's error.

How can a person allow himself the luxury of attempting spiritual perfection when a Jewish child is languishing in a pit!

When others are suffering—when Jewish girls and boys, men and women, are languishing in the pit of economic hardship, of low self-esteem, of alienation and emotional, physical, or religious pain—it is

2   *Shalom Rav*, p. 426.
3   *Bereishis* 37:25.
4   Ibid., v. 29.

not appropriate to concentrate on the finer details of spiritual perfection while ignoring them. The path of refinement into a G-d-fearing Jew must include sensitivity to the hardships of others and a commitment to help them.

Had Reuven been aware of this message, he would have stayed to ensure Yosef's safety and only then concentrated on his spiritual refinement. He wasn't, and as a result, Yosef was sold down to Egypt, and *galus* began.[5]

Although our wings must face upwards, our faces still need to be turned toward each other.

Unity

והבריח התיכון בתוך הקרשים מבריח מן הקצה אל הקצה.

And the middle bar amid the planks shall [extend and] penetrate from one end to the other end.[6]

The *Targum Yonasan* explains that this middle bar inside the planks was made out of wood that miraculously had rubber-like qualities that allowed it to bend, and it was one piece that encircled the entire *Mishkan*.

Rav Zeidel Epstein, Mashgiach of Yeshivas Torah Ohr, asks the obvious question: why was this miracle necessary? If it is essential, why did it only apply to the middle bar and not to the top and bottom bars that did not go straight through but were comprised of different pieces that joined together?

Rav Epstein answers that Hashem wanted to show us the level of *achdus* to which we have to strive.

---

5 Rabbi Y.Y. Jacobson, "When Religion Becomes Toxic and Full of Lies," minute 34:30.
6 *Shemos* 26:28.

We need to aspire to be one unified block—not simply different pieces that are stuck together, even if they are stuck together with the strongest glue.

Items that are stuck together may create something that is one, but they are not completely one and lack unity.

Something that is one continuous piece **is** *achdus*.

Such a level of unity is an ideal not readily achievable. So, the other bars were made up of multiple parts to assuage our fears and assure us that *any* level of joining together is a step in the right direction.

Slowly and surely, each act of unity will lead us to achieve the degree that we seek, which is to be united as one and not just joined as one.[7]

Spiritual and Material Focus

Rav Moshe Sternbuch quotes the Gemara that says: "הרוצה להעשיר יצפין והרוצה להחכים ידרים, וסמנך שלחן בצפון ומנורה בדרום—If one wishes to be wealthy, he should face the north, and someone who wishes to be wise should face the south,"[8] since the *Shulchan* was in the north, and the *Menorah* was in the south.

Rav Moshe Sternbuch points out that between the *Menorah* and the *Shulchan* stood the *Mizbei'ach Ha'ketores*—the Golden Altar on which the incense was offered. It represents fire, the fire of passion, the *mesirus nefesh* that is necessary to be successful in both spiritual and physical matters. It represents the dedication needed to set aside quality time for learning and working on one's *middos* in order to grow closer to Hashem, and the *mesirus nefesh* that it takes to use one's hard-earned finances to give *tzedakah* and perform *hachnasas orchim*.

The simple message of these *keilim* is that there is no such thing as a free lunch. Everything, whether it is physical or spiritual, requires hard work if you are going to be successful.

---

7   *L'titecha Elyon*, p. 452.
8   *Bava Basra* 25b.

Without the fire, the dedication, and the *mesirus nefesh* represented by the *Mizbei'ach*, then the physical blessings represented by the *Shulchan* and the spiritual bounty represented by the *Menorah* will be lost.[9]

Reb Saul Glasser noted that when a person enters the *Kodesh*, he faces the *Kodesh Hakodashim*, and his aim is toward spirituality and toward Torah. Therefore, as he walks, the *Shulchan* that represents physicality is on his right—the side of prominence—because if your focus is toward spirituality, then you can place a degree of importance on the physical.

However, as you turn to leave the *Kodesh*, turning your back on the *Kodesh Hakodashim* and making it no longer your focus, then the *Menorah*, representing spiritual blessing, is on your right, because you can no longer afford to emphasize the physical.

If our focus is toward the *Kodesh Hakodashim* and we are willing to put in the hard work and necessary *mesirus nefesh*, we have the recipe for spiritual success and the tools to enjoy material blessings.

---

9   *Taam V'Daas*, p. 181.

תצוה

Constantly Vigilant

באהל מועד מחוץ לפרוכת אשר על העדות יערך אתו אהרן ובניו מערב
עד בקר לפני ה׳ חקת עולם לדרתם מאת בני ישראל.

*In the Tent of Meeting, outside the dividing curtain that is in
front of the testimony, Aharon and his sons shall set it up before
Hashem from evening to morning; [it shall be] an everlasting
statute for their generations, from the children of Israel.*[1]

Rashi explains that when the *pasuk* says, מערב עד בקר, it means
that the Kohanim have to ensure that they place sufficient oil
into the *Menorah* to ensure that it remains lit from the evening
to the morning, even during the long winter nights.

Rav Yosef Zvi Dunner quotes Rabbeinu Ephraim, who asks what the
message is in this explanation of *Rashi*.

Rabbeinu Ephraim answers that we may have thought that a Kohen
would need to stand by the *Menorah* all night with a flask of oil on watch
in case the lamps needed "topping up."

Therefore, *Rashi* tells us that this wasn't necessary, as long as

---

1   *Shemos* 27:21.

sufficient oil was placed in the lamps at the beginning of the evening, the Kohanim didn't need to stand on watch the entire night.

Rav Dunner continues and says that this only applies to the lighting of the *Menorah* but not to what the *Menorah* represents, namely, the pure light of Torah. Whereas we did not need to watch all night to ensure that the oil burned as it should, and we could assume that if there was sufficient oil at the beginning of the night that everything went as planned, with Torah learning and spiritual growth, that is not the case.

When it comes to growth, we must never take our eye off the ball, and we always need to focus on achieving the goals that we set for ourselves. We continuously need to be on hand to "top up" our spiritual batteries if necessary. We cannot place a program of growth in place and then leave it to run automatically, because it won't. We must tend to it if we are to achieve success.[2]

I Need to Achieve— I Need to Move Forward

ויקחו אליך שמן זית זך כתית למאור.

And you shall command the children of Israel, and they shall take to you pure olive oil, crushed for lighting, to kindle the lamps continually.[3]

Rashi comments that כתית means that the olives were crushed in a mortar so that there was no sediment in the oil that they produced.

The requirement to use pure crushed oil only applied to the oil for lighting the *Menorah*; however, it was not necessary for the oil used for the *menachos*—the meal offerings.

---

2   *Mikdash Halevi*, p. 286.

3   *Shemos* 27:20.

The *sefer Chashavah L'tovah* writes that a person needs to have the attitude of כתית—having a crushed ego and displaying humility, the opposite of being proud and arrogant.

However, the obligation to see ourselves as כתית must not lead us to feel so broken that we do not want to do anything because we think that we have nothing to offer and just want to be left alone.

On the contrary, if we feel that we have not yet accomplished what we think we can, this should spur us on to make an extra effort to find an area in which we can excel.

Therefore, the Torah tell us that the oil must be כתית למאור—we must use כתית, the crushing of our negative ego, to enlighten the world, but not כתית למנחות, to use it as an excuse למנוחה—to rest and not attempt to change the world.

There is a fine line between humility and low self-esteem. While it is honorable to be humble, we should not hide behind humility to screen our low self-esteem.

We all have something to contribute.

We all have unique skills and talents.

We all must use them to make the world a better place.[4]

Arrogance vs. Healthy Self-Esteem

ועשית את הציץ...והיה על מצח אהרן.

And you shall make a Head-plate of pure gold...it shall be upon Aharon's forehead.[5]

The Talmud tells us that the *Tzitz* was placed on the *metzach*—the forehead of the Kohen Gadol, to atone for the sin of *azus metzach*—haughtiness.[6]

---

4   *Maayanah shel Torah*, p. 128.
5   *Shemos* 28:3
6   *Zevachim* 88b.

The *Chasam Sofer* points out that this is the reason why the *Tzitz* was the only one of the *bigdei kehunah* that had the words "*Kodesh La'Hashem*" on it. Why?

The *Chasam Sofer* explains that sin is only possible due to haughtiness. The sinner thinks, consciously or subconsciously, "Hashem tells me not to do something, but I know better, and therefore, I can override what Hashem has told me." There can be no greater expression of arrogance than this, and consequently, *azus metzach* is clearly something very negative.

However, we would not be able to perform any mitzvah without possessing some degree of *azus metzach*. The *yetzer hara* tells us not to perform mitzvos, and the wider world tells us not to perform mitzvos, sometimes our own family tells us not to perform mitzvos, and yet we manage to ignore all of them and fulfill the commandments! This can only be because we know better than them. It can only be because we have some arrogance.

Since *azus metzach* is sometimes negative and sometimes positive, the words "*Kodesh La'Hashem*" are written on the *Tzitz*.

We don't deny it, we don't totally negate it, but instead, we channel *azus metzach* to further our *avodas Hashem* and our relationship with Hashem. Our *azus metzach* needs to be *Kodesh La'Hashem*.

Hashem does not want us to negate, destroy, or remove the very characteristics that make us who we are. If, however, we tend toward certain negative features, we need to channel these to further our service to Him. Every characteristic that we have, and every action we take, should be *Kodesh La'Hashem*.[7]

---

7   *Nesivos Daas*, p. 576.

כי תשא

The Four Steps to Success

The *parashah* begins with the words כי תשא את ראש בני ישראל, which, when translated, literally mean, "When you lift up the heads of the Children of Israel."

This *parashah* contains the gravest of all the sins that the B'nei Yisrael committed during their stay in the desert—the *chet ha'eigel*—so how is it appropriate to talk about the Jewish People "raising their heads" in such a *parashah*?

The four main topics in the *parashah* are:

1. Shabbos
2. The *Mishkan*
3. The *machatzis ha'shekel*
4. The sin of the golden calf

Are these four random topics that happen to be mentioned together in one *parashah*, or are they grouped to deliver a particular message?

Rav Shimon Biton suggests that by arranging these topics together and starting the *parashah* with the words כי תשא, the Torah addresses two fundamental questions that everyone needs to ask himself regarding their direction in life.

The first question is: How can we take care to guard against falling into the seductive trap and warm embrace of the *yetzer hara*?

131

Second, if we do fall prey to the machinations of the *yetzer hara*, how should we react to avoid falling further? How do we extricate ourselves?

In answering the second question, the way to encourage the sinner to avoid further mistakes is not by rebuking or chastising him, but by emphasizing his greatness as a child of Avraham, Yitzchak, Yaakov, Sarah, Rivkah, Rachel, and Leah. Specifically in a *parashah* that deals with the greatest fall, we need to begin with כי תשא—raising up!

In answer to the first question, of how to avoid becoming entangled with the *yetzer hara* in the first place, the Torah gives us three answers by grouping three topics together in our *parashah*:

1. *Machatzis ha'shekel*—I am only half of the world, and other people complete it. In essence, everyone is one part of the same whole. I would not purposely damage my hand, saying that it is only part of my body; likewise, I will not do anything to hurt another Jew, as we are all part of the same whole.

   That is the foundation of all *mitzvos bein adam l'chaveiro*, and when the *yetzer hara* tries to tempt us to transgress any mitzvos between man and man, we need to remember the half-*shekel* and realize that hurting and damaging someone else ultimately pains and harms me.

2. *Mishkan*—the sanctity of space. Every person should ensure that they are in an environment that is conducive to spiritual growth. Our surroundings will play an essential role in pushing us onwards or holding us back.

3. Shabbos—the sanctity of time. Time is our most precious commodity, and we need to use it constructively by engaging in pursuits that encourage spiritual growth and mitzvah observance. If we are busy doing good, then we guarantee that there is no time to listen to the *yetzer hara*, and we will stay away from sin.

So, the three topics of *machatzis ha'shekel*, *Mishkan*, and Shabbos remind us of:

- The mitzvos between man and man
- The need to find a positive environment
- The need to keep busy with spiritual pursuits

The *parashah* then concludes with *chet ha'eigel* and comes full circle from where it began.

If the three topics teach us how to avoid sin, what happens if the *yetzer hara* entices us and we fall and sin?

The answer is כי תשא—we need to raise up the sinner.

After the sin of the golden calf, Moshe taught that the way to help people out of the vice-like grip of the *yetzer hara* is to elevate them by reminding them of their innate greatness.

The way to help the people out of the mistake of the *chet ha'eigel* was כי תשא את ראש בני ישראל—remind them who they are, from whom they descend, and the glorious future that awaits them.[1]

He Meant Well!

לך רד כי שחת עמך אשר העלית מארץ מצרים.

Go, descend, for your people that you have brought up from the land of Egypt have acted corruptly.[2]

The central event in our *parashah* is the *chet ha'eigel*—the sin of the golden calf.

The Gemara tells us that the sin was so grave that we still suffer its consequences; every punishment that Hashem visits on the world contains an element of punishment for the golden calf.[3]

Rabbi Shai Piron wonders what aspect of the *chet ha'eigel* was so disastrous that it turned into a mega-sin with ramifications that we feel even today.

In the *Kuzari*, Rabbi Yehudah Halevi suggests that the Jews felt that building the calf was justified and correct. The Jews wanted to serve Hashem, but they thought that they needed a physical medium

---

1 *Bein Adam LaParashah*, p. 337.
2 *Shemos* 32:7.
3 *Sanhedrin* 102a.

through which to do so. Their intentions were good, but their actions were mistaken.

The Jews did not sin with *avodah zarah* in the simplistic sense of the term but rather with an *avodah* that was *zarah* for our spiritual world. They had pure motives, but their actions were tragic.

If this was their sin, then we understand which element of the *chet ha'eigel* we are guilty of repeating, and why its ramifications are still being felt today. We often have the purest of motives, but our actions result in the impurest (*sic*) of outcomes.

Someone who is evil and knows that what he does is evil is less of a threat than someone convinced that he is saving the world but is actually destroying it.

The Izhbitzer Rebbe, on the words, לך רד כי שחת עמך, points out that the word רֵד is comprised of two letters that are enlarged in different places in the Torah.

The letter ר׳ is enlarged in the *pasuk* warning against serving *avodah zarah*, כי לא תשתחוה לאל אחר,[4] while we find a large ד׳ in the *pasuk*, שמע ישראל ה׳ אלוקינו ה׳ אחד.[5]

The significance is that we must never confuse the אחד for אחר. Sometimes, a person thinks he is serving Hashem when in fact he is acting at the behest of *avodah zarah*.

The difference between a ד׳ and a ר׳ is almost insignificant, but a small mistake can change an action from positive and welcome to harmful and destructive.

The challenge in life, says the Izhbitzer Rebbe, is not to distinguish between outright evil and good, for that is simple. The challenge is to ensure that we don't change אחד into אחר. Good is sometimes wrapped up in bad and vice-versa.

With all our good intentions, we may inadvertently give expression to evil while trying to defend what is good. We may think we are serving Hashem but end up building a golden calf.

---

4   *Shemos* 34:14.
5   *Devarim* 6:4.

We must view all of our actions with this in mind, and before we convince ourselves that we are saying שמע ישראל ה' אלוקינו ה' אחד, we need to ensure that our actions do not scream כי לא תשתחוה לאל אחר.[6]

Be Honest with Yourself!

When Moshe descended from the mountain after being told by Hashem that the people have sinned, he is greeted by the sight of the people dancing around a golden calf, rejoicing and declaring, אלה אלהיך ישראל.

The Klausenberger Rebbe notes that at this very instant, we see the greatness of Moshe Rabbeinu.

Rashi tells us that the Satan had shown the B'nei Yisrael a vision of a dead Moshe being carried to heaven. Believing that Moshe was dead, the people sought to replace him with a golden calf.

Moshe could have poured scorn on their actions by saying, "If you thought I was dead, why was it that you were rejoicing around the golden calf? Surely if you thought I was gone, the atmosphere while building the calf would have been sad and subdued. If you really felt that I was not going to return, you would have sat *shivah*, and mourned for a year, and yet what I see before me is more akin to a party than a wake!"

However, not only did Moshe refrain from rebuking them in this way, but when he returned to הקב"ה, he said that if You intend to destroy B'nei Yisrael, then, "מחני נא מספרך אשר כתבת—Erase me from Your book that You have written!" Even in the face of their seemingly ambivalent attitude toward Moshe's death, his one objective is to intercede with ה' on their behalf.

Here we see genuine leadership and the greatness of Moshe Rabbeinu.

The test of leadership is whether the leader acts purely and totally in the best interest of the people, leaving aside any element of self-interest or self-promotion.

---

6   *He'aros Shulayim*, p. 191.

Moshe Rabbeinu teaches us that whenever we find ourselves in a position of leadership—be it as parents, grandparents, teachers, or professionals—it is vital to always remember that the focus must be on the people we lead and their needs. We must never emphasize ourselves and how we can benefit from such a position.

The people may hurt us, upset us, even belittle us, but the focus needs to remain what is in the best interest of those people and how we best serve that interest.

Another important lesson along the same lines is that when the people gave the excuse that they had built the *eigel* because they thought that Moshe was dead, it was clear that this was not true. If it were true, they would not be dancing.

Why did they offer this as an excuse if it was obviously false?

Here we see the power of the *yetzer hara.*

The *yetzer hara* can convince us that our actions are permissible and sometimes even commendable when the truth is clearly the opposite, and this truth is sometimes made evident by our actions.

We need to be continually and honestly evaluating our actions. Is what I am about to do advisable, permitted, and positive? Or am I being deluded into thinking so, due to some weakness that has been exploited by the *yetzer hara?*

Am I truly in need of an intermediary now that Moshe Rabbeinu has seemingly died, or do I just want to serve *avodah zarah?* It is one or the other; there is no maybe.

May Hashem grant us the ability to make such an evaluation, to be honest about our intentions, and in that way, our actions will be permitted, positive, and pure.

ויקהל

How to Behave during the Coronavirus Pandemic

וכל הנשים אשר נשא לבן אתנה בחכמה טוו את העיזים.

And all the women whose hearts uplifted them with wisdom, spun the goat hair.[1]

When the Torah describes the preparations for the *Mishkan*, it emphasizes the wisdom of the women who spun the goat hair.

Rashi explains that the women did not spin the wool once it had been sheared off the goats' backs but rather while it was still growing on the goat, which required great skill and wisdom. Only once it was spun on the goats' backs was it cut and brought for use in the *Mishkan*.

Also, they prepared the *yerios*, the coverings for the *Mishkan*, even before they completed the poles that would be used to hold up these coverings.

Why did the women behave in this way?

Why did they spin the wool when it was still attached to the animal?

---

1   *Shemos* 35:26.

Why did they complete the coverings even though there were no poles finished on which to suspend them?

The Lubavitcher Rebbe explains that there were different levels of sacrifices brought in the Temple, and a "live" sacrifice was higher than one brought from something that grew from the ground. (We see an early example of this when Hashem accepted the sacrifice of Hevel, which was livestock, but rejected the produce that Kayin offered.)

Therefore, the *yerios* that were spun while still attached to the animal were of a higher level than those spun after the wool had been sheared off the animals' backs, because they were in essence coming from a live animal.

The women wanted to donate to the *Mishkan* something on the highest level, and so they spun the wool while it was still attached.

The Rebbe writes that from the actions of the women, we can learn two valuable lessons. First, when Hashem gives a person a particular skill or talent, he must know that it has been given to him to share with others and to use *l'shem shamayim*—in the service of Heaven to perfect himself and the entire world. Hashem did not instruct the women to spin the wool while it was still on the animals' backs, something that would require of them a high degree of skill and wisdom. The women, who possessed this talent, understood without being told that they needed to use these skills to fashion something for the *Mishkan*. Whatever the skill, talent, or ability with which Hashem has blessed a person, it needs to be used to further a relationship with Him and to benefit others.

The second lesson is that we must avoid causing distress to others. Usually, when building a structure, the walls are constructed first, followed by the roof. With regard to the *Mishkan*, the roof, i.e., the *yerios*, was completed, and only then the poles that held up the coverings, i.e., the walls, were made.

This deviation from standard practice was intended to minimize the suffering of the animals. To have their wool spun while still attached was probably uncomfortable for them, and it no doubt caused them a certain amount of distress. Therefore, once the wool had been spun, it was immediately removed to spare the animals any unnecessary pain.

The message is that to avoid pain, we can suspend the standard order of doing things. What is primary is our concern for the welfare of others, not continuing as usual.

In the light of the Coronavirus pandemic, the words of the Lubavitcher Rebbe are more relevant than ever.

Our usual way of life has been suspended, and everyone is affected.

Shuls that operated through wars and financial crises, where the sound of prayer had been heard every day for decades, have closed their doors.

Companies faced financial ruin, and people were locked in their houses, scared to venture outside.

If things are not continuing as normal, it is because our primary duty is to ensure that others do not suffer.

We stopped operating as usual in the hope that this "sacrifice" would ensure the safety of others, and if that is so, then normal is no longer important.[2]

---

2   *Shulchan Shabbos with the Lubavitcher Rebbe*, p. 101.

פקודי

When Is Prayer Appropriate?

וירא את כל המלאכה והנה עשו אתה...ויברך אתם משה.

Moshe saw the entire work, and behold! They had done it; as Hashem had commanded, so had they done. So Moshe blessed them.[1]

Rashi comments that the blessing that Moshe Rabbeinu gave the people when they completed the building of the *Mishkan* was: "יהי רצון שתשרה שכינה במעשה ידיכם—May it be the will of the Almighty that the Divine presence should rest on your work."

Rabbi David Hofstedter notes that at the end of the ימי המילואים—the inauguration of the *Mishkan*, Moshe gave the people the identical blessing of יהי רצון שתשרה שכינה במעשה ידיכם.[2] Why did the Jews need this blessing after Hashem had promised them that "ועשו לי מקדש ושכנתי בתוכם—Build a *Mishkan* and then I will dwell in [it]"?[3]

Once they had completed the structure, it was inevitable that Hashem would dwell in it, so why did Moshe have to give them a blessing to that effect?

---

1   *Shemos* 39:43.
2   *Vayikra* 9:23.
3   *Shemos* 25:8.

Second, why did Moshe repeat the blessing after the seven days of inauguration?

Rav Hofstedter suggests that we need to observe the state of mind of the Jewish People at each of these two events—the completion of the *Mishkan* and the end of the inaugural days.

When the Jews collected materials and then fashioned them into the vessels and structure of the *Mishkan*, there was a general feeling of joy and elation.

They had succeeded in fulfilling all of Hashem's instructions and had created a place where the *Shechinah* could reside.

By contrast, after seven days of inauguration during which Moshe had erected the *Mishkan*, but the *Shechinah* had not come down and rested in it, the people were sad and discouraged.

On both of these occasions, Moshe Rabbeinu blessed the people with the same blessing to teach us a valuable lesson.

First, even when success has been promised, and we are assured of reaping the rewards of our endeavors, we still need to pray for Divine assistance.

The *Ramchal* writes that even when Hashem has prepared bounty to rain on *Klal Yisrael*, they first need to act, to draw near to Him and request it, for if they do not pray that Hashem shower them with His glory, they will not receive it.[4]

So, Moshe Rabbeinu blesses the people that even though Hashem had assured them that once they build a *Mishkan* He will reside in it, nonetheless יהי רצון שתשרה שכינה במעשה ידיכם—only when you pray and draw close to Him will it happen.

The first lesson learned from Moshe Rabbeinu's blessing is the need to pray to Hashem, even when He has assured us of success.

The second occasion when Moshe Rabbeinu blessed the people was after the seven days of inauguration, and this time the mood of the people was not a happy one. They had just witnessed Moshe putting up and taking down the *Mishkan* for seven days, and there was no sign of the

4   *Derech Hashem* 4:5:1.

Shechinah. It seemed that Hashem was not attentive to and accepting of their prayers for success.

For this reason, Moshe repeats his prayer of יהי רצון שתשרה שכינה במעשה ידיכם to teach them that even when it seems that Hashem is not responding to our requests and that He is not listening to us, we must not give up and become despondent. When the chips seem to be down, that is precisely the time to renew our efforts to move closer to Him. It is precisely at that moment that a prayer of יהי רצון שתשרה שכינה במעשה ידיכם is most relevant.

Nowhere more than in regard to prayer is the saying, "If at first you don't succeed, try and try again" more relevant. Hashem always listens and always answers; we just may not always like the answer.

So, from the repeated blessing of Moshe Rabbeinu, we learn two lessons in the realm of prayer:

- First, do not take success, even guaranteed success, for granted. Pray to Hashem so that He will deliver that success.
- Second, even when it seems that He is not listening, He is! Prayer is the key even in the darkest moments.[5]

The Quality of Charity

אלה פקודי משכן המשכן העדות.

These are the numbers of the Mishkan, the Mishkan of the Testimony.[6]

The *Kli Yakar* asks why Moshe Rabbeinu made an accounting of all the gold and silver and materials that were used in the construction of the *Mishkan* before that construction was complete. After the accounting, the *parashah* tells us of the *bigdei kehunah* and how

---

they were made. Why did Moshe Rabbeinu not wait until everything, including the *bigdei kehunah*, was finished, and then make a reckoning or accounting?

Rabbi Menachem Chaim Merel suggests that sometimes people contribute sums of money to specific causes or institutions, and then for some reason that institution folds, and the person who donated comes to feel that his money would have been better spent elsewhere.

The quality of the mitzvah of tzedakah, however, is not affected by the end result of where the money ends up or how it is put to use; that is left for Hashem to judge. What is important regarding tzedakah is that the donation was made with the correct intention.

To teach us this message, Moshe Rabbeinu stops and gives an accounting before the *Mishkan* is completed to show that it is not important what happens to the money at the end of the project, but the intention and act of giving that took place at the beginning are what counts.

This explains why Moshe Rabbeinu blesses the people once the *Mishkan* is completed but before it is erected.[7] Moshe Rabbeinu wanted to show the people that they deserved a *berachah* for the work and effort that went into the *Mishkan*, which is independent of whether or not their work and effort bore the fruit of seeing the *Mishkan* assembled and working.

Our obligation is to perform the task. The success or failure of that task is in the hands of Hashem.[8]

---

7   *Shemos* 39:43.
8   *Minchas Chayeinu*, vol. 1, p. 193.

ספר
ויקרא

ויקרא

Hearing and Listening

וַיִּקְרָא אֶל מֹשֶׁה וַיְדַבֵּר ה׳ אֵלָיו מֵאֹהֶל מוֹעֵד לֵאמֹר.

And He called to Moshe, and Hashem spoke to him from the Tent of Meeting, saying.[1]

W hy doesn't the verse just say, 'וַיִּקְרָא ה׳ אֶל מֹשֶׁה וַיְדַבֵּר אֵלָיו וכו? Why is the *pasuk* broken up into וַיִּקְרָא אֶל מֹשֶׁה and then וַיְדַבֵּר ה׳ אֵלָיו?

Rashi writes on the words וַיִּקְרָא אֶל מֹשֶׁה that the sound of the call reached Moshe's ears and that the rest of *Klal Yisrael* did not hear it.

It seems obvious that if the sound of the call only reached Moshe's ears, then no one else heard it. If so, why is it necessary for *Rashi* to say both that the call only reached Moshe's ears and that *Klal Yisrael* did not hear it?

The answer is that the call of Hashem went out to everyone, but only Moshe picked it up. The rest of *Klal Yisrael*, who had not worked on themselves to the point of spiritual perfection, did not tune in.

Rashi uses very exact wording when he says that, concerning Moshe Rabbeinu, the sound was "מַגִּיעַ לְאָזְנָיו—it reached his ears," whereas in

---

1   *Vayikra* 1:1.

147

connection to *Klal Yisrael* the terms *Rashi* uses are שומעים לא ישראל וכל,
which means that the sound also reached their ears except that they
could not hear it, as they were not tuned in.

The call of Hashem goes out to all of us and reaches all of our ears. The
only question is if we can hear it.

> When Rav Shimon Schwab was a young man, he met the
> Chafetz Chaim, who by then was an old man, well-established
> as one of the great leaders of the Jewish People. The Chafetz
> Chaim took the young Rabbi Schwab by the hand and asked
> him what the difference was between Rabbi Schwab and the
> Chafetz Chaim.
>
> Rav Schwab was somewhat lost for words; he was a young man
> just starting out on his rabbinic career, whereas the Chafetz
> Chaim was the gadol ha'dor. The difference was quite apparent.
>
> Seeing the look of bewilderment on the young man's face, the
> Chafetz Chaim explained that the difference between them
> lay in their hands. As a Kohen, when the Beis Hamikdash is
> rebuilt, the Chafetz Chaim would use his hands in the Temple
> service, whereas Rabbi Schwab, not being a Kohen, would not
> be able to use his hands.
>
> The Chafetz Chaim added that the reason for this difference is
> because at the chet ha'eigel, after Moshe smashed the luchos, he
> descended from Mount Sinai and cried "אלי ה' מי—Whoever
> wants to follow Hashem come toward me!" The pasuk tells us,
> לוי בני כל אליו ויאספו—that out of all the tribes of Israel, the
> tribe of Levi alone heeded the call and followed Moshe.
>
> "It is because my ancestors not only heard the cry, but they were
> tuned into it and acted. That is why I will one day work in the
> Beis Hamikdash, and you will not," said the Chafetz Chaim.

There are times in the lives of every person when the cry of ה' מי
אלי rises up, and it will reach everyone's ears. The question is: Will
we hear it?

Thanks for Forcing Me!

אל פתח אהל מועד יקריב אתו לרצונו לפני ה'.

He shall bring it willingly to the entrance of the Tent of Meeting, before Hashem.[2]

Rashi tells us that the words יקריב אותו mean that we force a person to bring a sacrifice. However, the word לרצונו teaches us that a sacrifice is only valid if brought willingly. How can it be forced and willing at the same time? The answer is that we force him until he agrees willingly.

The *Chasam Sofer* explains the possibility of forcing someone to bring a sacrifice willingly in the following way:

Imagine a Jew who lives far from the Beis Hamikdash and is busy all day long working hard to make a living and till the land. After being engaged in these activities for a prolonged period, the subtlety of spiritual endeavors may be lost on him—to the point that he may view them as a burden.

However, if we bring him to the Holy City, where the air is saturated with the words of Torah and spiritual yearnings, and he sees for perhaps the first time in a long while the Kohanim in the Temple performing their service and hears the Leviim singing their songs of praise, then his heart will be overwhelmed with a desire to grow closer to Hashem and observe His commandments.

The atmosphere automatically has a positive effect and melts even the most stubborn of hearts.

Therefore, the *pasuk* reads that if someone is refusing to bring a sacrifice, then אל פתח אהל מועד—force him to come to the entrance of the

אוהל מועד and let it work its magic. The natural outcome will be "יקריב
אתו לרצונו לפני ה'—he will willingly offer it up to Hashem."

The message is that we need to attract Jews to living a Torah lifestyle not by forcing or legislating against them, but by showing them the majestic beauty of living a Torah life. If we manage to do so, then any opposition that people may have will simply melt away. We need to start by ensuring that we are in love with Hashem and His Torah, and then others will automatically be drawn to follow suit.[3]

Do I Smell Nice?

עלה הוא אשה ריח ניחוח לה'.

It is a burnt offering, a fire offering [with] a pleasing fragrance to Hashem.[4]

The Torah refers to the acceptance of the *korban* using the phrase ריח ניחוח לה', a sweet-smelling aroma or fragrance to Hashem. What does this phrase mean?

Rabbi Shalom Rosner quotes Rav Yaakov Tzvi Mecklenberg, who suggests a unique approach in his commentary, *Hakesav V'Hakabbalah*.

ריח ניחוח does not describe the scent of the *korban*, but rather it describes the person who offers it.

A ריח ניחוח is a pleasant fragrance; if one enters a home on Erev Shabbos, he can smell that there is something tasty cooking. As he walks further into the house, the aroma becomes stronger and stronger until he reaches the kitchen and lifts off the pot cover, finally discovering the source of the scent.

The smell hit him immediately upon opening the door, and it informed him that something was coming—that there was something tasty to anticipate.

---

3   *Talelei Oros*, p. 46.
4   *Vayikra* 1:13.

Similarly, if you walk into a garden and you immediately smell a flower, the scent informs you that there is a sweet-smelling flower in the vicinity.

When we offer a *korban*, we provide a ריח ניחוח. It is a sweet-smelling "aroma" that we put out to Hashem, saying, "Hashem, I am putting out a delicate 'scent' now, but I am going to improve even more."

I am going to use this to lead me to change my actions for the better.

Just like a smell precedes the item, so too, the *korban* is our ריח ניחוח. We provide a good smell to Hashem as a foreshadowing of what is going to transpire in the future.

Our actions have to mirror what we just did—we brought a ריח ניחוח, so we need to make sure that our actions improve as well.

Anybody who offers a *korban* should contemplate *teshuvah* to return and get closer to Hashem.

The sacrifices we offer should lead us to further our connection to Hashem, placing our finer "fragrance" before Him.

Given the difficult situation that the Coronavirus pandemic and its aftermath have created, we must all strengthen our study of Torah and acts of *chessed*, intensifying our ריח נחוח before Hashem so that we can experience His mercy and merit salvation.[5]

---

5   *Torah Tidbits, Vayikra* 5780.

צו

Parenting, Shabbos Hagadol, and Lighting the Torch

arashas Tzav is often read on the Shabbos before Pesach, called
Shabbos Hagadol. Is there any connection between the two, or
is it merely by chance that they overlap?

In the eighth chapter of *Sefer Vayikra*, the Torah describes the inauguration of Aharon as the Kohen Gadol and of his sons as Kohanim to serve in the Temple.

What is striking is that the consecration of Aharon and his sons took place in one ceremony.

The *pasuk* says, "קח את אהרן ובניו אתו"—Take Aharon and his sons with him and consecrate them."[1]

And then again, in *pasuk* ו, we read, "ויקרב משה את אהרן ואת בניו וירחץ אתם במים—And Moshe brought Aharon and his sons forward and immersed them in water."

Throughout the chapter, the Torah refers to אהרן ובניו—Aharon and his children as one group who were inaugurated into service at the same time and in the same ceremony.

---

1   *Vayikra* 8:2.

The sanctity of the Kohen Gadol and his office was higher than that of a regular Kohen. This difference was clearly displayed through the extra ceremonial robes that he wore, by the type of service that he performed, and, most of all, by the fact that once a year, he alone was permitted to enter the Holy of Holies.

Accordingly, we would not have been surprised if Moshe had first inaugurated Aharon's sons as regular priests, and then consecrated Aharon in a special ceremony befitting his level and status.

Why was there only one joint ceremony?

By connecting Aharon and his sons in their elevation to holiness, the Torah seems to be telling us that a person is measured not only by how much *they* have grown and achieved with their life, but also by how much they have managed to pass on to their children.

Children do not have to become carbon copies of their parents. Still, parents hope that they will be successful in imparting fundamental values and beliefs that will join them and their children together forever.

This is the connection between *Parashas Tzav* and Shabbos Hagadol.

As we enter Pesach, we do so as parents with a responsibility and opportunity to share with our children the fundamental values of *hakaras ha'tov*, *emunah*, *bitachon*, and so much more.

We, as parents, will do our part to try to inspire, and it is up to the next generation to take that torch forward and blaze a burning path for themselves and for the future.[2]

---

2   *Bein Adam LaParashah*, p. 42.

It All Starts and Ends with Thinking of Others

וְעָרַךְ עָלֶיהָ הָעֹלָה וְהִקְטִיר עָלֶיהָ חֶלְבֵי הַשְּׁלָמִים.

The Kohen shall kindle wood upon it every morning, and upon it he shall arrange the burnt offering and cause the fats of the peace offerings to [go up in] smoke upon it.[3]

The Gemara states that the first sacrifice brought in the morning was the *tamid shel shachar*.[4]

The last sacrifice offered at the end of the day was the *tamid shel bein ha'arbayim*.

Nothing could be brought before the *tamid shel shachar*, and nothing could be sacrificed after the *tamid shel bein ha'arbayim*.

Rabbi Yitzchak Yaakov Raines writes that we should notice that the first and last sacrifices offered in the Beis Hamikdash were communal *korbanos tzibbur*. Between them, people brought their individual offerings and discharged their private duties, *korbanos yachid*.

The message is that while we may be busy during most of the day earning *our* income, working at *our* work, performing *our* private mitzvos, and concentrating on ourselves, all our activities need to be framed in the broader context of benefiting others.

We need to start and end the day with a sacrifice that is for others as well.[5]

---

3   *Vayikra* 6:5.
4   *Pesachim* 55b.
5   *Parpera'os LaTorah*, p. 32.

Lights, Think, and Action!

דבר אל אהרן ואל בניו...במקום אשר תשחט העלה תשחט החטאת.

Speak to Aharon and to his sons, saying, "...The sin offering shall be slaughtered before Hashem in the place where the burnt offering is slaughtered."[6]

This *pasuk* instructs that just as the *Korban Olah* is slaughtered in the north of the Beis Hamikdash, so too, the *Korban Chatas* needs to be slaughtered in the north.

The *Avnei Neizer* explains that the *Korban Olah* is slaughtered in the north because it comes to atone for the negative thoughts that led to the sinful act. These thoughts are hidden within our minds. Therefore, the slaughter of the animal is in the צפון—the north, which is derived from the Hebrew word צפון—hidden.

Just as the thoughts are hidden, so too, the place that we slaughter represents that which is hidden.

If so, why is the *Korban Chatas* slaughtered in the north? The *Korban Chatas* is not brought to atone for sinful **thoughts**. It is brought to atone for sinful **actions**. Actions, by definition, are in the open and revealed. They are the opposite of צפון, so why are they brought in the north?

The *Shem MiShmuel*, son of the *Avnei Neizer*, answers that no one sins without first thinking. Thoughts enter our mind and entice us to sin. Even if we manage to suspend acting upon that thought for a period of time, if we do subsequently act, it is due to those original thoughts.

So even though the *Korban Chatas* is being brought to atone for the act, it is slaughtered in the north, the צפון, to impress upon us that no action is born in a vacuum. Our actions are the result of sinful thoughts, and if we overcome having those hidden, sinful thoughts, we will not be led to sin.

The Satmar Rebbe adds that this idea is alluded to in the words of our *pasuk*. The *pasuk* says, במקום אשר תשחט העלה תשחט החטאת, which

6   *Vayikra* 6:18.

he interprets to mean: במקום—the same place within us—אשר תשחט
העלה—that is responsible for us having to bring an *Olah*, namely our
mind and thoughts—תשחט החטאת—is the same place that is ultimately
responsible for us having to bring a *Chatas*.

Everything begins in the mind. If we manage to lead our mind and
thoughts away from that which is negative and forbidden, we will avoid
performing those *actions* that are negative and forbidden.[7]

---

7   *Talelei Oros*, p. 124.

שמיני

I Am Delighted for You!

ויהי ביום השמיני קרא משה לאהרן ולבניו ולזקני ישראל.

And it was on the eighth day, Moshe called to Aharon and his sons and to the Elders of Yisrael.[1]

Rabbeinu Bachya cites a Midrash that connects ויהי ביום השמיני and the burning bush. The reason why Aharon was appointed to be the Kohen Gadol was due to his happiness when he heard that Moshe had been chosen as the leader, as it says, "אמר רבי שמעון בן יוחאי הלב ששמח בגדולת אחיו ילבש אורים ותומים—Rabbi Shimon Bar Yochai says that the heart that rejoiced when his brother was elevated to greatness shall wear the *Urim V'Tumim.*" Now was that moment when Aharon was to take over.

The *Midrash Tanchuma* states that at the time when Aharon was appointed as the Kohen Gadol and his children as Kohanim, Moshe Rabbeinu said to him, "שכשם ששמחת בגדולתי כך אני שמח בגדולתך—In the same way that you were happy for me when I was appointed

---

1   *Vayikra* 9:1.

157

leader, so too I am glad for you now that you have been appointed Kohen Gadol."[2]

The *Ohr Hachaim Hakadosh* proves this point from the way that Moshe Rabbeinu behaved when appointing Aharon.

Suppose you are jealous or do not wish a certain person to be appointed to a high office, and yet you are the one that has to appoint him. In that case, you are in all likelihood going to make sure that the appointment process is long and stretched out in order to delay the inevitable. Second, when the actual time comes for the inauguration, you will perform it in stages, again to delay the inevitable and to save you the pain of seeing him appointed. Finally, you will try to attract as little attention as possible to the inauguration.

Moshe Rabbeinu, however, acted in the completely opposite way when it came to appointing Aharon and his sons. First, he appointed them immediately when the time came for doing so. ויהי ביום השמיני—as soon as it was day on the eighth day, Moshe Rabbeinu called for Aharon and his sons, without delay.

Second, he did not appoint them in stages but קרא לאהרן ולבניו, even though seeing them all together only reinforced the message that not only was Moshe not going to be the Kohen Gadol, but also that his children would not be Kohanim. Nonetheless, the appointment was made in one go.

Finally, the appointment was made in front of the Elders in order that they would act as witnesses that the appointment had been sanctioned by Hashem.

From his behavior, we can see clearly that Moshe Rabbeinu was happy for Aharon and his sons.

Likewise, it befits us to be happy for other people's success—to celebrate with them at their *simchas*, and to rejoice with them for their good fortune.

---

2   *Tanchuma, Shemini* 3.

You Reap What You Sow

ויהי ביום השמיני קרא משה לאהרן ולבניו וכו׳.
And it was on the eighth day, Moshe called to Aharon and his sons and to the Elders of Yisrael.[3]

Rashi writes that ויהי ביום השמיני refers to the eighth day of the ימי המילואים. The *Kli Yakar* asks that it is stated in a different *pasuk* that there were only seven days of inauguration, not eight, as it says, שבעת ימים ימלא את ידכם.[4]

The *Kli Yakar* answers that we are being told the reason why Hashem appeared on this day specifically, as it says, כי היום ה׳ נראה אליכם,[5] namely, because it was day eight.

The number eight represents that which is above nature, that which is *kadosh*, and therefore, as opposed to the previous seven days that were *chol*, the eighth day is *kadosh*, and that is why Hashem appeared. That is the meaning of ויהי ביום השמיני. Hashem had not appeared on the previous seven days, and He did appear on day eight.

As an aside, Rabbeinu Bachya highlights several items in the *Mishkan* and Beis Hamikdash that were associated with the number eight.

For example:

- Eight *bigdei kehunah*.
- The anointing oil and the *ketores* incense each have four fragrant ingredients, together equalling eight.
- There were eight poles—two each on the *Aron, Shulchan*, and two *Mizbechos*.
- An animal must remain for seven days with its mother after being born before being eligible to be brought as a korban on day eight.

---

3   *Vayikra* 9:1.
4   Ibid. 8:33.
5   Ibid. 9:4.

- The Leviim had eight different songs that they sang to accompany the sacrifices.

This shows the supernatural nature of the *Mishkan* and the Beis Hamikdash.

The Lubavitcher Rebbe notes that the *Kli Yakar* hasn't answered the question. If the number eight is higher spiritually than the previous seven, and if it is in a league of its own, then the eighth day has no connection to the previous seven. If so, why call it יום השמיני, which automatically associates it with the previous seven?

The Rebbe answers that while it is true that the number eight represents a level of spirituality beyond human comprehension, and is given to us as a gift, it will only be given to us if we have worked and grown during the previous seven days.

It was the previous seven days of the *milu'im* that paved the way for the eighth day of *kedushah*. The two go hand-in-hand, and the latter can only happen as a result of the former.

That is why the Torah says, ויהי ביום השמיני, because as a result of the work of the previous seven days, we were gifted with the supernatural spirituality of the eighth.

The Rebbe then suggests that this idea can be found in Shabbos, whose *kedushah* surpasses that of the other days of the week, and yet the Gemara says: מי שטרח בערב שבת יאכל בשבת,[6] our ability to recognize and benefit from the *kedushah* of Shabbos depends on the effort that we have put into the preceding days of the week.

Similarly, although we are told to count fifty days of *sefiras ha'omer*, we actually only count forty-nine. The Rebbe gives the same explanation: If we have worked on ourselves in the previous forty-nine days, then the fiftieth level is gifted to us, but that sublime level is dependent on the previous forty-nine days of work and effort.[7]

---

6   *Avodah Zarah* 3a.
7   *Otzar Likutei Sichos*, p. 139.

The same idea can also be applied to a *bris milah*, which occurs on the eighth day of a boy's life. The extra level is gifted to the baby and his parents due to the previous efforts that the parents have invested in living a Torah life and serving Hashem.

These efforts result in Hashem gifting their baby the ability to experience *kedushah* at the start of his life—with all our prayers that he continues to live a life of Torah and mitzvos and to experience *kedushah* and spirituality until 120.

The Sale of Yosef, the Mishkan, and What Binds Them

ואל בנ״י תדבר לאמר קחו שעיר עיזים לחטאת ועגל וכבש בני שנה תמימים לעולה.

And to the children of Yisrael you shall speak, saying, "Take a he-goat as a sin offering; and a calf and a lamb, [both] in their first year and [both] unblemished, as a burnt offering."[8]

Rabbeinu Bachya asks why the people brought more sacrifices than Aharon. They brought a he-goat for a sin-offering, a calf and sheep in their first year as a burnt offering, and a bull and a ram for a peace offering. Aharon brought a young bull as a sin offering and a ram as a burnt offering, but he did not bring a he-goat. Why not?

Rabbeinu Bachya answers by quoting the Midrash that says that at this time, B'nei Yisrael were atoning for two sins: one that involved a *se'ir*—a he-goat, and the other that involved an *eigel*—a calf.

In *Bereishis*, it says that after the brothers sold Yosef, they had to present a story to their father Yaakov. So, they slaughtered a he-goat

---

8   *Vayikra* 9:3.

and dipped Yosef's coat of many colors in its blood so that their father would think that a wild animal had consumed Yosef.[9]

Therefore, the B'nei Yisrael brought a he-goat to atone for the sale of Yosef, which was a national sin perpetrated by the brothers, who were the nation of Israel at that time.

As an individual, Aharon did not need to bring a sacrifice that atoned for the nation.

The *Oznayim La'Torah* asks that if the B'nei Yisrael needed to bring a sacrifice to atone for the sale of Yosef, why didn't they bring it as soon as they went free from Egypt?

The reason why we went down to Egypt and became slaves in the first place was due to the sale of Yosef, so the minute we were redeemed from that slavery and left Egypt would seem to be the opportune moment to atone for that sale by bringing a sacrifice. Why did it have to wait until the *Mishkan* was built?

The *Oznayim La'Torah* explains that an overriding theme of the *Mishkan* was the unity of *Klal Yisrael*—everyone donated the materials equally, everyone gave a *machatzis ha'shekel* toward its operating costs, and everyone encamped around the *Mishkan*. It was the national focal point, and its focus was unity.

When we now focus on unity, we can atone for sins caused by a lack of unity, and one of those was the sale of Yosef by a divided family of brothers.

Therefore, rather than bring the sacrifice immediately upon leaving Egypt, it was offered up in an atmosphere of unity when the regret over lack of unity that caused Yosef to be sold would be paramount and the *teshuvah* done would be sincere.

The *Hagahos Maharid* also asks why the sale of Yosef suddenly needs a sacrifice to be brought to atone for it. The incident of the *eigel* was fairly recent and directly connected, according to some authorities, to the building of the *Mishkan*. But why deal with the sale of Yosef now?

---

9   *Bereishis* 37:31–32.

Why at this juncture do B'nei Yisrael bring a sacrifice for the sin of the sale of Yosef?

The *Hagahos Maharid* answers that one of the justifications that the brothers had for "disposing" of Yosef was that they saw that in the future that he would have a descendant by the name of Yeravam ben Navat, who would place golden calves in a Temple that he made and cause the people to transgress the sin of idolatry. For that reason, the brothers decided to "remove" Yosef and in that way avoid Yeravam ben Navat being born.

That reasoning, faulty as it may be, is all well and good as long as the brothers or their descendants refrain from involving themselves in idolatry, but once they also worship idols, then their reasoning around Yosef's sale becomes totally invalid, and they have to bring a sacrifice to atone for that sale.

Therefore, following the *chet ha'eigel*, not only do B'nei Yisrael have to bring a sacrifice to atone for the sin of the *eigel* itself, but they also have to bring a sacrifice for the sale of Yosef, for their rationale has now been proven to be false.[10]

---

10   *Maayanah shel Torah*, p. 44.

תזריע

Peace and Truth

אדם כי יהיה בעור בשרו שאת או ספחת...לנגע צרעת והובא אל אהרן
הכהן...

*If a man has a seis, a sapachas, or a baheres on the skin of his
flesh, and it forms a lesion of tzaraas on the skin of his flesh,
he shall be brought to Aharon the Kohen or to one of his sons
the Kohanim.[1]*

The Rebbe of Alexander writes that *tzaraas* is brought as a result
of speaking *lashon hara*. Often, those who spoke this *lashon hara*
did so with the justification that it is essential to tell the truth.
However, their zeal to protect *emes* led them to speak *lashon hara*, an
outcome of which is *machlokes*.

Therefore, the Torah says that they have to be brought to Aharon
HaKohen because, while their righteous defense of truth led to con-
frontation and strife, Aharon's approach to life was precisely the opposite. Aharon HaKohen was prepared to bend the facts to achieve *shalom*.

The *Avos D'Rabi Nosson* teaches us that when two people had argued
and were angry with each other, Aharon would go and sit with one

---

1   *Vayikra* 13:2.

of them and say that he had just seen the other, that the other was distraught over the pain he had caused, and that he is looking to make amends. Aharon would then go to the second person involved in the dispute and say the same thing about his antagonist. The result would be that the next time these two enemies met each other, they would apologize, and their friendship would be resumed.

Was each side truly distraught about their argument? Were they sincerely looking to mend the unpleasant situation between them? The *Avos D'Rabi Nosson* does not say. But, since Aharon HaKohen's approach to life was that *achdus* and *shalom* should reign supreme in *Klal Yisrael*, he took the measures necessary to ensure that this would indeed be the case.[2]

The Torah shows us that if there is a battle between *emes* and *shalom*, our overriding value is to ensure that there is *achdus* and *shalom* in our marriages, in our families, and in our communities.

If by defending *emes* you speak *lashon hara*, then the result is *tzaraas*. If by defending *shalom* you are "generous" with the truth, then the result is that you become appointed the Kohen Gadol.[3]

I'm Not Perfect, but I'm Great!

אדם כי יהיה בעור בשרו שאת או ספחת...

If a man has a seis, a sapachas, or a baheres on the skin of his flesh, and it forms a lesion of tzaraas on the skin of his flesh...[4]

The *Netziv* cites the *Zohar's* comment that out of all the words that the Torah uses to describe a person, the word אדם is the highest form.

---

2   *Avos D'Rabi Nosson* 12:3.
3   *Otzar Chaim*, p. 73.
4   *Vayikra* 13:2.

Against this backdrop, the *Netziv* wonders why the Torah uses this term to describe someone who has *tzaraas*, as the verse says, אדם כי יהיה בעור בשרו...לנגע צרעת.

A person is afflicted with *tzaraas* primarily because he spoke *lashon hara* or was stingy.

Why is a person who has exhibited these negative traits and been punished for it described as אדם, which is reserved for someone who is on a very high level?[5]

Rabbi Nissan Alpert suggests the following answer to the question of the *Netziv*.

We usually assume that the difference between a great person and a regular person is that the great person has no faults, whereas the ordinary person has flaws. The reality is that everyone has faults. If so, what differentiates a great person from everyone else?

A great person is someone who is aware that he has faults and attempts to overcome and correct those faults. A regular person is someone who has weaknesses and is content to remain with those weaknesses.

When a person is afflicted with *tzaraas* and realizes that it came to him as a result of some flaw in his behavior, and והובא אל הכהן he comes to the Kohen to be advised as to how to correct his defect, such a person is indeed great, deserving of the title אדם.

No one is born great, but a person who strives to improve and aspires for greatness is great—whether or not they manage to achieve and reach the goals they have set.

The person who accepts his flaws and is content to live with his faults can never be great.

As Rabbi Isaac Bernstein stated in the name of a certain Rosh Yeshiva: "The minimum that Hashem expects from us is our maximum."

We need to aim for greatness and not accept any of our imperfections.

---

5   Rabbi Isaac Bernstein, *Tazria*, series 1.

מצורע

It's Wrong, Plain Wrong

זאת תהיה תורת המצורע.

This shall be the law of the person afflicted with tzaraas.[1]

he word *metzora* (מצורע) is an acronym for מוציא שם רע. The *Baal Shem Tov* would say that someone who speaks *lashon hara* is מוציא את הרע משורשו—extracting the evil from its root. What did he mean by this?

It has been explained in the following way:

We are taught that any negative character trait should be channeled in the service of Hashem. Someone who loves blood should become a *shochet* or a *mohel*, etc. However, there is one negative trait that is impossible to channel positively, and that is speaking *lashon hara* and *rechilus*.

Someone who speaks negatively about someone else doesn't derive any physical or material benefit as a result. They simply enjoy talking negatively, tale-bearing, or gossiping about someone else.

Such a negative character trait has no positive outlet.

This is because it is not a human trait; it isn't even an animal trait.

---

1   *Vayikra* 14:2.

Animals only act if they are going to benefit from such an act. They attack for food or to protect their young or for territory, but they do not act out of spite.

To speak *lashon hara* is evil. There are no mitigating factors, and one cannot claim to have benefitted in any way other than from enjoying a good piece of gossip.

It is, as the *Baal Shem Tov* noted, "מוציא את הרע משורשו—rooted in evil!"[2]

True Humility

וצוה הכהן ולקח...שתי צפרים...ועץ ארז ושני תולעת ואזב.

Then the Kohen shall order the person to be cleansed to take two live, clean birds, a cedar stick, a strip of crimson [wool], and hyssop.[3]

Rashi says that the sin of speaking *lashon hara* is a result of *gasus ruach*—haughtiness, and that is why an *eitz erez*—a cedar, is included as part of the atonement of the *metzora*.

The *Sifsei Chachamim* explains that the cedar tree is the highest of all the trees, and thus it represents haughtiness.

In the same manner, *Rashi* says that the hyssop is part of the atonement process because it represents the lowest of all trees. It represents the humility that would have acted as a deterrent from speaking *lashon hara* and will hopefully cause the speaker to avoid repeating the mistake in the future.

The *Shem MiShmuel* asks why we need cedar wood that reminds the transgressor of his past misdemeanors. He is trying to make amends and surely doesn't want the past rubbed in his face!

---

2   *Otzar Chaim*, p. 84.

3   *Vayikra* 14:4.

Second, this flies in the face of the principle of אין קטיגור נעשה סנגור—the accuser cannot become the defender. If the cedar represents that which caused him to sin, how can it be part of his atonement process?

The *Shem MiShmuel* cites his father, the *Avnei Neizer*, who said that there are two types of humility.

- There is a humility born as a result of the realization of man's lowliness when considered against the majestic magnificence of the Almighty.
- Then there is the humility when one is afflicted with poverty or depression that makes him feel worthless.

In neither case is one exhibiting any arrogance, but one type of humility is healthy and productive, while the other is only short-term, unhealthy and non-productive.

If my humility is a result of a warped impression of reality, then I need to be able to see the cedarwood.

I need to understand that as important as humility is, it must not be based on a misconception of who I am but on a realization of my real value.

I am like the cedarwood, and yet I am humble in the knowledge that I am nothing compared to the Almighty.

That is the reason why the cedarwood that represents haughtiness is included in the atonement process of the *metzora*.

The *metzora's* mistake is that as a result of arrogance, he spoke *lashon hara*.

From this mistake, he has to learn and undertake to be humble. But it is crucial that he undertakes humility in a healthy way—the way of the *erez*—with a clear picture of his talents, capabilities, and abilities, and at the same time be humble.

The lesson is an important one regarding humility. Having the right kind of humility does not mean to deny our talents and abilities, but rather to acknowledge that we are talented and unique. We have exceptional skills and gifts, but at the same time, we employ them with humility.[4]

---

4   Rabbi Avraham Rivlin, *Iyunei Parashah*, p. 173.

Speak!

וצוה הכהן ולקח...שתי צפרים...ועץ ארז ושני תולעת ואזב.

Then the Kohen shall order the person to be cleansed to take two live, clean birds, a cedar stick, a strip of crimson [wool], and hyssop.[5]

ashi says that *tzaraas* is a result of *lashon hara*, which is an act of unnecessary "twittering" of words, so the sacrifice that is brought are two "twittering" birds.

The *Apirion* asks that we can understand why it is necessary to bring birds to hint to the *metzora* that he is in this situation because he "twittered" like a bird, but why must he bring two? One should be enough to deliver that message.

The *Apirion* suggests that had the *metzora* only brought one bird, he would have thought that it is to atone for his loose lips, and thus from now on, he is going to be quiet and not talk! In that way, he will avoid any future transgressions of *lashon hara*.

Therefore, a second bird is brought that remains alive. This indicates to the *metzora* that while careless talk can cause destruction, positive words create life.

The *pasuk* says, "החיים והמות ביד הלשון—Life and death are in the hand of the tongue,"[6] which means that speech has the power of life as well—to learn, speak words of Torah, perform *chessed* with speech, etc.

Hashem does not want us to be silent; He just instructs us how to use the power of our speech correctly.

Therefore, two birds are brought: one to remind the *metzora* that he is in his predicament because of his "twittering," i.e., his negative and harmful speech, and the second bird that is not killed but set free shows

---

5   *Vayikra* 14:4.
6   *Mishlei* 28:11.

that we are supposed to speak, but only in a way that brings life through the learning of Torah and the observance of mitzvos.[7]

Rabbi Moshe Sternbuch notes that there are two types of people who speak *lashon hara*. Some speak negatively in private and would be mortified if they were ever found out, and some have no compunction about speaking *lashon hara* openly and in public.

This is the reason why two birds are brought. One of them is sent "על פני השדה"—to the face of the field," a reference to those who openly speak *lashon hara*. The other bird that is slaughtered represents those who speak *lashon hara* in private.

In addition, the bird that is sent free is dipped in the blood of the bird that is slaughtered so that he carries it with him when he is set free על פני השדה. This shows that even *lashon hara* that you speak in private and about which you think no one will know, will become public.[8]

---

7 *Talelei Oros*, p. 282.
8 *Taam V'Daas*, p. 80.

אחרי מות

The Times They Are A-changing!

דבר אל אהרן אחיך ואל יבא בכל עת אל הקדש.

*And Hashem said to Moshe: "Speak to your brother Aharon,
that he should not come at all times into the Holy."*[1]

The *Panim Yafos*, Rabbi Pinchas Horowitz, writes that this
pasuk is to be read literally and that it is an instruction for all
generations.

The Torah is *kadosh*, Judaism is *kadosh*, and halachah is *kadosh*. All the
principles by which a Jew lives his life are *kadosh*.

Do not measure that which is *kadosh* against בכל עת—that which
is popular.

Therefore, ואל יבא בכל עת אל הקודש—do not approach that which is
kadosh with the fads and fashions of the times in which you live.

Do not hold up everything that we hold dear, everything that is
kadosh, and ask if it is in keeping with the times, but hold up the times,
the morals, the lifestyles of the present and see if they are in keeping
with everything *kadosh*.[2]

---

1   *Vayikra* 16:2.
2   *Otzar Chaim*, p. 100.

172

Rabbi Shimshon Raphael Hirsch echoes this idea when he explains the Gemara that says that when we stand before the Heavenly Court after 120 years, one of the questions that we will be asked is "קבעת עיתים לתורה?"[3]

The standard explanation of the question is whether we allotted a fixed time for Torah study; was our relationship with *limud Trah* haphazard, or were we dedicated enough to engage in Torah learning on a fixed basis?

Rav Hirsch explains that the question can also be interpreted to mean whether we showed that the Torah is alive, vibrant, and relevant to the times in which we lived. "קבעת עיתים"—Did you fix the times in which you lived; "לתורה"—to show how everything the Torah stands for is relevant and applicable?

We must not fall into the trap of adjusting the Torah to meet the demands of the times, but we must adapt the requirements, fads, fashions, and behaviors of the time to align with the Torah.

Do I Really Care?

וידבר ה׳ אל משה אחרי מות שני בני אהרן.

And Hashem spoke to Aharon after the death of Aharon's two sons.[4]

The *Yerushalmi* explains that the deaths of Nadav and Avihu are mentioned next to the Temple service of Yom Kippur to teach us that in the same way as Yom Kippur atones for Am Yisrael, so too, the death of *tzaddikim* atones for Am Yisrael.

By the same token, says the *Yerushalmi*, the death of Miriam is placed next to the laws of the *parah adumah* to teach that in the same way as

---

3   *Shabbos* 31a.
4   *Vayikra* 16:1.

the *parah adumah* afforded atonement to the Jewish People, so too, the death of Miriam affords atonement.[5]

The *Chasam Sofer* wonders why the *Yerushalmi* needs to bring two examples—Nadav and Avihu, and Miriam—in order to teach us the same thing. Why isn't one sufficient?

The *Chasam Sofer* answers by suggesting that there are two types of atonement achieved through the death of a *tzaddik*.

The first is when a community has strayed from Hashem. The death of a *tzaddik* can act as an atonement for that entire community, but only on a communal level, not an individual one.

The second type of atonement offered by the death of a *tzaddik* is on an individual level, and that takes place when every individual is affected and moved to *teshuvah* as a result of that *tzaddik*'s death.

The *Yalkut Shimoni* in *Parashas Chukas* tells us that when Miriam died, B'nei Yisrael did not eulogize her in a way that was befitting to her spiritual level, instead they became embroiled in complaints over the lack of water at Mei Merivah.

As a result, the death of Miriam acted as atonement for the community, but not for the individuals.

This is why the death of Miriam is placed next to the *parah adumah*, because the *parah adumah* was not brought by each individual but by the community, and her death offered collective atonement.

By contrast, by the deaths of Nadav and Avihu, the *pasuk* states that וַאֲחֵיכֶם כָּל בֵּית יִשְׂרָאֵל יִבְכּוּ אֶת הַשְּׂרֵפָה אֲשֶׁר שָׂרַף ה'[6]—every *individual* was affected by their deaths, and therefore their deaths offered atonement for everyone's individual sins.

This is why the deaths of Nadav and Avihu are placed next to the *avodah* of Yom Kippur, because Yom Kippur atones on an individual level, in the same way as the deaths of Nadav and Avihu were also an atonement for the individual.

The death of a *tzaddik* is an opportunity to receive atonement. How personal that atonement will be depends on how the death of that

---

5   *Yoma* 1:1.
6   *Vayikra* 10:6.

tzaddik affects each individual, how much they internalize the lessons that the *tzaddik* taught, and how much they undertake to try and emulate the *tzaddik* in the future.[7]

---

7   *Talelei Oros*, p. 301.

קדושים

We Are in This Together

דבר אל כל עדת בני ישראל ואמרת אלהם קדושים תהיו כי קדוש אני ה׳
אלוקיכם.

Speak to the entire congregation of the children of Yisrael, and say to them, "You shall be holy, for I, Hashem, your God, am holy."[1]

The commentators offer different explanations as to why the instruction of קדושים תהיו needed to be expressed with the introduction of אל כל עדת בני ישראל, to "all the congregation of B'nei Yisrael," and not the regular אל בני ישראל.

Rashi suggests that since "רוב גופי תורה תלויין בה—The main substance of the Torah is dependent on it," i.e., our fulfilling קדושים תהיו, it needed to be instructed to everyone gathered together in one place. What are these רוב גופי תורה?

The *Torah Temimah* suggests that *Rashi* is referring to the mitzvah of ואהבת לרעך כמוך, which we find in this *parashah*,[2] which Rabbi Akiva said is a "כלל גדול בתורה—an all-encompassing obligation of the Torah."

---

1   *Vayikra* 19:2.
2   Ibid. 19:18.

Therefore, since everything hinges on loving your friend as yourself, everyone needed to hear the *parashah* of קדושים תהיו all together.

The *Chasam Sofer* writes that Hashem does not want us to achieve a life of holiness by removing ourselves from society. Instead, the instruction of קדושים תהיו is given when we are all gathered together. This teaches us that holiness is only found in our actions as a community.

It is easy to be a *tzaddik* when there is no one around to pester you, to annoy you, or to disagree with you. The test is how we behave within society and how we deal with the challenges that living in society presents.

The *Sefas Emes* adds that קדושים תהיו was presented to the community so that we realize that only when we act united as a community can קדושה be attained. If each section of the community only works on perfecting themselves and is not worried about how they can help different parts of the community achieve success, then there can be no קדושה, and no one attains sanctity. Only by working as כל עדת בני ישראל, i.e., as one united congregation, can we successfully achieve קדושים תהיו.

Finally, the *Alshich* suggests that קדושים תהיו needed to be presented to the people gathered all together to emphasize that everyone can live a life of sanctity. It isn't a realm reserved for the select few, but rather it is within reach for every single Jew. Had the Torah followed the usual prescription of דבר אל בני ישראל, there would have been those who, when hearing the words קדושים תהיו, would have said that Moshe wasn't really referring to him. How could he be expected to live a life of sanctity? After all, he was just a simple Jew.

However, when all the people gathered together and heard the words קדושים תהיו together, they realized that it applies to everyone.[3]

---

3   *Parpera'os LaTorah*, p. 133.

When Will I Be Holy?

דבר אל כל עדת בנ"י...קדושים תהיו כי קדוש אני ה' אלקיכם.

Speak to the entire congregation of the children of Yisrael, and say to them, "You shall be holy, for I, Hashem, your G-d, am holy."[4]

R abbi Paysach Krohn says that sometimes we feel that it is important to live a Torah-observant life because if we look at the alternative, it appears to us as stale, unspiritual, unfulfilling, and meaningless. While this may or may not be true, the opening words in our *parashah* tell us that this is the incorrect approach.

The opening words are קדושים תהיו כי קדוש אני ה' אלקיכם, and they say that we need to live an ethical, worthwhile, and spiritual life, כי קדוש אני ה' אלקיכם—for no other reason than that Hashem is *kadosh*. Even if the alternative lifestyles were honest, genuine, and fulfilling, we would still choose to live a Torah life, a life of spiritual growth, and a life of cultivating a relationship with The Almighty for no other reason than כי קדוש אני ה' אלקיכם!

We measure ourselves not by what we are not, but by what we are!

The *mefarshim* ask why the words קדושים תהיו are stated in the plural and not the singular tense. The *Alshich* suggests that this is to emphasize that real *kedushah*, real spiritual growth, and establishing a genuine relationship with Hashem, are only achievable as part of a community. *Kedushah* is not found by excluding oneself from interaction with other human beings for fear of speaking *lashon hara*. Spiritual growth is not achieved by isolating oneself and not facing the challenges that regular social interaction brings. Instead, *kedushah* is found when we are part of a collective, when we act in the plural—קדושים תהיו. We interact, are part of, and contribute to Am Yisrael, and all the while we overcome the challenges that threaten *kedushah*.

---

4   *Vayikra* 19:2.

Rabbi Yechezkel Halberstam, the son of the *Divrei Chaim* of Tzanz, asks why the word תהיו is in the future tense. Why doesn't the Torah say "קדושים היו—Be holy," in the imperative form?

Rabbi Yechezkel explains that the Torah is informing us that we have a promise from Hashem that in the future we will be *kedoshim v'tehorim*. We will merit redemption, as the *Rambam* says that the Torah promises that we will all eventually do *teshuvah* and be redeemed.[5]

Hence, קדושים תהיו—do not become distraught, nervous, or pressured that your efforts will be in vain and that you will not attain *kedushah* and the benefits that accompany it. You will, we all will, and Mashiach will herald in an era of sanctity and holiness.

May this moment arrive very soon.

But I Gave Good Advice!

ולפני עור לא תתן מכשול.

Do not place a stumbling block before someone who is blind.[6]

The simple explanation of these words would follow the translation; namely, one is forbidden to place a stumbling block in front of a person who is visually challenged.

There does not seem to be any difficulty in understanding the *pasuk's* instruction.

If one sees a blind man walking down the road and places something in that person's way to cause him to stumble, he violates ולפני עור לא תתן מכשול.

However, *Rashi*, quoting the *Toras Kohanim*, explains these words to mean that if someone is blind in a particular matter, you must not give him advice that is not appropriate.

---

5   *Rambam, Mishneh Torah, Teshuvah* 7:5, cited in *Parpera'os LaTorah*, p. 134.
6   *Vayikra* 19:14.

The Lubavitcher Rebbe wonders why *Rashi* abandons the straightforward explanation of the *pasuk*. Why explain that *iver* means someone who is blind in a particular matter rather than as someone who is visually challenged, which is certainly the simple meaning.

Second, the word *michshol* means a physical stumbling block. Why does *Rashi* say that it refers to "advice that is not appropriate for him"?

Rashi then gives an example of advice that is not appropriate for him: One should not say, "Sell your field and buy yourself a donkey, and you maneuver around him and take the field from him."

The Rebbe asks three questions on this part of *Rashi*:

1. Why does *Rashi* need to bring an example of what constitutes "advice that is not appropriate for him"? Surely we can work it out for ourselves.

2. If *Rashi* wants to bring an example of "advice that is not appropriate for him," why did he choose this example out of the thousands that he could have brought?

3. In *Toras Kohanim*, which is *Rashi*'s source, it brings three examples of "advice that is not appropriate for him":

   • Do not tell someone to set out on a journey early in the morning when you know bandits will thereby capture him.

   • Do not tell someone to go on a journey in the afternoon when you know this will cause sunstroke.

   • Do not tell someone to sell his field and buy a donkey, and then you go and take the field.

Why did *Rashi* ignore two of the three examples brought in *Toras Kohanim* and only quote the case of the field and the donkey?

The Rebbe begins his answer by saying that when a *pasuk* seems to repeat information contained in an earlier *pasuk*, we need to find a justification for the repetition. The justification will usually take the form of a new insight that this *pasuk* provides that was not apparent in the first. Therefore, the straightforward explanation of the *pasuk*—do not place a *michshol* in front of a blind person—would seem to be a repetition of previous *pesukim* warning against damaging a person.

Parashas Mishpatim is full of such cases of damages. For example, the Torah warns against uncovering a pit or digging a hole and not covering it. One who does so is liable if an animal or person falls into the pit and is damaged.[7] This is a clear example of placing a *michshol*.

Our *pasuk*, therefore, would seem to be a repetition of the injunction not to cause damage via a *michshol*.

Therefore, *Rashi* explains that our *pasuk* adds a new dimension of not giving bad advice, which was not included in the *pasuk* talking about the uncovered pit.

We now understand why *Rashi* could not include the first two examples brought by the *Toras Kohanim*. Subjecting someone to bandits or sunstroke are examples of damages caused by a stumbling block, which would be included in the earlier *pasuk* of uncovering a pit. They are not part of the new dimension of giving bad advice.

The only example that *Rashi* can use is one of advising him to sell his field and buy a donkey. This case is not included in the previous prohibition of causing damage because it is not **inevitable** damage.

For some, a field is more useful than a donkey. For others, their circumstances demand a donkey over a field. This case is subjective.

If so, why is this forbidden?

The clue is in the last words of *Rashi*: "You maneuver around him and take the field from him." When a person advises another, he must focus solely on what is best for the person he is advising, divesting himself of any thoughts of personal gain. It is forbidden to advise someone to sell his field and buy a donkey, and then you buy that field, because it is not advice that is "הוגנת לו—appropriate for the other person," and this makes it unfit.

Even if your advice causes no monetary or other damage, since it was not given with the sole interest of the person being advised, it falls under the prohibition of ולפני עור לא תתן מכשול.

If someone is "blind" in a particular matter and turns to you for advice, he assumes that you will have **only** his interests at heart when

---

7   *Shemos* 21:33.

advising him. From here we see how far-reaching our *ahavas Yisrael* needs to be. It is not sufficient that someone else benefits from your advice and leadership. Your sole interest needs to be the other person, and you need to divest yourself of any thoughts of personal gain that may accrue from your advice.

This is the *chiddush* of the *pasuk*, says the Rebbe, namely that ולפני עור לא תתן מכשול does not refer to causing damage but applies even when one is remiss in his *ahavas Yisrael* and stands to gain personally from the advice he is giving.

Now we understand *Rashi*:

- The *pasuk* cannot be interpreted literally, as this has been covered in earlier *pesukim*.
- The *pasuk* is not discussing giving damaging advice, and therefore, the first two examples of the *Toras Kohanim* are omitted.
- The *pasuk* is referring to advice that, while beneficial to the one asking for it, wasn't given solely with him in mind—עצה שאינה הוגנת לו—and the *chiddush* is that this is a violation of the duty to live with *ahavas Yisrael*![8]

---

8   *Otzar Likutei Sichos*, p. 335.

אמור

I Believe with a Complete Belief...

ששת ימים תעשה מלאכה וביום השביעי שבת שבתון מקרא קדש.

For six days, work may be performed, but on the seventh day, it is a complete rest day.[1]

The *perek* begins with an introduction about the Festivals—מועדי ה' אשר תקראו אתם מקראי קדש—and then seems to take a detour and discuss Shabbos before returning to the theme of the *chagim*. *Rashi* explains that Shabbos is placed in the middle of the Festivals to teach us that anyone who profanes the Festivals it is as if he has desecrated Shabbos, and anyone who observes the Festivals it is as if he has observed Shabbos.

The question is why this is so. What is the connection between observing the Festivals and Shabbos?

Rav Moshe Feinstein explains that Shabbos and the Festivals represent the two elements of faith. The first is that Hashem created the world, and the second is that He directs the world and controls nature. By resting on Shabbos, we attest to the fact that Hashem created the

---

1   *Vayikra* 23:3.

183

world in six days and on the seventh created Shabbos. By observing the Festivals, we attest to the fact that Hashem controls nature.

- Pesach attests to the fact that He took us out of Egypt with miracles that showed His mastery over nature.
- Shavuos is dedicating to remembering that Hashem then gave us the Torah—the handbook for living within the physical world.
- Sukkos demonstrates that during the forty years in the desert, Hashem protected us from nature with the Clouds of Glory.

Placing Shabbos next to the Festivals shows us that they are both parts of one *emunah*, and you can't have one without the other. Believing that Hashem created the world and not believing that He controls it are incompatible.

Therefore, one who observes the Festivals—thus showing his belief in Hashem as controller of nature—automatically observes the Shabbos—the faith in Hashem as the Creator, and the same in reverse.

Our relationship with the Almighty needs to be whole. It needs to be a relationship based not only on belief in Hashem as the Creator but also in His involvment in every aspect of the world as a whole and my life specifically. My observance of the festivals, in addition to Shabbos, shows that I have a personal relationship with the Creator of the world![2]

2   *Kol Ram*, p. 140.

When Is Yom Tov Over?

וְאָמַרְתָּ אֲלֵהֶם מוֹעֲדֵי ה׳ אֲשֶׁר תִּקְרְאוּ אֹתָם מִקְרָאֵי קֹדֶשׁ, אֵלֶּה הֵם מוֹעֲדָי.

Speak to the children of Yisrael and say to them, "Hashem's appointed [holy days] that you shall designate as holy occasions. These are My appointed [holy days]."[3]

The *Seforno* notes that the Gemara discusses the aspect of the Festivals being חציו לה׳ חציו לכם, meaning that there is a spiritual aspect to the festival, but there is also a physical aspect of eating, family, etc. The danger lies when we concentrate solely on the לכם aspect and spend so much time eating, sleeping, and socializing that we miss the spiritual point of the festival entirely.

Therefore, the *pasuk* says: מוֹעֲדֵי ה׳ אֲשֶׁר תִּקְרְאוּ אֹתָם מִקְרָאֵי קֹדֶשׁ—the festivals that you designate as **holy** convocations, and not that you ignore the spiritual lessons and opportunities of the festival, אֵלֶּה הֵם מוֹעֲדָי—those are My type of festivals, says Hashem. Those are the festivals that Hashem is interested in, and that is the way we must celebrate them.

Too often, we hear complaints that it is another long Shabbos, or that the *chag* seems to go on and on. If we embrace the spiritual opportunities for Torah learning, etc. that these days present, then we would not make such a complaint!

---

3   *Vayikra* 23:2.

Shabbos, Teshuvah, and the Garden of Eden

ששת ימים תעשה מלאכה וביום השביעי שבת שבתון מקרא קדש.

For six days, work may be performed, but on the seventh day, it is a complete rest day.[4]

The *Midrash Rabbah* says that Adam HaRishon met Kayin and asked him what happened in his judgment for killing his brother. Kayin replied that he had repented, and as a result his punishment had "cooled." Adam was so impressed with the power of *teshuvah*, which was news to him, that he immediately declared מזמור שיר ליום השבת!

What is the connection between Adam's epiphany that *teshuvah* is valid and his declaration of מזמור שיר ליום השבת?

Rabbi Tzvi Hirsch Rabinowitz, Av Beis Din of Kovno, explains with a parable:

Before the days of computers and departments dedicated to bookkeeping, a large, successful factory would usually have one day a week when it closed production and concentrated on paperwork and administration, such as how much money came in, how much was owed to suppliers, etc.

However, if the factory incurs debts and ceases to operate, it does not need a day to work out the accounts, because it has nothing and owes everything.

Initially, Adam thought that there was nothing one could do to mend the damage caused by sin.

He thought it was spiritual bankruptcy, and there was no point in spending time examining his actions, as there was nothing he could do to make amends.

---

4   *Vayikra* 23:3.

After hearing from Kayin that there is something that he could do to make amends and pay his debts, he cried out, מזמור שיר ליום השבת. He needed a day off to sort out his spiritual accounts. That's what Shabbos is for.

It is time we should spend examining our actions of the previous week and undertaking to improve them in the coming week.

Shabbos is proof of the power of teshuvah, for if we were not capable of doing teshuvah, we would not need a day off to make a spiritual reckoning. The very fact that Hashem gave us Shabbos demonstrates that we can and must mend our ways. Let us use Shabbos properly and emerge focused on ensuring that the following week will be an improvement over the previous one.[5]

Teach, Teach, Teach

אמר אל הכהנים בני אהרן ואמרת אלהם לנפש לא יטמא בעמיו.

Speak to the Kohanim, the sons of Aharon, and say to them: "Let none [of you] defile himself for a dead person among his people."[6]

Rashi notes that there seems to be a redundancy in the *pasuk*, it uses the expression אמר twice. He explains that this is להזהיר הגדלים על הקטנים—that when it comes to the laws of avoiding *tumas meis*, adults need to ensure that the young children avoid coming into contact with a dead body.

The Lubavitcher Rebbe quotes the Gemara that states with regards to three mitzvos, the Torah specifically instructs adults to warn the children:

5   *Peninim MiShulchan Gavoha*, p. 187.
6   *Vayikra* 21:1.

1. אכילת שקצים—Eating insects
2. אכילת דם Eating blood
3. טומאת מת לכהנים—Kohanim coming in contact with a dead body[7]

The obligation to ensure that children don't violate the Torah applies to all of the mitzvos, so why are these three examples chosen?

The Lubavitcher Rebbe suggests that each of these prohibitions represents a unique group of prohibitions.

The prohibition against eating insects is one which, by nature, most people would avoid. Eating insects is repulsive, and therefore, even without a specific prohibition in the Torah, we would have stayed away from consuming them.

The prohibition against eating blood stems from when we became accustomed to eating blood in Egypt after living there for two hundred and ten years and were influenced by Egyptian culture, which used blood as part of their idol worship.

The prohibition for Kohanim to come into contact with a dead body is unique in that it represents a group of prohibitions that are not based on human logic but have been instructed to us by Hashem.

The Lubavitcher Rebbe says that the Torah specifically instructs us to train our children regarding these three prohibitions so that we absorb three essential principles in *chinuch*.

First, from the prohibition not to eat *shekatzim*—insects, we learn that even if someone has fallen so low that he is involved in actions that should naturally be repulsive, we must not give up on him. We must educate, instruct, and inspire him to forsake these behaviors. From the prohibition of eating blood, we learn that even if you think that someone's immoral acts have gone on for so long that they have become an unbreakable habit, we must continue with our efforts to bring him back to the proper path. He can and will change if we believe in him. Finally, from איסור טומאת מת לכהנים, we see that it is possible to educate people regarding matters that are above human logic and comprehension. People can attune themselves to issues of *kedushah* and *taharah*.

---

7   *Yevamos* 114a.

If the Torah gives us instruction to do something, it is a clear sign that we can do it. If the Torah specifically gives us the instruction to educate, it is a clear sign that we can educate. Even if someone is so lost as to go against nature, even if it has been going on for so long as to have become a habit, and even if the material is above human intuition, we must not give up on teaching, instructing, and inspiring.[8]

---

8   *Shulchan Shabbos with the Lubavitcher Rebbe*, p. 137.

בהר

Knock, Knock, Knocking on Mashiach's Door

וחשב עם קנהו משנת המכרו לו עד שנת היובל.

He shall calculate with his purchaser [the number of years] from the year of his being sold to him until the Yovel year.[1]

When a non-Jew acquires a Jew as an *eved*, he pays the purchase price, and the Jew is his until *Yovel*. When the Jew's family wants to redeem their relative, the redemption price is commensurate with the time left to his servitude. The closer the redemption is to *Yovel*, the less there will be to pay to redeem the Jew, and the longer there is until *Yovel*, the more expensive his redemption.

Therefore, if the non-Jew bought the *eved* fifty years before *Yovel* and paid fifty shekels for his labor, then this works out at one shekel a year until *Yovel*. Thus, if we redeem him with forty-five years left to *Yovel*, we would need to pay the master forty-five shekels for the Jew's redemption, whereas if we redeem him five years before *Yovel*, we would only need to pay five shekels.

---

1   *Vayikra* 25:50.

The Chafetz Chaim used this concept to answer a question about bringing Mashiach.

If the *tzaddikim* of previous generations, who were on a higher spiritual level than we are today, were unable to bring Mashiach, what chance does our generation have of bringing him? If the great Tanna'im, Amora'im, Geonim, Rishonim, and Acharonim did not manage to bring Mashiach, do we genuinely think that we can?

The Chafetz Chaim explained that Hashem has a fixed time as to when Mashiach will come. In order to bring Mashiach early, we must perform many good deeds and learn Torah. The further away we are from the intended date, the more Torah and *maasim tovim* we need to make Mashiach's arrival immanent. The closer we get to that date, however, the closer we are to the time when Mashiach MUST arrive, so the less Torah and *maasim tovim* we need to plug the gap.

We are in the *ikvesa d'Meshicha*...we can hear the footsteps of Mashiach...he is around the corner...he is banging on the door...he's urging us to open it and let him in! If he is so near, the amount of Torah and *maasim tovim* needed to open that door is much less than in previous generations, and therefore, we can and must do everything in our ability and on our level to bring him.[2]

2   *Taam V'Daas*, p. 166.

G-d vs. Me

יובל היא שנת החמישים שנה תהיה לכם לא תזרעו ולא תקצרו את ספיחיה
ולא תבצרו את נזריה.

*This fiftieth year shall be a Yovel for you; you shall not sow,
reap its aftergrowth, or pick [its grapes] that you had set aside
[for yourself].*[3]

Rabbi Yosef Zvi Dunner writes that if we examine the *Yovel* year,
we will see that there are primarily two mitzvos associated with
it that at first glance seem to be unrelated.
The first is the return of property to its ancestral owner, and the
second is the prohibition against working the land, as in a *shemittah*
year. However, a more in-depth examination will reveal that these two
mitzvos are intrinsically connected.

When a person receives his ancestral field again—the same field
that he was forced to sell due to economic difficulty—he is obviously
thrilled. His natural desire would be to set to work immediately on his
newly returned land. This has been his dream during all the years that
he waited for its return. It is therefore at this point that Hashem tells
him that he is not permitted to work his land, reminding him that he
does not own the property and cannot do with it as he pleases.

All land ultimately belongs to Hashem. It is only entrusted to us for
a limited time in order for us to use it to serve Him. Therefore, the mitzvah to return the land, and the prohibition to work it, serve to highlight
that Hashem is the true owner of everything.[4]

There is, however, another message that we can learn from these two
aspects of the *Yovel* year.

Sometimes, what fuels us to serve Hashem is not what Hashem wants
us to do but what we feel like doing. If our mood, desires, and wishes
happen to align with what Hashem demands, we end up observing

---

3   *Vayikra* 25:11.
4   *Mikdash Halevi*, p. 387.

Hashem's commandments. However, in a clash between what I want to do and what Hashem requires of me, who wins? The landowner desires to begin working his returned land immediately. Hashem forbids him to do so during *Yovel*. There is a clash; who will win? The aim in life is to tune one's desires so that they automatically align with what Hashem demands.[5]

An example of how one needs to be in control of one's emotions and desires is found in an incident recorded about Rav Dessler.[6]

During the Second World War, Rav Dessler was in England while his wife and daughter were in Australia. In total, they were separated for six years. Contact between the two countries was difficult, and the only method of communication was through writing letters, which even then was sporadic.

One morning, a letter arrived from his wife and daughter. From the shape of the envelope, it was clear that there were photographs enclosed. The mere sight of the letter set off powerful emotional reactions in Rav Dessler. Any other person would not have wasted a second and would have torn open the envelope immediately to see the photographs and read the letter enclosed. Rav Dessler, however, placed the letter on the mantlepiece and waited a full ten minutes before opening it.

Any strong desire must be controlled, for if not, the *yetzer hara* has an opening to gain a foothold. Everything that we experience must be controlled and used to further our relationship with Hashem.

---

5   *Avos* 2:4.
6   *Rav Dessler* (Artscroll), p. 184.

Double Goodness!

שש שנים תזרע שדך...ובשנה השביעית שבת שבתון יהיה לארץ שבת לה׳.

You may sow your field for six years...But in the seventh year, the land shall have a complete rest, a Sabbath to the Lord.[7]

T he *Meshech Chochmah* notes that the Torah instructs us to work the land for six years and to rest on the seventh. This is parallel to working for six days of the week and resting on Shabbos.

In the description of Creation in *Parashas Bereishis*, the words "כי טוב—It was good," are mentioned twice on the third day and twice on the sixth day.[8]

This is known as יום שנכפל בו כי טוב, and as a result, it is seen as auspicious to celebrate a wedding or other *simchah* on a Tuesday or on a Friday. These are days associated explicitly with everything טוב.

The parallel to day three and day six of creation are years three and six of the *shemittah* cycle.

Where is the particular association with טוב in these years?

The *Meshech Chochmah* points out that these are the years in which we are instructed to give a special tithe to the poor, called *Maaser Ani*. As part of one's annual distribution of *terumos* and *maaseros*, in years three and six, one needs to separate a tithe from one's crop and give it to the poor. It is this *Maaser Ani* that is parallel to the double expression of כי טוב that is found on days three and six of creation.

The message is that we can only enjoy the blessing, and things can only be טוב, if we share them with others less fortunate than ourselves.[9]

---

7   *Vayikra* 25:3–4.
8   *Bereishis* 1:10, 12, 25, 31.
9   *Parpera'os LaTorah*, p. 193.

בחוקותי

All We Are Saying Is
Give Peace a Chance

ונתתי שלום בארץ ושכבתם ואין מחריד.

And I will grant peace in the Land, and you will lie down with no one to frighten [you].[1]

ashi explains that the previous *pesukim* have described the physical plenty that will accrue as a result of listening to Hashem and following His Torah. As a result of this plenty, says *Rashi*, a person may be moved to ask: "What worth is having plenty of food and drink if there is no peace?" Therefore, in this subsequent *pasuk*, Hashem promises that ונתתי שלום בארץ.

From here, we see that "השלום שקול כנגד הכל"—Peace is equivalent to the total of all the other blessings."

Rav Moshe Feinstein suggests that the peace *Rashi* refers to is not peace between countries and the absence of war. If we were talking about wars, how could we say that we have all the food and drink that we need? At times of war, there are inevitable food shortages. Production is affected, and rationing is the norm. Besides, we do not need *Rashi*

---

1   *Vayikra* 26:6.

to tell us that peace from armed conflict is equal to any other blessing; modern history is proof of the destruction that war brings.

Therefore, Rav Moshe explains that peace refers to peace between each other. While we may have the blessing of food and drink, if communities are not at peace with each other, then what is it all worth?

Families may be blessed with an abundance of material wealth, but if parents cannot sit down and enjoy those blessing together with their children, grandchildren, and family, what benefit does the wealth serve? Therefore, the true blessing of peace—the peace that is שקול כנגד הכל—is the peace, tranquility, and harmony that reigns between people inside a country, communities, and at the heart of families.[2]

But That Was Then, and This Is Now!

איש כי יפלא נדר בערכך נפשות לה׳.

When a man expresses a vow, [pledging the] value of lives to Hashem.[3]

The *Kli Yakar* explains that the reason why the section dealing with vows is placed next to the *klalos* is that we very often make vows, especially vows to donate, when we are facing *tzaros*, facing some hardship or other. Then, human nature is that once the crisis has blown over, we forget all about the vows that we made.

This is comparable to the reed that, while the storm is raging, is bent over by the wind. However, once the storm has passed, the reed returns to its upright and proud position.

So too, when the storm is raging and we face troubles, we are humble and make vows to donate, yet when the storm blows over, and we are no longer facing any *tzaros*, we seem to forget the vows that we have made.

---

2   *Kol Ram*, p. 171.
3   *Vayikra* 27:2.

Immediately after the *klalos*, we find vows, because that is what people do when faced with a crisis. To impress upon us the importance of keeping our promises after the tribulations are completed, the subjects are connected.

The *Baal Haturim* explains, along the same lines, that if you add up all the shekel amounts mentioned in this passage (50+30+20+10+5+3+15+10), it totals 143, which equals the forty-five curses found in our *parashah* plus the ninety-eight curses in *Parashas Ki Savo*. This shows that the curses and the vows are connected, and hence, the section dealing with vows follows the curses.

The *Chozeh MiLublin* suggests another connection between the curses and vows. After hearing all the terrible curses that will befall Am Yisrael, a person may think that he is worthless, merely an object onto which Hashem will pour His scorn.

Therefore, immediately after the *klalos*, the Torah tells us that not only are we not worthless, but that everyone has a worth *l'hekdesh*, even when it comes to spiritual matters.

No matter what crisis we have just endured, be it national or private, we always need to remember that we have value, worth, and purpose. We need to dust ourselves off, connect with our self-worth and self-esteem, and redouble our efforts to forge a relationship with Hashem through Torah and mitzvos.[4]

---

4   *Otzar Chaim*, p. 200.

ספר
במדבר

במדבר

Education Begins at Home

ויפקד אתם משה על פי ה' כאשר צוה.

And Moses counted them according to Hashem's word, just as he was commanded.[1]

ashi explains that since the Leviim had to be counted from the age of one month old, and not from twenty years old like the rest of *Klal Yisrael*, Moshe Rabbeinu was faced with a problem. It would have been immodest for Moshe to enter the tents to count the babies. So how would he know how many Levite babies there were?

Hashem told Moshe to do what he had to do—and that He would take care of the rest. Moshe waited outside the tents while the *Shechinah* preceded him, and the *Shechinah* announced to him how many babies were in each tent.

This is why the *pasuk* says, על פי ה', for the counting was done literally by Hashem.

Dayan Moshe Swift uses this *Rashi* to teach us a vital lesson in *chinuch*:

If you want a Jewish child to be counted outside of the home, you must ensure that the *Shechinah* precedes him into the home. If we want

---

1   *Bamidbar* 3:16.

our children to continue along the path of Torah and mitzvos when they are outside of our direct control and influence, then we must ensure that we bring them up in a home were the values of Torah and mitzvos permeate every brick and guide every act. If we want our children to avoid speaking *lashon hara* and *rechilus*, then we have to ensure that our homes are free of such damaging talk. If we want the next generation to thrive on a Shabbos atmosphere with a table full of *divrei Torah, zemiros*, and guests, then we have to ensure that we give them such a table to emulate. And if we want our families to give back to the community, to play roles as leaders, innovators and educators, then they must first see all of that at home.

If you want a Jewish child to be counted outside of the house, first make sure that the *Shechinah* is to be found in that home![2]

Early Caring Education

פקד את בני לוי...כל זכר מבן חדש ומעלה.

Count the children of Levi...all males from the age of one month and upward.[3]

Unlike the rest of B'nei Yisrael, who were counted from age twenty and upwards, the Leviim were counted from one month old. *Rashi* explains that after one month, the child is old enough to be considered as "שומר משמרת הקודש—guardians of the holy charge." How can a month-old baby be considered for משמרת הקדש? What does this mean?

Later in the *parashah*, we read:

והחנים לפני המשכן קדמה לפני אהל מועד מזרחה משה ואהרן ובניו שמרים משמרת המקדש למשמרת בני ישראל והזר הקרב יומת.

---

2   *Peninim on the Torah*, third series, p. 182.
3   *Bamidbar* 3:15.

Moshe and Aharon and his sons camped in the east, and they were the guardians in charge of the Sanctuary, for the charge of the Children of Yisrael, and any non-Levi who approaches shall die.[4]

Why are we being told that any non-Levi who approaches shall die? The *parashah* is describing the camping arrangements around the *Mishkan*. How is this law related to the camping formation of the Leviim?

The answer is that the Leviim encamped surrounding the *Mishkan* to act as a buffer between the *Mishkan* and the rest of the people. If any non-Levi accidentally wandered toward the hallowed area of the *Mishkan*, the Leviim would be there to stop him. This is what the *pasuk* means when it says that the משמרת המקדש was למשמרת בני ישראל—the way the Leviim encamped was to guard and protect B'nei Yisrael and ensure that "הזר הקרב יומת—A stranger who approaches shall die" would never happen.

If your whole *raison d'etre* is to look out for the welfare of others and to have the interests of others first and foremost in your mind, then if you want to pass this on to the next generation, you can't begin to educate them only from age twenty and upwards.

If you want your children to grow up caring, worrying for, and helping others, they need to be educated in this direction from the moment they are born! Since the primary concern of the Leviim was the rest of *Klal Yisrael*—as reflected in the way they encamped around the *Mishkan*—they needed to be counted from the earliest viable age,[5] i.e., of one month and upwards, because that is when the education of what being a Levi meant began. Likewise, if we wish to raise children who care for others, they need to be educated in this regard from the moment they are born; we cannot wait until they have reached twenty and older, for by then it will be too late.

4   Ibid., v. 38.
5   *Rashi*, ibid., v. 15.

נשא

Oops...I Didn't Mean to Do It!

ויהי ביום כלות משה להקים את המשכן.

And it was that on the day that Moshe finished erecting the Mishkan.[1]

Rashi writes that even though Betzalel, Oholiav, and the *chachmei lev* were the ones who actually built the *Mishkan*, nonetheless the *pasuk* attributes it to Moshe: "לפי שמסר נפשו עליו לראות תבנית כל דבר ודבר...ולא טעה בתבנית אחד—Because he dedicated himself to know the exact dimensions of every artifact...no mistakes were made."

The *Meilitz Yosher* wonders what the connection is between the fact that Moshe dedicated himself and the fact that no mistakes were made. *Rashi* could have simply said that the *Mishkan* is attributed to Moshe because of his dedication. What is *Rashi* adding by saying that no mistakes were made?

The *Meilitz Yosher* answers that the two are directly connected. Mistakes happen because we are not sufficiently focused on the task at hand. If we dedicate ourselves to the task, prepare accordingly, and concentrate when performing it, mistakes will not happen.

---

1   *Bamibar* 7:1.

While to err may be human, to not prepare sufficiently or not adequately concentrate while performing a task is not being human; it is being negligent and setting yourself up to make mistakes.

Therefore, *Rashi* connects the two: The reason why Moshe is credited with the building of the *Mishkan* and the reason why no mistakes happened is because Moshe was dedicated and focused on the task at hand.[2]

While this is an important lesson for our daily life, it is no less important in our relationship with Hashem. If we take our relationship with Him seriously, we will prepare to ensure that we don't accidentally break Shabbos or violate any of the laws. If we prepare correctly and concentrate on our mitzvah performance, then we will not make the mistakes that can adversely affect our mitzvos. If we desire to be error-free in all our actions and relationships, then we need to approach them with the preparation they deserve and to concentrate while we are engaged in them.

Here We Go Again!

ויקרבו הנשאים את חנוכת המזבח.

The princes brought [offerings for] the dedication of the Altar.[3]

Why does the Torah repeat the details of the sacrifices brought by each of the Nesiim when they all brought the same thing? Why didn't the Torah just list their names and then write that they each brought the same thing, obviating the need to list everything more than once?

The Alter of Kelm suggests that the reason why the Torah repeats the sacrifice of each Nasi is to tell us that when a group of people perform a mitzvah together at the same time as a community, Hashem does not

2   *Talelei Oros*, p. 88.
3   *Bamidbar* 7:10.

only relate to the group but is happy with each individual as if he is the only one performing the mitzvah.

Sometimes, we feel that our participation in communal activities is at best irrelevant or unnecessary.

The *parashah* teaches us that many people may be engaged in the same mitzvah at the same time, yet Hashem loves each and every one of them as individuals.[4]

The Lubavitcher Rebbe says that here is an essential message as to the place of every individual in society in general. We are often obliged to perform the same acts as everyone else. We all need to say the same prayers and perform the same mitzvos. Yet, the repetition of the details of the sacrifices teaches us that within the standard practices, we need to inject our personal mark.

The *Ramban* quotes the Midrash that says that even though each Nasi brought the same thing, they each had different things in mind as they brought it![5]

The Torah is not looking for us to be clones of each other, even if outwardly we are all doing the same thing.

This is highlighted in prayer. Although we may repeat the same words three times daily, we need to find a way to make each time different and concentrate on a different aspect.[6]

4   *Talelei Oros*, p. 96.
5   *Bamidbar Rabbah* 13:14.
6   *Le'hachayos es Hayom*, p. 329.

If We Could Only
Put Plaques on Chicken!

ויקרבו הנשאים את חנוכת המזבח.

The princes brought [offerings for] the dedication of the Altar.[7]

T he *Oznayim LaTorah* notes that the Nesiim's donation to the *Mizbei'ach* was more significant than their contribution to the building of the *Mishkan*.

Usually, the opposite is true. Anyone who has been involved in fund-raising will testify that it is easier to solicit donations for the cost of a building than it is to raise money to pay the electricity bill, because when donating for a building, people can see the tangible results of their donations. Someone once told me that if only we could place plaques on cooked chickens, no teachers would go hungry. We often emphasize the means and ignore the cause. While the means was the physical building of the *Mishkan*, the cause was the sacrifices. They were the *raison d'etre* of the entire *Mishkan* enterprise. Therefore, it is to the *Nesi'im*'s credit that they emphasized the sacrifices over the *Mishkan*'s construction.

Perhaps we can use this insight of the *Oznayim LaTorah* to explain the Nesiim's actions at the time of the building of the *Mishkan* in a more positive light.

In *Parashas Vayakhel*, the Torah lists the materials donated by Am Yisrael to be used in the construction of the *Mishkan*. The people who brought their donations last were the Nesiim.[8] *Rashi* explains that they waited until everyone had brought their donations and were then going to donate what was still needed. The problem was that everyone else gave everything that was required, and none of the basic materials were left to be donated, so they were left donating the stones for the breastplate. This is seen as a criticism of the Nesiim, and they are viewed as being lazy. Consequently, the word נשאים is written *chaser*

---

7   *Bamidbar* 7:10.
8   *Shemos* 37:27.

(without a second letter ") in *Parashas Vayakhel,* indicating that there was something amiss in their behavior. *Rashi* then suggests that the reason why the Nesiim were so quick to donate for the *Mizbei'ach* at its inauguration was to atone for their earlier error.

Using the explanation of the *Oznayim LaTorah*, perhaps we can suggest a different reason for the Nesiim's behavior. The Nesiim knew that when it came to donating to the physical construction of the *Mishkan*, there would be no shortage of people willing to give. After all, who wouldn't want to donate when they could point to a part of the structure and show that they donated the gold or silver that went into building it?

They therefore gave at the end, knowing that there would be no shortage.

However, when it came to sacrifices that would be burnt on the Altar, where there would be no plaque to show family and friends, it was then that the Nesiim showed the way and taught that the sacrifices were the cause and the physical building the effect.

Their delay when donating to the construction of the physical edifice and their enthusiasm to donate for the sacrifices can be seen in a positive light. It can teach us an essential lesson in the mitzvah of tzedakah to communal causes.

If, however, this suggestion as to the Nesiim's behavior is correct, why is their name written *chaser* in *Parashas Vayakhel?* If there is no criticism, why is there something amiss with the spelling of their name? Perhaps we can suggest that while their actions may have been praiseworthy in theory, the fact remains that Hashem Himself, through Moshe, had requested donations to the *Mishkan.* When we have a request from Hashem, we do not play police officers and analyze who will give what and that we will give last, etc. If Hashem commands, then we react; the analysis can come later. If we delay the fulfillment of the command and engage in analysis, even if that analysis is correct, our actions are negligent and lacking.

בהעלותך

Always Look on the Bright Side of Life!

בהעלותך את הנרות אל מול פני המנורה.

When you light the lamps, the seven lamps shall cast their light toward the face of the Menorah.[1]

At the beginning of the *parashah*, Hashem teaches Moshe Rabbeinu the laws connected to the lighting of the *Menorah* and instructs him to teach these laws to Aharon HaKohen, which he does.

It then says that "ויעש כן אהרן אל מול פני המנורה העלה נרתה—Aharon did so, toward the face of the *Menorah*, he kindled its lamps."[2]

On these words, *Rashi* makes a startling comment: "להגיד שבחו של אהרן שלא שינה—These words are said in praise of Aharon that he didn't change," and followed the instructions that his brother Moshe had given him. What is *Rashi* trying to tell us? Would we think for a moment that Aharon would ignore the Divine command and act differently? What does *Rashi* mean?

---

1   *Bamidbar* 8:2.
2   Ibid., v. 3.

The Torah is telling us בהעלתך—If you want an *aliyah*, if you're going to elevate your life and be successful, then את הנרות—always look to the light; always see things positively, be optimistic, and be brave.

- Not everything in life goes the way we want it to, but hopefully most things do.
- Not every person we meet will treat us fairly and kindly, but hopefully most people will.
- Not every dream and aspiration that we have for the future will come to fruition, but *b'ezras Hashem* most of them will.

בהעלתך—If we want to be happy and successful, then את הנרות—look at the light and be positive. There is much about which we can be negative, cynical, and pessimistic, but happiness and success are derived from looking at the *neiros* and having the attitude that no matter what, we will succeed.

Perhaps this is the message that *Rashi* is teaching us concerning Aharon HaKohen. Who more than Aharon was justified in thinking that perhaps the odds were stacked against him? When he was young, his parents separated. His younger brother was thrown into a river. He was passed over as leader of the B'nei Yisrael in favor of that younger brother. He suffered the loss of two children, and finally, he was denied entry into Eretz Yisrael! Aharon had good reason to be negative, pessimistic, and cynical, yet the *pasuk* says, ויעש כן אהרן העלה—he elevated his life. And how? נרותה—He always looked at the positive side of things, he was אוהב שלום ורודף שלום[3] by always teaching people to be positive, optimistic, and brave.

That is the praise of Aharon HaKohen—that despite good reason, he did not change from Moshe's instruction of בהעלתך—of elevating himself and always looking את הנרות.

---

3   See *Avos* 1:12.

Hashem Loves Us— Even When We Fall!

ויהי בנסוע הארון ויאמר משה...ובנחה יאמר...

So it was, whenever the ark set out, Moshe would say...And when it came to rest, he would say...[4]

If we look in a *Sefer Torah*, we will see that these two *pesukim* are bracketed with an inverted letter נ. *Rashi* explains that this is to alert us to the fact that these two *pesukim* do not belong here. The reason why Hashem placed them here is to break up two episodes where the Jews displayed less than satisfactory behavior. When Am Yisrael left Har Sinai, they did so like a school pupil "escaping" at the end of the day. Instead of trying to delay their leave as long as possible to absorb the atmosphere of the Sinai experience for a few extra moments, the Jews bolted as soon as they were instructed to travel. This showed that they perhaps did not appreciate the true significance of the Divine revelation and *Kabbalas HaTorah*, and their behavior was not looked upon favorably by Hashem.

The second unsavory episode was that of the *misonenim*, when the Jews complained to Moshe about the *mann* and displayed a lack of appreciation for the miraculous sustenance that Hashem provided.

So that these two happenings should not be read in one continuous flow, Hashem inserted these two *pesukim* into the Torah to create a break in the narrative.

The Alter from Slabodka makes a fascinating comment related to this *Rashi*. He challenges us to look at the two *pesukim* that Hashem uses as His buffer. These two *pesukim* describe how when the *Aron* travels, the enemies of *Klal Yisrael* will be scattered and will flee from us.

Why were these *pesukim* used as the buffer?

Of all the *pesukim* that could have been inserted to break up the flow of negativity, why choose these two?

The Alter from Slabodka answers that these two were chosen not just to act as a buffer, but to deliver a message as well. The message is that even when we have fallen and have acted inappropriately, Hashem will still take our side and protect us. Even if we are engaged in negativity, He will still smash our enemies and scatter them. His love for us is so great that it is more durable than our misbehavior.

Rabbi Dov Katz, a student of the Alter from Slabodka, adds that now we can understand why these two *pesukim* are bracketed with two inverted letter 'נs and not any other letter of the alphabet. The Gemara tells us that the only letter missing from the *Ashrei* chapter of *Tehillim* is the letter 'נ. This is because the letter נ stands for *nefilah* (נפילה)—falling, i.e., when someone falls and behaves in a manner that is at odds with Hashem's wishes. Such sentiment has no place in a prayer devoted to praising Hashem's glory.[5]

It is precisely for this reason that this letter is chosen to bracket these two *pesukim* and is inverted. We should never think that because we are experiencing a *nefilah*—a moment of challenge in our relationship with Hashem—that He abandons us. The opposite is true. During the times of challenge themselves, Hashem declares how much He loves us. As we fall, He takes the נ of *nefilah* and turns it upside down and inside out to declare that our *nefilah* can and will be reversed, and that He loves us no matter what. This is the message of the placement of ויהי בנסוע הארון and the two letter 'נs.

In the middle of a crisis, when we have moved away from Hashem and His Torah and when we are struggling with our relationship with the Almighty, we need to remember that He is on our side and loves us. When we are running away from *Kabbalas HaTorah*, complaining, and showing ingratitude, Hashem will show us His love with two inverted letter 'נs and ויהי בנסוע הארון![6]

---

5   *Berachos* 4b.
6   *L'titecha Elyon*, p. 164.

שלח לך

Reaching Up or Pressing Down?

כי תבאו אל ארץ מושבתיכם אשר אני נתן לכם...ויין לנסך רביעית ההין תעשה.

Speak to the children of Yisrael and say to them: "When you arrive in the Land of your dwelling place, which I am giving you...And a quarter of a hin of wine for a libation, you shall prepare."[1]

The Lubavitcher Rebbe teaches that there are two ways in which a person may desire to serve Hashem. He may wish to connect so strongly with spirituality and soar upwards to Heaven so seriously that he almost wants to divest himself of anything physical, which he sees as an impediment to achieving his goals. Alternatively, a person may be moved in the opposite direction and receive inspiration from above, driving him down to earth to engage in the physical world with the goal of sanctifying mundane existence. A sacrifice that is burnt on the Altar until its blood and fats have risen in smoke represents the first method of aspiring upwards. On the other hand, the

---

1   *Bamidbar* 15:2, 5.

wine libations are poured downwards, and they represent the path of inspiration from above.

The spies saw interaction with the physicality of living in Eretz Yisrael as a challenge to their desire to divest themselves of physicality. They did not see the necessity to plow, sow, water, reap, etc., as the ideal way to be G-dly. This is what led them to spread their slanderous report about the Land of Israel. The sin of the spies, who excelled in their desire to aspire upwards, is therefore followed by the libations, which represents the ability to engage in this world. The message of the *nesachim* comes to counter the mistaken outlook of the spies.

Spirituality is to be found from the top-down, i.e., by learning the Torah and the spiritual lessons it contains, and then applying what we have learned in our day-to-day activities in this physical world.[2]

The need to look upon physicality as an opportunity to engage with spirituality, and to raise everything as part of our relationship with Hashem, is also found in our *parashah* in the *pasuk* related to the mitzvah of separating challah. The *pasuk* reads:

בבאכם אל הארץ אשר אני מביא אתכם שמה ראשית ערסתכם חלה
תרימו תרומה.

When you come to the Land to which I bring you…the first of your kneading you shall set aside.[3]

The *Avodas Yisrael* writes in the name of Reb Zusha that humans were created with the need to eat and drink so that they would elevate these mundane actions. Therefore, before eating, people need to contemplate that Hashem could have created them without the need to eat. If Hashem created them with this need, it is because Hashem wants us to elevate the act of eating. We need to eat in purity and holiness, and not just to satisfy our appetite.

2   *Kol Menachem* 959.
3   *Bamidbar* 15:18, 21.

This what the Torah means when it says:

- בבואכם אל הארץ—When you approach earthly, physical activities, remember:
- אשר אני מביא אתכם שמה—It was I who created you in this way.
- תרימו תרומה לה׳—You will elevate all acts of physicality into actions that serve Hashem.[4]

Stick Together!

ראשית עריסתכם תרימו תרומה.

The first portion of your dough, you shall separate a loaf for a gift.[5]

The *Shem MiShmuel* writes that any tithe that we are instructed to separate is an acknowledgment and thanks to Hashem for the new produce with which He has blessed us. The mitzvah of challah, though, is different. There is no product here; it is flour and water mixed together. It is not a new crop, but rather a fruit already grown that has been turned into flour. Why do I need to acknowledge Hashem at this stage, if I have already acknowledged Him when the wheat was harvested?

The message of *hafrashas challah* is that two items (flour and water) combined together form one entity of dough. We separate challah to atone for the lack of unity in *Klal Yisrael*, behaving like separate entities that do not mix and join together.

By separating a part of the mixture and elevating it, we accept to act with unity and promote harmony amongst us.

Seen through this idea, the taking of challah is not an act of thanks to Hashem but an act of emphasizing the need for us to live in unity

4   *Maayanah shel Torah*, p. 73.
5   *Bamidbar* 15:20.

with each other. This is one of the reasons why the mitzvah of *hafrashas challah* was given after the sin of the spies.

The spies caused *machlokes* amongst the Jewish People, and *hafrashas challah* highlights the need for *achdus*.[6]

Rav Unsdorfer of Petach Tikvah explains the question in the *Mah Nishtanah* of הלילה הזה כלנו מסובין—that all other nights we eat sitting upright or leaning, but on this night we only lean—in the following way:

Chazal often refer to *galus* as "night." Therefore, the child is asking מה נשתנה הלילה הזה—Why is this exile different from all the others? The exile in Egypt lasted two hundred and ten years. The exile in Babylon was for seventy years. Our present exile is over nineteen hundred years long and still going! Why hasn't it ended? The answer is הלילה הזה כלנו מסובין! The halachah is that on Shabbos, it is forbidden to knead flour and water together to make a dough. However, it is permitted to knead water and *subin*—bran, together because the *subin* does not stick together. The reason why this *galus* has lasted longer than all the others is because הלילה הזה כלנו מסובין—we are all like *subin* and do not stick together. The key to ending this present exile is unity. Without it, the *galus* will continue and become longer and longer.[7]

Sticks and Stones

שלח לך אנשים ויתורו את ארץ כנען.

Send for yourself men and they will spy out the Land of Canaan.[8]

The *parashah* of the spies follows the *parashah* of Miriam. *Rashi* explains that Miriam was punished for misusing her speech, and "these *resha'im* (i.e., the spies) saw this happen and did not

---

6 *Yagdil Torah*, p. 203.
7 *Sheva D'Nechamasa, Haggadah shel Pesach*, p. 72.
8 *Bamidbar* 13:2.

learn from it." The Talmud tells us in the name of Rav Elazar ben Parta that we can see how severe the sin of *lashon hara* is from the fact that the spies spoke against an inanimate object, i.e., the Land of Israel, and were punished so severely.[9] But if they only spoke against "wood and stones," as the Gemara calls it, how are they expected to learn from the case of Miriam? She did not speak against "wood and stones" but rather against her brother, Moshe, and perhaps that is why she was punished. Maybe the spies **did** take the case of Miriam to heart and would have learned from her that it is absolutely forbidden to speak *lashon hara* against another human being, but how are they supposed to learn from Miriam that speaking out against the holy "wood and stones" is forbidden?

Rav Shlomo Gantzfried, author of the *Kitzur Shulchan Aruch*, answers that when we speak against other people and thereby upset them, damage them, and hurt their feelings, we have transgressed a *mitzvah bein adam l'chaveiro*. However, that only applies to a regular person. A person such as Moshe Rabbeinu, who was the humblest of all men, would never be offended when someone spoke against him. There would be no hurt feelings, for he was, as it were, "wood and stones." Therefore, when Miriam spoke against Moshe Rabbeinu, it was like talking against "wood and stones," and yet she was punished. These spies saw this and did not take *mussar*, and therefore they too are punished for speaking against "wood and stones."

Rav Yerucham of Mir asks: The worst thing that the spies are guilty of is not learning from what happened to Miriam? Surely their real problem is that they spoke negatively against Eretz Yisrael, thus leading to their own deaths and the deaths of an entire generation in the desert. Why is *Rashi* so concerned that the spies saw what happened to Miriam and didn't take *mussar* from it?

Rav Yerucham answers that after every event that we experience, see, or hear, we are supposed to ask ourselves, "Why did I see or hear that? What am I supposed to learn and internalize from what I have just

9   *Arachin* 15a.

seen, heard, or experienced?" The fact that the spies failed to do so after what happened with Miriam led them to the sin of speaking *lashon hara* against Eretz Yisrael.

Therefore, *Rashi* is highlighting the underlying reason for their sin. They did not stop to ask themselves why they had just witnessed Miriam's punishment. They failed to learn from what they had witnessed.

Things do not happen to us by chance, and we need to be sensitive and learn from all our experiences.[10]

---

10   *Talelei Oros*, p. 177.

קרח

Where's the Beef?

R abbi Isaac Bernstein notes that when we conclude saying the *Shema*, it is forbidden to interrupt between the final words אני ה׳ אלקיכם and the first word אמת of the next paragraph.

It is so vital that *emes* is attached to Hashem that we are not permitted to talk, hint, or make any verbal or non-verbal communication that interrupts the flow of אני ה׳ אלקיכם אמת.

If so, why is it not written so in the Torah? At the end of *Parashas Shelach*, the last *pasuk* reads אני ה׳ אלקיכם and does not continue with the word אמת. If it is so important to have this continuous flow in the *Shema*, why is it not found in the Torah?

Rabbi Isaac Bernstein answers that if the Torah had written אני ה׳ אלקיכם אמת, then the connecting word between the end of *Parashas Shelach* and the beginning of *Parashas Korach* would have been the word *emes*, and we cannot associate the rebellion of Korach with *emes* in any shape or form.

There was not a shred of truth in any of Korach's claims. It would be fair to suggest that Korach himself didn't believe them. His was a rebellion against the authority of Moshe Rabbeinu as a result of Korach not receiving the *kavod*—the honor that he felt he deserved. Therefore, the last word of *Parashas Shelach* cannot be the word *emes*, as Korach's rebellion has no association with the truth.[1]

Echoing the same theme, the *Levushei S'rad* asks why the paragraph dealing with the *matanos kehunah*—the twenty-four gifts that non-Kohanim give the Kohanim, is placed immediately following Korach's rebellion. The twenty-four gifts would be better placed in *Sefer Vayikra* where we deal with the sacrifices, or at the time of the inauguration of the Kohanim. Why are they placed here, following the rebellion of Korach and his followers?

The *Levushei S'rad* answers that the *matanos kehunah* are placed next to the rebellion of Korach so that we should understand that this was the real motivation behind the revolt.

Korach talked in hallowed terms: כל העדה כלם קדושים ובתוכם ה׳—I'm not doing this for myself, I am doing this for the honor of Hashem! His real displeasure was that he would be financially worse off, as he wouldn't receive the twenty-four *matanos kehunah*.

The *emes* did not feature in Korach's mind. Instead, it was self-interest that fuelled Korach's desire to challenge Moshe Rabbeinu, with the disastrous consequences that it brought.

Every rebellion starts with a leader preaching lofty ideals. How do we know whether he is genuine and sincere or has sinister intentions that he masks by talking in hallowed terms? The answer lies in examining his actions and those of his followers. If the leaders are genuine and sincere, then their true followers will behave in a way that reflects those lofty ideals and spiritual ambitions.

If, however, the ideals are not matched in practice, and instead of peace and harmony the rebellion brings chaos, violence, and hate, then we have to question whether there were, perhaps, other motivations.

Korach talked the talk but didn't walk the walk, and that resulted in tragic consequences for him and his followers.[2]

1   Rabbi Isaac Bernstein, *Parashas Korach*, series 2.
2   *Meorah shel Torah*, p. 90.

0–60 In?

ולבני לוי הנה נתתי כל מעשר בישראל לנחלה חלף עבדתם אשר הם
עבדים את עבדת אהל מועד.

*And to the descendants of Levi, I have given all tithes of Yisrael
as an inheritance, in exchange for their service that they perform—the service of the Tent of Meeting.*[3]

The *Ohr Sameach* writes that this *pasuk* tells us that the Leviim
did not own a portion in the Land of Israel, but were instead supported by the rest of the nation in return for their
Temple service.

The *Ohr Sameach* quotes the *Rambam*,[4] who says that Shmuel HaNavi
and David HaMelech split the Leviim into twenty-four *mishma-
ros*—watches, with one watch serving in the Temple each week.

Each watch was further divided into groups, called *batei avos*, and the
heads of the *batei avos* decided which Leviim from within the *batei avos*
would work on each day.

What transpires is that in a regular year that has around fifty weeks,
each *mishmar* was on duty for two weeks, and each individual Levi
worked for only two days out of the year!

If so, why did the rest of the nation have to support the Leviim financially? The Leviim had plenty of time when they were not on duty to
find a job and support themselves!

The *Ohr Sameach* suggests that to be adequately prepared for their
two days of Temple work, the Leviim needed the rest of the year. For
twenty-three weeks of the year, the Levi needed to purify, sanctify, re-
fine, and elevate himself so that he was ready for his two days of service.

To work in the Temple assisting the Kohanim takes preparation. One
cannot simply travel from 0–60 in a few seconds.

---

3   *Bamidbar* 18:21.
4   *Rambam, Mishneh Torah, Klei Ha'mikdash* 3:9.

Therefore, the Leviim needed to prepare, and consequently, they were supported by the rest of the nation.[5]

Rav Aharon Kotler asks that if the Leviim needed to be supported so that they could prepare for their two days of Service, why wasn't *maaser* distributed in an orderly and equal fashion? The farmers would decide which Levi they would give their *maaser*, which could result in some Leviim receiving more than others. Also, there are a few tactics that people can employ to ensure that their produce is exempt from *maaseros*, for example, if the food is brought into the house through the roof as opposed to the door.

All of this meant that any particular Levi could not be assured that he would receive sufficient produce. So how was he meant to prepare for his two days?

Rav Kotler answers that as a result of their elevated status, there was a real fear that the Leviim may take themselves too seriously and become arrogant. Since it was the duty of the people to support the Leviim, there was a worry that far from feeling indebted and obliged to the people, the Leviim would think that they deserved it by right and would become aloof. This would cause the opposite effect of what was intended. Rather than growing in spirituality and serving the people, they would become arrogant, and such a person cannot be spiritual. Therefore, to keep the Leviim on their toes, they never knew exactly from where their *maaser* would come, and if indeed they would receive any *maaser* at all. This instilled within them a level of humility, which is the springboard for any spiritual growth.[6]

The two messages, therefore, are that spirituality takes work. One who desires a close relationship with Hashem needs to be prepared to put in the effort and toil. Without hard work, there cannot be spiritual growth. Second, the critical factor in achieving that spiritual growth is humility; it ensures that the hard work invested in spiritual growth pays dividends.

5   *Talelei Oros*, p. 307.
6   *Peninim Mishulchan Gavoha*, p. 157.

Sweet and Bitter!

ויצא פרח ויצץ ציץ ויגמל שקדים.

It gave forth blossoms, sprouted buds, and produced ripe almonds.[7]

The final sign that Hashem gave to show that the appointment of Aharon as the Kohen Gadol was legitimate and that Korach's claims were unfounded was that Aharon's staff blossomed with almonds, while none of the other tribes' sticks blossomed.

Rabbi Shlomo Zalman Kook, who was the father of HaRav Avraham Yitzchak HaKohen Kook, once found himself in a shul that was experiencing a severe *machlokes*, and they approached him to see if he could bring peace between the two warring sides.

Rav Shlomo Zalman Kook mounted the *bimah* and asked a question from this week's *parashah*:

Why was it, he asked, that the flower that blossomed on Aharon's stick was almonds? Why not any other flower? *Rashi* answers that almonds flower very quickly, but Rav Shlomo Zalman Kook offered another explanation.

In the first chapter of *Masechta Maaseros*, we are told that there are two different types of almonds. The first type is sweet-tasting at its beginning but bitter by the time it fully ripens, and the second type is precisely the opposite—initially bitter but sweet when ripe. The reason why the almond was chosen to flower on the staff of Aharon was to teach us that this is the inevitable outcome of *machlokes*. It starts off all juicy and sweet, and everyone is keen to find out who is on which side, "what happened today in shul," "who spoke to whom," etc. But, inevitably, by the time we reach the end, all we are left with is bitterness. Old friends no longer talk to each other, the authority of leaders is eroded, and communities can be destroyed.

---

7   *Bamidbar* 17:23.

When it comes to the search for peace, however, the opposite is true. At first, it may be bitter. Each side may have to make painful concessions. By the end though, one gets the sweet taste of peace with all the beauty and blessings that it brings.

The almond was chosen to highlight the adverse long-term effects of *machlokes* in contrast to the long-term benefits of *shalom*.[8] Rabbi Yehoshua ibn Shuav, one of the Rishonim, quotes a Chazal that says that the almonds that grew on Aharon's staff were bitter and sweet. On one side of the staff grew sweet-tasting almonds, while on the other side grew bitter almonds, which fits perfectly with the message taught by Rabbi Shlomo Zalman HaKohen Kook.[9]

---

8   *Otzar Chaim*, p. 98.
9   *Minchas Chayeinu*, vol. 3, p. 387.

חקת

Meat and Milk and Red Cows!

זאת חקת התורה אשר צוה ה'...ויקחו אליך פרה אדומה.

*This is the statute of the Torah that the Hashem com-
manded...take for you a perfectly red unblemished cow, upon
which no yoke was laid.[1]*

The expression זאת חקת התורה is found in only one other place,
and that is after the war with Midian. Hashem commands B'nei
Yisrael to purify themselves and the vessels that they captured
from Midyan, and in this context, the *pasuk* says: זאת חקת התורה אשר צוה
ה' את משה.[2]

The *Meshech Chochmah* explains that the connection between the two
is that in our *parashah*, we are instructed concerning the *parah adumah*,
for which no reason is given, and likewise, the *parashah* after the war
with Midyan deals with the laws of kashrus, for which no explanation is given.

Rabbi Shimon Biton suggests that in today's world, we are accustomed to every question having an answer. We encourage our children

---

1   *Bamidbar* 19:2.
2   Ibid. 31:21.

to be inquisitive, to ask questions, and to search for answers. We take nothing for granted or at face value. We are educated, intelligent, and have a duty to use our intellect to make informed decisions.

However, life's experiences teach us, and as we grow older, it becomes more and more apparent that not every question has a simple answer. Some deep and essential questions seemingly have no answers at all.

Our *parashah* tells us that when educating our children, we need to make them open to the possibility that for some questions, there are no answers. But if there are no answers, why do we follow such practices? גזירה היא מלפני ואין לך רשות להרהר אחריה; if we understood Hashem fully, we would be Hashem.

We need to be able to say זאת חקת התורה, my performance in this area of Torah is dependent on nothing other than the fact that I was commanded to do so by Hashem.

Perhaps this is why we have two examples of זאת חקת התורה. One is in connection to kashrus / eating, which is an activity in which even the very young are engaged. This is to show that we need to educate the young that not everything has a ready-made answer and that one needs to be able to submit to a higher power.

One might think that only someone whose mind has not yet developed, who perhaps lacks a certain level of sophistication, needs to be ready to submit to a higher power. Once that child's mind has matured, developed, and expanded, then only that which is understood by the intellect needs be observed, and that which has no reason need not be heeded altogether.

To counter this mentality, the Torah specifies the case of *parah adumah*, whose very essence could, theoretically, only be understood by the mature mind, and still it says, זאת חקת התורה. Even adults, who are ostensibly experienced, educated, and wise, must also be ready and able to say, גזירה היא מלפני ואין לך רשות להרהר אחריה.[3]

3 *Bein Adam LaParashah*, p. 212.

I Can't Hear You When You Shout!

וְדִבַּרְתֶּם אֶל הַסֶּלַע לְעֵינֵיהֶם וְנָתַן מֵימָיו.

And speak to the rock in their presence so that it will give forth its water.[4]

someone once remarked that וְדִבַּרְתֶּם אֶל הַסֶּלַע can be used with regards to people who are so removed from Torah and mitzvos that they have become as hard as a rock and resist anything that has to do with religion. When interacting with such people, the Torah tells us, וְדִבַּרְתֶּם אֶל הַסֶּלַע—you need to speak to them, and then וְנָתַן מֵימָיו—water, which is analogous with Torah, will flow from them like a river.

No one has been alerted to the beauty of Torah by having it shoved down his throat, and no one has fallen in love with Hashem and His mitzvos because he was shouted at for not fulfilling them. וְדִבַּרְתֶּם אֶל הַסֶּלַע—engage people in a civil dialogue. Warm, friendly, and genuine exchanges of ideas can melt the heart of even the hardest stone.[5]

However, while dialogue is to be encouraged, the Torah uses the word וְדִבַּרְתֶּם, which reflects a strong type of speech, as opposed to וַאֲמַרְתֶּם, which would indicate a softer, gentler way of communicating. If we are being urged to engage in friendly communication with those for whom religion is a heavy, dried-up rock, then the Torah should have said, וַאֲמַרְתֶּם אֶל הַסֶּלַע. What is the significance of the expression וְדִבַּרְתֶּם?

The message being relayed by the use of the word וְדִבַּרְתֶּם is that even as we communicate and befriend those who are estranged from a Torah way of life, or who may be strongly opposed to a Torah way of life, we must stand firm in our principles and be unapologetic for our unwavering dedication to Hashem and His Torah.

We must be able to say, "I love who you are, but I hate what you are doing."

---

4   *Bamidbar* 20:8.
5   *Otzar Chaim*, p. 109.

If we are prepared to ויְדַבֵּר, then we can affect even the סֶלַע.

Engage, debate, talk, and befriend, but do so knowing that מֹשֶׁה אֱמֶת ותורתו אמת.

To Life, to Life, L'Chaim!

שִׁמְעוּ נָא הַמֹּרִים.

Now, listen, you rebels.[6]

The *Rambam* suggests that Moshe's error at Mei Merivah was not that he hit the rock but that he became angry and called the people *morim*—rebels.[7]

The effect that a person of Moshe's stature has on the people is immeasurable. Therefore, Moshe becoming angry, lashing out at the people, and calling them rebels had a negative effect of far greater proportions than the act itself.

When the people saw how upset Moshe was with them, they automatically thought that Hashem was likewise annoyed with them for requesting water.

However, if we look at the *pesukim* that relate how Hashem instructed Moshe, it is all said very calmly and without any hint of anger: "קַח אֶת הַמַּטֶּה וְהַקְהֵל אֶת הָעֵדָה אַתָּה וְאַהֲרֹן אָחִיךָ וְדִבַּרְתֶּם אֶל הַסֶּלַע...וְהוֹצֵאתָ לָהֶם מַיִם—Take the staff and assemble the congregation, you and your brother Aharon, and speak to the rock in their presence so that it will give forth its water." No anger!

So, according to the *Rambam*, there is no sin associated with Moshe's hitting the rock except for the anger that he displayed when he said, שִׁמְעוּ נָא הַמֹּרִים.

The question we need to ask is why was it that Moshe Rabbeinu, who consistently defended B'nei Yisrael when they ran afoul of Hashem,

---

6   *Bamidbar* 20:10.

7   *Rambam, Shemonah Perakim*, end of *perek* 4.

suddenly got angry and called them rebels? Does this not seem very uncharacteristic of what we know about Moshe Rabbeinu? What had B'nei Yisrael said or done to bring about this reaction?

Rav Yitzchak HaKohen Rappaport suggests that when the Jews demanded life, and their desire was for food or something associated with living, Moshe defended them.

However, here they say, "ולו גוענו בגוע אחינו—If only we had perished as our brethren perished before Hashem."[8]

Their desire is not life but the opposite, and for such a hope, there is no defense. Moshe cannot defend their wish to die. We have nothing more precious than life itself.

As long as B'nei Yisrael demanded what they thought was beneficial for living, Moshe Rabbeinu defended their mistakes. However, once they relinquished the desire to live and gave in to pessimism, hopelessness, and talk of perishing, their mistakes can no longer be defended.[9]

---

8   *Bamidbar* 20:3.
9   *Otzar Chaim*, p. 110.

בלק

Single vs. Plural

וירא בלק בן ציפור את כל אשר עשה ישראל לאמרי.

Balak, the son of Tzippor, saw all that Yisrael had done to the Emorites.[1]

t the end of *Parashas Chukas*, we read about two military victories: the victory over Sichon, King of the Emorites,[2] and over Og, King of the Bashan.[3]

The question, therefore, is why at the beginning of our *parashah* does it only mention the war against the Emorites?

Why is Balak not troubled by the victory of the Jews over Og, King of the Bashan?

As a general rule, wherever the Torah refers to the Jewish People as "Yisrael," in the singular, it alludes to the fact that at that moment, the Jews were united together as a single person.

The most famous example would be when the Jews arrived at Mount Sinai prior to receiving the Torah, where the *pasuk* says, ויחן שם ישראל

---

1   *Bamidbar* 22:2.
2   Ibid. 21:21.
3   Ibid., v. 33.

כנגד ההר,[4] on which *Rashi* comments, "כאיש אחד, בלב אחד—Like one man with one heart."

At the battle with Og, the *pasuk* says, "ויכו אותו ואת בניו ואת כל עמו—They struck him, his sons, and his whole nation," with the word ויכו in the plural. This is in contrast to the battle with Sichon, where the Torah writes, ויכהו ישראל—i.e., in the singular.

The battle against Sichon was fought when the Jews unified and united.

It was this unity that Balak feared. The Jews' victories did not trouble him, as he could outsmart them in war. He had superior weapons and armies. The fact that the Jews had defeated Og militarily was not a cause for alarm.

However, the fact that they had become united frightened Balak and caused him to act.

This is alluded to in the reason given in the *pasuk* for Balak's alarm: "ויגר מואב מפני העם מאד כי רב הוא—Moav became very frightened of the people because it was numerous."[5]

The *pasuk* does not say "כי רבים הם—For they were numerous," i.e., in the plural, but rather כי רב הוא—in the singular.

Balak understood that when the Jews are united, no one can stand in their way.

Balak understood that the key to Jewish success and survival is unity.

Balak, the enemy of *Klal Yisrael*, understood this fundamental truth. Do we?

---

4   *Shemos* 19:2.
5   *Bamidbar* 22:3.

I Can See Everything So Clearly Now!

לא הביט און ביעקב ולא ראה עמל בישראל ה׳ אלוקיו עמו ותרועת
מלך בו.

He does not look at evil in Yaakov, and has seen no perversity in Yisrael; Hashem, his G-d, is with him, and he has the King's friendship.[6]

Rebbe Levi Yitzchak of Berditchev interprets the *pasuk* so beautifully when he says that someone who has a strong relationship with Hashem will not look for the negative in fellow Jews. Instead, he will continuously seek out something positive, some merit, some talent, and something good in every person. That is the sign that someone is truly G-d-fearing.

This is the alluded to in the *pasuk*: "לא הביט און ביעקב ולא ראה עמל בישראל—Someone who sees no iniquity in Yaakov and no perversity in Yisrael," a person who always seeks out the positive and ignores the negative, we can be sure that with such a person, "ה׳ אלוקיו עמו ותרועת מלך בו—Hashem is with him, and the friendship of the King is in him."[7]

But how can we achieve such a lofty level? Based on the Kotzker Rebbe, we can explain in the following way.

After the initial attempt to curse the people failed, Balak tells Bilaam to relocate to a position where he will only be able to see part of Am Yisrael but not all of them: "אפס קצהו תראה וכלו לא תראה וקבנו לי משם—However, you will see its edge but not see all of it, and you will curse it for me from there."[8]

The Kotzker Rebbe says that this teaches us that if you only look at part of the story or situation—at the קצה, then תראה—you will see something negative, something wrong. However, if you know the

---

6   Ibid. 23:21.
7   *Otzar Chaim*, p. 131.
8   *Bamidbar* 23:13.

full story (כלו), then לא תראה, suddenly you can't see that negativity, because every question you had now falls away.

This is true concerning our relationship with Hashem, where many of our fundamental questions of faith are due to the fact that we can't see the whole picture and the entire plan that He has for us. It is also true in our relationships with others, where we don't know the complete story and therefore misinterpret people's actions, leading to a breakdown in relationships.

There is always a reason as to why people act the way they do, and it may be as simple as cultural differences; whereby a compliment in one place may be seen as rude or insulting in another. Before we get insulted, look at the complete picture. By doing so, we will not think negatively of others, and as a result, it will be said, לא הביט און ביעקב ולא ראה עמל בישראל ה' אלוקיו עמו.[9]

Why Are You Here?

כעת יאמר ליעקב ולישראל מה פעל א-ל. הן עם כלביא יקום וכארי יתנשא.

In time, it will be said to Yaakov and Yisrael, "What has G-d wrought?" Behold! The people will arise like a lion cub and raise itself like a lion.[10]

Rabbi Avraham of Slonim explains that today, when we meet a friend, we ask him, "How is business?" and inquire as to the success or otherwise of his physical business dealings. כעת—there will come a time when two Jews will meet, and their primary line of inquiry will be, מה פעל א-ל, what have you done for Hashem today, how is your spiritual business?[11]

9   *Maayanah shel Torah*, p. 112.
10 *Bamidbar* 23:23–24.
11 *Otzar Chaim*, p. 133.

Rabbi Nosson Wachtfogel quotes *Rashi*, who explains that this *pasuk* refers to the fact that Jews rise from their sleep, like a lion, ready to perform mitzvos. The first law in the *Shulchan Aruch* is the instruction to rise with eagerness in the morning to perform the work of Hashem. Rabbi Wachtfogel notes that if this is what Bilaam means when he says, עם כלביא יקום וכארי יתנשא, then it turns out that what impresses Bilaam and what he is led to praise is not the fact that *Klal Yisrael* observe the mitzvos but rather the way that they observe them.

It is not the fact that they perform the mitzvos but that they execute them with eagerness and with readiness—"like a lion they rise up."

In other words, it is not necessarily important what you do, as much as the way that you do it.[12]

Rabbi Yitzchak Elchanan Spektor once headed a delegation of rabbis to the Russian Interior Minister to persuade him to repeal some anti-Jewish decrees. Just before the meeting, the Deputy Minister, a known anti-Semite, approached Rabbi Spektor and asked him what the reason was for the Jewish People having been created. What do they contribute to society? They serve no purpose, and the world would be better off without them and the problems they bring.

When Rabbi Spektor heard these words, he was immediately filled with joy, which left the Deputy Minister confused. He explained himself by quoting our *pasuk*: כעת יאמר ליעקב ולישראל, at that time when they say about the Jews, מה פעל א-ל why did Hashem bother to create them, then this is a sign of that the rest of the *pasuk* will be fulfilled: "הן עם כלביא יקום וכארי יתנשא—Behold! The people will arise like a lion cub and raise itself like a lion."

The ultimate indication that victory is close at hand is not when the nations of the world disagree with our actions, but when they challenge our very right to exist.[13]

The Chafetz Chaim notes that the word מה has two connotations: first, it is a simple question, as in "מה ה' שואל מעמך—What does Hashem

---

12   *L'titecha Elyon*, p. 386.

13   *V'Karasa LaShabbos Oneg*, vol. 1, p. 240.

request from you," and second, it is an expression of wonderment, as in "מה טובו אהלך—Wow! How goodly are you tents etc."

The Chafetz Chaim explains that at present, all we have is questions concerning Hashem's actions, such as מה פעל א-ל—how could Hashem allow such a thing to happen? We do not understand much of what we have experienced as individuals and as a nation.

Today, when the Divine plan has not been revealed to us, מה פעל א-ל is a question. However, כעת יאמר ליעקב ולישראל—there will eventually come a time when we will be able to see how all of world history fits into one Divine plan. We will be able to put all the pieces together and form one clear picture. At that moment, we will say מה פעל א-ל as a declaration of wonderment! "I can't believe the wonder of the design, plan, and outcome!"[14]

---

14 *Peninim MiShulchan Gavoha*, p. 206.

פנחס

Play It Again, Sam!

את הכבש אחד תעשה בבקר ואת הכבש השני תעשה בין הערבים.

One lamb you will do in the morning, and the second lamb you will do in the evening.[1]

Rabbi Yosef HaLevi Dunner quotes a Midrash that says:

- According to Ben Zoma, the *pasuk* that best encapsulates the essence of Judaism is שמע ישראל ה' אלקינו ה' אחד.
- Ben Nanas says that the *pasuk* that best encapsulates the essence of Judaism is ואהבת לרעך כמוך.
- Finally, Rabbi Shimon ben Pazi suggests that the most inclusive *pasuk* of the tenets of Judaism is את הכבש אחד תעשה בבוקר ואת הכבש השני תעשה בין הערבים.[2]

We can fully understand why one would suggest that *Shema Yisrael* encapsulates everything important in Judaism. The bedrock of Judaism is monotheism.

---

1 *Bamidbar* 27:4.
2 Although Rav Dunner quotes the *Ein Yaakov*, who says that he could not find such a Midrash, Rav Dunner proceeds to develop his idea based on this Midrash.

We can also understand why Ben Nanas suggests that it is ואהבת
לרעך כמוך. After all, it was about this *pasuk* that Rabbi Akiva said, זה
כלל גדול בתורה. Without love for our fellow man, our Judaism is severely
deficient.

However, what does Rabbi Shimon ben Pazi mean when he suggests
that the instruction to bring a *Korban Tamid* every morning and evening is the most important? How does this *pasuk* contain a message
that encompasses what it means to be a Jew?

Rabbi Yosef HaLevi Dunner suggests that the answer can be summed
up in one word—consistency.

The *Korban Tamid* is brought every day—every morning and every evening.

It does not depend on our mood or how busy we are. It does not stop
due to *simchas* and is not interrupted by tragedy.

Every day, day after day, the *Korban Tamid* is brought.

This is why the two lambs that were offered—one in the morning and
one in the evening—had to be the same. It underscores that our service
of Hashem needs to be the same, no matter what the circumstances.

The morning represents times of joy, when everything is clear, and
the evening is compared to times of challenge, when everything seems
dark. Nonetheless, it is the same *Korban Tamid* that is sacrificed at
both times.[3]

Our relationship with Hashem is no different than any long-term
relationship that we may have with a fellow human being.

In every relationship, there will be ups and downs. Every relationship
will have moments of closeness and others of distance.

The key to a successful relationship is the consistency needed to
be true to the other, no matter what the current situation may be.
Through consistency and sticking together through all the challenges,
the relationship will flourish.

---

3   *Mikdash Halevi*, p. 497.

If we want to build a long-lasting and enduring relationship with the Creator of the world, we need to exhibit consistency. Consistency of purpose and consistency of action will lead to a constant relationship with Hashem.

Don't Wait, Don't Delay

כבשים בני שנה תמימים שנים ליום עולה תמיד.

Two unblemished lambs in their first year, each day, as a continual burnt offering.[4]

Rabbi Yitzchak of Drohovitz writes that the word "כבשים—lambs," can also be read to suggest things which are hidden (כבושים).

We can therefore read the *pasuk* in the following way: כבושים—Anger that a person has hidden in his heart toward someone else, do not leave it; שנה תמימה—for a whole year, dealing with it only around the time of Yom Kippur. שנים ליום—Rather, twice a day, once in the morning when you awake, and again in the evening before going to sleep; עולה תמיד—offer up and sacrifice the anger, and then your heart will be pure to serve Hashem and your fellow man.[5]

We must not allow negative feelings toward others to fester; rather, we must consistently act to remove them from our hearts.

---

4   *Bamidbar* 28:3.
5   *Otzar Chaim*, p. 157.

Books, Shtenders, and Leadership

ויאמר ה׳ אל משה קח לך את יהושע בן נון...וסמכת את ידך עליו.

Hashem said to Moshe, "Take for yourself Yehoshua, the son of Nun, a man of spirit, and you shall lay your hand upon him."[6]

T he Talmud tells us that Moshe's face was comparable to the sun, whereas Yehoshua's was like the moon.[7] When Yehoshua was appointed leader, the elders said, "אוי לה לאותה בושה אוי לה לאותה כלימה—Woe to us is the embarrassment and disgrace." The simple understanding of this statement is that they were bemoaning the state of the people who had lost a leader of the caliber of Moshe Rabbeinu only to have him replaced by Yehoshua, who they felt was not of the same stature.

The *Chida*, however, interprets this Gemara differently, and explains that on the *pasuk* that says, "ומשרתו יהושע בן נון נער לא ימוש מתוך האהל—His servant, Yehoshua son of Nun, a lad, would not depart from within the tent,"[8] we are taught that Yehoshua used to organize and arrange the tables and chairs in the *beis midrash* of Moshe Rabbeinu. He would tidy up after the *shiur* and do all the menial jobs that no one else was interested in or were too embarrassed to do, and it was in this merit that Yehoshua was appointed leader after Moshe.

Therefore, when Yehoshua was appointed, the elders said, אוי לה לאותה בושה אוי לה לאותה כלימה, woe to us is that embarrassment, because had we bothered to become involved in those jobs that we thought were beneath us, we might have been appointed leader!

Rav Moshe Sternbuch asks that while being the one who engages in all the menial tasks, such as arranging the chairs and tables for the *shiur*, may be an admirable attribute, how is it a sign of leadership? Why is this the reason Yehoshua merited following Moshe Rabbeinu as the leader?

---

6   *Bamidbar* 27:18.
7   *Bava Basra* 75a.
8   *Shemos* 33:11.

Rav Sternbuch answers that it is a sign that Yehoshua was willing to serve everyone—from the greatest of the great down to the "regular" members of *Klal Yisrael*. Just as a chair does not distinguish whether the person sitting on it is a *tzaddik* or a *rasha*, so too, Yehoshua would not distinguish. In the same way as a table does not differentiate between a scholar and an ignoramus when it comes to supporting his books, so too, Yehoshua would not differentiate.

A true leader needs to serve everyone and is not the exclusive domain of the rich and influential. By clearing up the *beis midrash*, Yehoshua showed that he appreciated this lesson and deserved to be the next leader.

מטות

A Part of, Not Apart From

הנה קמתם תחת אבותיכם תרבות אנשים חטאים.

And behold, you have now risen in place of your fathers as a society of sinful people.[1]

The *Targum* explains this *pasuk* to mean that Moshe is telling the B'nei Gad and B'nei Reuven that they had become *talmidim* of the spies. In the same way that the spies did not wish to enter Eretz Yisrael, so too, you, their students, do not want to enter the Promised Land and prefer to remain on the other side of the Jordan River.

The Lubavitcher Rebbe asks why at first Moshe Rabbeinu compares their request to the actions of the spies and then, when they assure him that they are willing to take part in the conquest of Eretz Yisrael, he relents and agrees to their request. What has changed in the meantime?

The Lubavitcher Rebbe explains that their request to remain and tend to their sheep was a request to be left to the tranquility of life as a shepherd, which is a life conducive to spiritual contemplation and growth. This is why the Avos were all shepherds, as the profession leaves plenty of time to think and grow spiritually.

1   *Bamidbar* 32:14.

This is the connection between their request and the actions of the spies. Their motivation was also to avoid the brutal reality of engaging with this world, as would be the case if they entered Eretz Yisrael. They preferred the spiritual bliss of life in the desert and the miracles that accompanied it.

The spies' motivation was considered a sin because, after *Matan Torah*, our challenge is to engage with this world and to elevate it, not to withdraw from it. This was the mistake of the spies, and Moshe thought that these two tribes were guilty of the same error. If so, what made Moshe change his mind, and why did he permit them to settle on the other side of the Jordan?

The answer is that for the Jewish People to fulfill its purpose, we need two types of people:

1. Those who elevate the physical and infuse it with spirituality
2. Those who dedicate themselves solely to the spiritual and the learning of Torah

The mistake of the spies was not that they wanted to dedicate themselves solely to Torah. Their mistake was that they wished for *everyone* to dedicate themselves strictly to spiritual pursuits and to withdraw from engaging with this world.

When the B'nei Gad and B'nei Reuven showed willingness to fight for the land, Moshe understood that they did not intend that their way of life was meant for everyone. They showed that they did not intend to sever their connection with the rest of the people, and therefore, Moshe agreed to their request.

Am Yisrael needs to have people who dedicate themselves solely to the pursuit of Torah knowledge, but that dedication needs to be as part of the people, not apart from it. They need to be involved and take their share of communal responsibility and influence everyone else with their Torah.[2]

---

2   *Shulchan Shabbos with the Lubavitcher Rebbe*, p. 185.

Hard Work, Not a Quick Fix

האחיכם יבאו למלחמה ואתם תשבו פה.

Shall your brethren go to war while you stay here?[3]

When blessing the tribe of Gad at the end of his life, Moshe says: "וירא ראשית לו כי שם חלקת מחקק ספון—He chose the first portion for himself, for that is where the lawgiver's plot is hidden."[4]

Rashi tells us that Gad requested to be given a portion in the lands of Sichon and Og because they knew that Moshe Rabbeinu would be buried there, and they wanted to be near him.

If this was their rationale, why was Moshe Rabbeinu so harsh with them when they made their request? Also, why did they not give this as their rationale? Why did they say instead that it was due to their large flocks and their need for pasture? Rabbi Baruch Shimon Shneurson suggests that although their primary rationale was to remain close to where Moshe Rabbeinu would be buried, they didn't mention this out of respect for Moshe. Instead, they blamed it on their wealth. This is why they didn't reply when Moshe told them off, because to do so would reveal their true rationale, which they did not wish to do.

The fact remains, however, that their request for part of Eiver HaYarden as opposed to a portion in Eretz Yisrael is seen as a grave mistake, driven by greed and wealth. If all they really wanted was to be near the place of Moshe's internment, what was so grave (pardon the pun) about that?

The lesson that needs to be learned here is that to genuinely get close to Hashem, we do not need to seek external *segulos*. Rather, we need to work hard, perfecting ourselves by listening to what Hashem wants from us.

---

3   *Bamidbar* 32:6.
4   *Devarim* 33:21.

B'nei Gad did not want the hard work of self-perfection that is represented by living in Eretz Yisrael and working hard to keep the mitzvos. What they wanted was a *segulah*, an address near the grave of Moshe Rabbeinu, which they felt would help them achieve high levels of spirituality without the need for any of the hard work that usually accompanies it. Every time they needed a spiritual "fix," they simply had to pop in to the area of Moshe's gravesite, and that would inspire them.

While this may be positive as *part* of one's relationship with Hashem, the relationship cannot be predicated on it.[5]

Perhaps the reason why the location of Moshe's grave is unknown is to highlight this message. One cannot swap Eretz Yisrael and its demands for a life dedicated to the hard work of *avodas Hashem* for some external spiritual experience, such as living near the grave of Moshe Rabbeinu.

---

5   *Talelei Oros*, p. 278.

מסעי

Good Journeys

אלה מסעי בני ישראל אשר יצאו מארץ מצרים לצבאתם ביד משה ואהרן.

These are the journeys of the children of Israel who left the land of Egypt in their legions, under the charge of Moshe and Aharon.[1]

The *Ohr Hachaim Hakadosh* refers us to the opening *pasuk* of *Parashas Mishpatim*, which begins with the words: "ואלה המשפטים אשר תשים לפניהם—And these are the ordinances that you shall place before them."[2] *Rashi* there comments that the word אלה indicates that the Torah is about to invalidate what was just said, but ואלה comes to build upon that which preceded it.

The beginning of our *parashah*, which deals with the journeys of *Klal Yisrael* from Egypt, does not have a letter ו, and therefore it is coming לפסול—to invalidate any other journeys except for the ones mentioned in this *parashah*.

Which other journeys are being referred to that have been invalidated?

---

1   *Bamidbar* 33:1.
2   *Shemos* 21:1.

The *Ohr Hachaim Hakadosh* answers that they are journeys that are not "ביד משה ואהרן—By the hand of Moshe and Aharon." These jour- neys, and these journeys alone, which are ביד משה ואהרן, i.e., that are in accordance with Hashem's will and His Torah, these alone can be termed מסעי בני ישראל. But any journey that we take, every action, every move that isn't ביד משה ואהרן, i.e., that isn't according to our *mesorah*, and that doesn't conform to Torah and halachah, these are *pasul*—invalid.[3]

Why Didn't You Tell Me?

ויצו משה את בני ישראל על פי ה׳ לאמר כן מטה בני יוסף דברים.

Moshe commanded the children of Yisrael according to the word of Hashem, saying, "The tribe of Yosef's descendants speaks justly."

Rabbi Mordechai Gifter notes that both here and when the daughters of Tzelophchad initially present their case,[4] before Hashem tells Moshe what the law is, He introduces His decision by noting that the question was a good one: כן בנות צלפחד דברת, and כן מטה בני יוסף דברים.

Why is this? Why doesn't Hashem tell Moshe His decision without any introduction?

Rav Gifter suggests that we are being taught a valuable lesson in ed- ucation. When someone does something good, we must first acknowl- edge it, and only afterwards continue to deal with any of the formalities that may be needed. If our children do something good, we need to give them positive feedback so that they know that what they did was right and that it is appreciated.

Too often, we may *shep nachas* but forget to tell our children that we are *shepping nachas*. The *pasuk* comes to teach us that just benefiting

---

3   *Otzar Chaim*, p. 182.
4   *Bamidbar* 27:7.

from someone's actions is not sufficient. We have to inform them that what they did was excellent and how much we enjoyed it.[5]

I Can Make a Difference

זה הדבר אשר צוה ה' לבנות צלפחד לאמר לטוב בעיניהם תהיינה לנשים אך למשפחת מטה אביהם תהיינה לנשים.

This is the word that Hashem has commanded regarding Tzelophchad's daughters: Let them marry whomever they please, but they shall marry only to the family of their father's tribe.[6]

The Lubavitcher Rebbe notes that we are introduced to the laws of inheritance as a direct result of the B'nos Tzelophchad and their inquiry to Moshe regarding their eligibility to inherit. The Rebbe asks that this seems to be an almost backhanded way of introducing a crucial area of civil law. Why was it introduced in this way?

The lesson the Torah teaches us is that we should never think that our private actions have no broader effects. B'nos Tzelophchad had an individual problem. Were they entitled to inheritance? They could have said, "Why should we bother troubling Moshe? Surely, he has better things to worry about." But it was important to them. They loved Eretz Yisrael and needed an answer to their inquiry, and so they took their question to Moshe Rabbeinu. As a result of their private longing for Eretz Yisrael, we were introduced to the laws of inheritance.

We must never feel that what we do as individuals does not have an effect.[7]

5 *Talelei Oros*, p. 330.
6 *Bamidbar* 36:6.
7 *Le'hachayos es Hayom*, p. 398.

ספר
דברים

דברים

A Defending Critic

אלה הדברים אשר דבר משה אל כל ישראל.

These are the words that Moses spoke to all of Yisrael.[1]

Rabbi Shlomo Kluger notes that usually, when the Torah uses the word אלה, it comes to exclude something else. It is as if the Torah writes, "these, but not those."

What is being excluded in this opening *pasuk* of *Sefer Devarim*?

Rabbi Kluger quotes the *pasuk* in *Mishlei* that says:

"מוכיח אדם אחרי חן ימצא—One who reproves someone will find favor."[2]

On this *pasuk*, the Midrash remarks that Rabbi Yehudah, son of Rabbi Simon, wondered about the meaning of the word אחרי in the *pasuk*. Hashem says that Moshe reprimanded Me אחרי—on behalf of the B'nei Yisrael, and rebuked the B'nei Yisrael—concerning their behavior toward Me.

Moshe's criticizing and reminding B'nei Yisrael of their sins was only when he spoke to them. When he spoke to Hashem on their behalf,

---

1 *Devarim* 1:1.
2 *Mishlei* 28:23.

though, he always fought in their corner, presenting their defense and attempting to gain them The Almighty's favor.

We can now understand what the word אלה excludes.

אלה הדברים אשר דבר משה אל כל ישראל—These are the words of criticism that Moshe spoke, because he was talking to the Children of Israel. However, when he spoke of the people to Hashem, he did not highlight their shortcomings, but rather always emphasized their greatness.[3]

With this insight, we can now revisit the *pasuk* in *Mishlei*. Why is it that "מוכיח אדם אחרי חן ימצא—one who reproves someone will find favor"? People do not usually appreciate being told off or criticized, even if it is meant well and is constructive criticism. So why will they "find favor"?

The answer is that if I know that the person rebuking me always defends me in front of other people, and I know that he would never make an unkind remark about me to others, then I am happy to accept his criticism. Even constructive criticism is hard to hear from a stranger. Even if the person offering advice means it for my benefit, I will only accept it wholeheartedly if I know that he is my greatest supporter in front of everyone else. The Jewish People knew that Moshe Rabbeinu sang their praises before Hashem, and as a result, they would accept his criticism.

Before we rush to offer advice and any form of criticism to anyone else, let us first ensure that we are his leading defender and foremost supporter.

---

3   *Talelei Oros*, p. 8.

Be Careful of Scared People!

אתם עברים בגבול אחיכם בני עשו הישבים בשעיר וייראו מכם ונשמרתם
מאד.

You are about to pass through the boundary of your kinsmen,
the children of Eisav, who dwell in Se'ir, and they will be afraid
of you. Be very careful.[4]

The *Be'er Yosef* says that there seems to be a contradiction in
the *pasuk*.

If the B'nei Eisav fear B'nei Yisrael, why do B'nei Yisrael need
to be very careful?

We are wary of people who do not fear us, not those who do.

The *Be'er Yosef* explains that indeed, we need to be careful of people
who fear us!

If you start up with someone who feels helpless and afraid, he has
nothing to lose by fighting, and he therefore can call upon unknown
reserves that can propel him to achieve almost superhuman results.

Hence, the *pasuk* is warning B'nei Yisrael that B'nei Eisav are so afraid
that they have nothing to lose. In such a situation, they have the potential to be even more dangerous than enemies who do not fear you.[5]

Rabbi Yissachar Frand explains that this is why when the Jewish army
waged war and surrounded a city, they always left one side of the city
open and did not wholly besiege it.

Intuitively, we would say that this seems self-defeating. What purpose
is there in surrounding a city only to leave one side open?

The answer is that if you surround a city on all sides, the inhabitants
feel that they have no way out. They therefore have nothing to lose and
summon hidden reserves with which to fight.

---

4   *Devarim* 2:4.
5   *Talelei Oros*, p. 57.

If, however, they see that one side of the city is not surrounded, human nature dictates that rather than fight a war that they probably cannot win, they'll choose to escape via the open side of the city.

Rabbi Frand used this idea to explain a story that took place in the old Soviet Russia:

> At one of the clandestine, underground bris milah ceremonies, after the circumcision had been completed, the mother cuddled the baby, kissed him, and then fainted. After the mother had been revived, she explained that, as everyone could see, the baby was a few months old and not the usual eight-day-old baby that has a bris. The reason for this was that the baby was born with a skin condition that needed to clear up before he could have his bris.
>
> The mother was so nervous that as the time passed, she would lose the strength to perform an illegal bris that she made an oath that she would not show the baby any love or affection until he had a bris. Consequently, when she finally cuddled and kissed him, it was the first time since the baby was born.

Rabbi Frand wondered: how could a woman, who had very little Jewish education and lived under a regime that had outlawed Jewish practices, have the strength to behave in such a way? The answer is that when there is no way out, no other options available, human nature draws on reserves that we cannot usually access and can achieve what seems to be almost impossible.

The *Be'er Yosef* concludes that the idea of not instilling too much fear in one's enemies also applies on a personal and individual level as well. The Gemara warns against instilling too much fear into one's household:[6] לעולם אל יטיל אדם אימה יתירה בתוך ביתו.

If our homes are ones where the children are overly afraid of their parents, this will eventually lead to the children distancing and breaking connections with their parents, for after all, what do they have to lose?

---

6   *Gittin* 6b.

Appreciate and Thank

אוכל תשברו מאתם בכסף ואכלתם, וגם מים תכרו מאתם בכסף ושתיתם.

You shall buy food from them with money, that you may eat, and also water you shall buy from them with money, that you may drink.[7]

For forty years of travel in the desert, Hashem provided for the people. And now, when the finish line of Eretz Yisrael is in sight, Hashem suddenly makes them pay for their food and drink. Why?

The *Oznayim LaTorah* compares it to a prince whose father provides him with food and lodgings, and the prince shows no appreciation toward his father and takes it all for granted. What does the father do? He sends the prince on holiday to a hotel and makes the prince pay for the stay. When the prince asks his father why he is doing this, the king answers that he wants the prince to learn how much it costs to eat and stay at someone else's expense, and then maybe the prince will show some gratitude to his father.

For forty years, Hashem provided for B'nei Yisrael, and all He received in return was moaning and grumbling. Now, Hashem wished to educate His people and let them see for themselves what goes into providing for that amount of people. Perhaps they will now show some gratitude.

This is why the *pasuk* that instructs the B'nei Yisrael to pay for their food and drink is followed by one that reminds them that in all their years in the desert, ה׳ אלוקיך עמך **לא חסרת דבר**. Hashem has provided for your every need, now go and understand what that should mean to you.

Let us take a moment to think of those who have spent their lives providing for us. Appreciate and thank them.

---

7   *Devarim* 2:6.

Why Did You Forget Your Manners?

ותקרבון אלי כלכם.

And you all drew near to me.[8]

When rebuking *Klal Yisrael* with regards to the sin of the
spies, *Rashi* tells us that Moshe Rabbeinu admonishes
them over their disorderliness. Unlike their approach at
the time of *Matan Torah*, where the leaders and the elders approached
first, and only then the youngsters, when it came to the spies, it was
a case of "ותקרבון אלי כלכם—Everyone approached me," with the children
pushing the elders and the elders, in turn, pushing the leaders, with
everyone showing a lack of *derech eretz*.

While showing a lack of *derech eretz* is obviously something negative,
in light of the disastrous consequences of the sin of the spies—the
entire generation dying, Tishah B'Av forever becoming associated with
tragedies, etc.—why is Moshe Rabbeinu highlighting a seemingly inci-
dental issue? The lack of discipline in the way the people approached
and requested to send spies into Eretz Yisrael seems trivial compared
to the sin of the spies itself!

The *Chiddushei HaRim* notes that it is not by chance that Moshe
Rabbeinu makes a comparison between their behavior at the sin of the
spies and their behavior at *Matan Torah*.

Perhaps we can excuse the way that B'nei Yisrael approached Moshe
Rabbeinu at the time of the spies by suggesting that it was merely
a reaction to how important they felt that the situation was, and in
their urgency, they forgot their manners, and everyone started to push
each other.

If so, says Moshe Rabbeinu to the people, how was it that you were
able to remain so calm, collected, and civilized at *Matan Torah*? Was
Matan Torah not an instance of supreme importance? Wouldn't your
urgency to hear the word of Hashem also cause you to forget your

---

8   Ibid. 1:22.

manners and to start pushing? If you managed to behave with the proper decorum and dignity at *Matan Torah*, but did not manage to at the sin of the spies, it is a sign that Hashem and His Torah are just not that important to you.

This is why Moshe Rabbeinu mentions the lack of *derech eretz* at the time of the spies, because not only is he rebuking them over the sin of the spies but also over the lack of urgency and importance they showed at *Matan Torah*.[9]

Rav Yaakov Kamenetsky adds that the fact that everyone approached Moshe Rabbeinu at the time of the spies, when usually it would have been the leaders or the troublemakers, shows that a certain level of panic had set in among *Klal Yisrael* over their proposed entry into Eretz Yisrael, and this was worthy of rebuke. When Hashem has promised His nation that he will take them from Egypt and lead them into Eretz Yisrael, whatever happens along that journey cannot be met with panic, for that shows a lack of trust and a flaw in our relationship with Hashem. If Hashem says something, then Hashem will do it, and we need to remain faithful to that knowledge, no matter what He throws at us along the way.[10]

Thus, the lack of *derech eretz* at the time of the spies is worthy of rebuke either because it showed that Torah was not seen as all that important, or because it showed a level of panic that has no place in the make-up of a people who have a strong relationship with Hashem.

As this *parashah* usually precedes Tishah B'Av, let us commit ourselves fully to Hashem and His Torah and show how important it is to us, especially *bein adam l'chaveiro*. Let us avoid the mistakes that led to Tishah B'Av by reaffirming our loyalty to His promise that He will lead us קוממיות לארצינו.

---

9   *Talelei Oros*, p. 45.
10   *Peninim Mishulchan Gavoha*, p. 26.

ואתחנן

Did You Want to If You Could?

אנכי עמד בין ה׳ וביניכם...כי יראתם מפני האש ולא עליתם בהר.

And I stood between Hashem and you...for you were afraid of the fire, and you did not go up on the mountain saying.[1]

From this *pasuk*, it would seem that Moshe Rabbeinu stood between the people and Hashem because the people were afraid of the fire, and for that reason they did not ascend Har Sinai.

It would seem that had they not been afraid of the fire, then Moshe Rabbeinu would not have had to stand between the people and Hashem, and they would have climbed up the mountain and received the Torah.

However, at *Maamad Har Sinai* itself, Hashem explicitly forbade the people from even touching the edge of the mountain:

והגבלת את העם סביב לאמר השמרו לכם עלות ההר ונגע בקצהו, כל הנגע בהר מות יומת.

You shall set boundaries for the people round about, saying, "Beware of ascending the mountain or touching its edge; whoever touches the mountain shall surely die."[2]

---

1   *Devarim* 5:5.
2   *Shemos* 19:12.

How do we explain this apparent contradiction? Rabbi Amnon Bezek suggests that Moshe Rabbeinu was reprimanding the people from a different angle. Moshe Rabbeinu told the people that they refrained from ascending the mountain, but not because it was forbidden to do so. He had to stand between them and Hashem because they were afraid of the fire; they didn't sufficiently desire to go up and receive the Torah. Had they had a burning desire to receive the Torah and have a direct experience of Hashem, they would not have been afraid of the fire. Moshe's point was that even if it had been permitted to ascend, they wouldn't have wanted to, because they did not sufficiently want it. Accordingly, whether or not it actually was permitted was not the issue.[3]

During the Coronavirus pandemic, we have been deprived of many of the mitzvos that we almost took for granted. We haven't been able to daven in a minyan, *hachnasas orchim* has been almost impossible, etc. The question is: Are we relieved that we could not perform these mitzvos, because we never really wanted to perform them in the first place, or do we crave the opportunities to perform these mitzvos and are upset that they have been taken away from us?

Moshe Rabbeinu tells us that if we genuinely wish to climb the mountain but refrain only because we have been barred, we will still merit to see the glory of Hashem.

Concerning mitzvah observance, we may not always be **able** to, but we must show that we always **want** to.

---

3   *Nekudas Pesichah*, p. 393.

I Get in the Way of Me

אנכי עמד בין ה' וביניכם בעת ההיא.

I stood between Hashem and you at that time.[4]

The Maggid of Mezhritz explains the *pasuk* in the following way. When Moshe Rabbeinu says אנכי עמד בין ה' וביניכם, he is giving us a message for all generations—that the main impediment in the relationship between us and Hashem is אנכי, our overindulgence in the self.

אנכי עמד בין ה' וביניכם means that our self-centeredness, our inability to see anything other than what **we** want and desire, and our unwillingness to divest of the self for the attainment of a higher cause is the main reason why we find it difficult to fulfill our full potential in our relationship with Hashem and His Torah.[5]

The same idea is found when Avraham Avinu instructs Eliezer to find a wife for his son Yitzchak. He instructs Eliezer not to take a girl from the daughters of Canaan: "לא תקח אשה לבני מבנות הכנעני אשר אנכי יושב בקרבו—Do not take a wife for my son from the daughters of Canaan, among whom I dwell."[6]

We all know that Avraham Avinu lived in Canaan. Why is it necessary to add the words אשר אנכי יושב בקרבו?

The answer is that Avraham Avinu was explaining to Eliezer what was wrong with B'nos Canaan and why they were unfit as a wife for Yitzchak. The reason was that אנכי יושב בקרבו—they were full of אנכי, self-centeredness and selfishness, and they were therefore not fit to be the mothers of the Jewish People.

We need to remove the "I" and make room for Hashem to enter.

When Yaakov Avinu ran away from Eisav, he lay down to sleep and placed the stones around his head. When he awoke, he said: אכן יש ה'

---

4   *Devarim* 5:5.
5   *Otzar Chaim*, p. 44.
6   *Bereishis* 24:4.

אנכי לא ידעתי—במקום הזה ואנכי לא ידעתי—Why was Hashem in this place? Because אנכי לא ידעתי—the overindulgence in the אנכי had been removed.[7]

Nonetheless, doing something for myself is not always negative; it can be positive.

The *Aseres Hadibros* begin with the word אנכי and end with the word לרעך. When the something I did for myself is used to help others—when we start with אנכי in order to end up with לרעך—then this is not only commendable but is the reason for our very existence.[8]

In the *berachah* for the host that we insert into *Birkas Hamazon*, we bless the host that ויהיו נכסיו מוצלחים וקרובים לעיר, which we usually understand to mean that the host should be successful in business and not have to travel far in order to conduct that business.

Rav Kook suggests an alternative explanation. The words קרובים לעיר do not mean that the business should be conducted "close to the city," but rather that the property that he acquires as a result of his business activities should be קרובים לעיר—made available to the city so that the community can benefit from them. In this way, the אנכי, the "I" that assisted me to own these properties, should be intended לרעך, for the benefit of others. In that way, what may have impeded my relationship with Hashem can become a foundation stone that supports it.

---

7   Ibid. 28:16.
8   *Parpera'os LaTorah*, p. 39.

עקב

Tread on the Land,
and Don't Become Complacent

והיה עקב תשמעון את המשפטים האלה.

And it will be, because you will heed these ordinances.[1]

On the first *pasuk* in this week's *parashah*, *Rashi* comments that if we observe the easy mitzvos that people trample on with their heels (עקב), then the rest of the *pasuk*, namely "ושמר ה' אלוקיך לך את הברית ואת החסד—Hashem will keep for you the covenant and the kindness [that He swore to your forefathers]" will also be fulfilled.

How is it possible to say that there are mitzvos that people relate to as *kal*—easy and therefore trample on them? The Mishnah in *Pirkei Avos* states clearly that one has to be as careful with the observance of מצוות קלות—light mitzvos, as he is with מצוות חמורות—strict mitzvos,[2] because we do not know the rewards for each mitzvah, and what we consider a light or easy mitzvah may generate significant rewards.

So why would it be that people would trample any mitzvah underfoot?

1   *Devarim* 7:12.
2   *Avos* 2:1.

The Kotzker Rebbe suggests that *Rashi* is very literal, and when he says that we have to observe the mitzvos that "דש בעקביו—One tramples with one's heel," it refers to a mitzvah where the mitzvah is to trample something with one's foot, i.e., to walk the length and breadth of a country and connect with the land and the mitzvos associated with it. In other words, *Rashi* is referring to "מצוות ישוב ארץ ישראל—The mitzvah to settle Eretz Yisrael."

According to this reading, the verse is saying: והיה עקב תשמעון את המשפטים האלה—if you observe the mitzvah that is associated with treading on it with your heel, i.e., living in Israel, then ושמר ה' א' לך את הברית ואת החסד.[3]

Perhaps we can suggest an additional approach.

The Talmud states that a Kohen whose hands are disfigured or covered in paint should not perform *Birkas Kohanim*, because people will look at his hands during *Birkas Kohanim*. The *Shechinah* rests on the Kohanim's hands during *Birkas Kohanim*, and it is thus inappropriate to look at them. However, says the Gemara, if it is a case where דש בעירו, which *Rashi* explains to mean that everyone is used to seeing his hands in such a state, then it is permitted for the Kohen to recite *Birkas Kohanim*.[4]

We see that the word דש can refer to something that one is used to. When *Rashi* describes mitzvos as being דש בעקביו, he is referring to those mitzvos that we perform so frequently that we have grown accustomed to them and perform them perfunctorily. We no longer are excited by them.

The Torah tells us והיה עקב תשמעון את המשפטים האלה—if you observe those mitzvos that have become routine and habit, and you do so in the proper way, i.e., with excitement, then ושמר ה' אלוקיך לך את הברית ואת החסד.

We need to inject passion and excitement into the performance of all mitzvos, not just those that come around once a year, but, perhaps more importantly, into those mitzvos that we perform monthly, daily, hourly, or even on a minute-to-minute basis.

3   *Parpera'os LaTorah*, p. 63.
4   *Megillah* 24b.

Diminishing Marginal Utility

וְאָכַלְתָּ וְשָׂבָעְתָּ וּבֵרַכְתָּ אֶת ה׳ אֱלֹקֶיךָ עַל הָאָרֶץ הַטֹּבָה אֲשֶׁר נָתַן לָךְ.

*And you will eat and be sated, and you shall bless Hashem,
your G-d, for the good land He has given you.*[5]

The Gemara states that the *pasuk* of וְאָכַלְתָּ וְשָׂבָעְתָּ וּבֵרַכְתָּ is the source for *Birkas Hamazon*. Where is the source for making a *berachah* before we eat? The Gemara says that it is a *kal va'chomer*: If I am obligated to make a blessing when I am satiated, I am certainly obligated to make a blessing when obtaining food when I am hungry.[6]

Elsewhere, the Gemara asks from where we derive that we must recite a *berachah* before learning Torah,[7] and answers from the *pasuk* of כִּי שֵׁם ה׳ אֶקְרָא הָבוּ גֹדֶל לֵאלֹקֵינוּ.[8]

The Vilna Gaon asks why it is that we need a textual source to teach us that we need to make a *berachah* **after** we eat, whereas in regards to *Birkas Hatorah*, we need a textual source for why we make a blessing **before** we learn?

In other words, with regards to eating, it is intuitive that we make a *berachah* **before** we eat, and we need a Scriptural source for making a blessing after we eat.

But with regarding to learning, it is obvious we make one **after**, but need a source for making one before. Why?

The *Gra* answers that from here we see the difference between physical and spiritual pleasure. With physical pleasure, the chief enjoyment and *hanaah* is to be found **before** a person has engaged in a particular desire. Once he has had his fill, any pleasure soon subsides. Before one eats a meal, a person is hungry and in need of nourishment, and he eagerly anticipates the tasty meal before him. However, once the food has been eaten and the hunger satiated, he is in no rush to eat any

---

5   *Devarim* 8:10.
6   *Berachos* 48b.
7   Ibid. 21a.
8   *Devarim* 32:3.

more. Any physical pleasure works in the same way. The anticipation of and the engagement in the desire itself is where the most enjoyment is found. Afterwards, the enjoyment is minimal if at all.

Spiritual pleasure is the exact opposite. Before one engages in a spiritual pursuit, be it Torah learning or any other mitzvah, one isn't drawn to it in the same way as he may be toward a good meal. However, once a person has experienced the eternal bliss of spiritual pursuits, he wants more and more.

Therefore, when it comes to physical pleasures, obviously one has to make a *berachah* beforehand, because that is when the most benefit is derived. It is after one is full and satiated and wants no more of that pleasure that we need to be told to make a *berachah acharonah*. Spiritual pleasures, on the other hand, obviously need a blessing **after** they have been achieved, because they leave you wanting more and more. It is beforehand that we need to be told to make a *berachah*, as that is when we are hesitant to draw nearer to them.

What emerges from this insight of the *Gra* is that after we have engaged in a spiritual endeavor, it should leave us wanting more and more. If this is not the case—that after we have completed the endeavor we are glad to have gotten it out of the way—then our mitzvos, rather than being spiritual activities, are in actuality only physical ones.

ראה

Ceteris Paribus
(All Other Things Being Equal)

וְנָתַתָּ אֶת הַבְּרָכָה עַל הַר גְּרִזִּים וְאֶת הַקְּלָלָה עַל הַר עֵיבָל.

You shall place those blessing upon Mount Gerizim, and those cursing upon Mount Eval.[1]

What is the symbolism of the blessings and curses being told to B'nei Yisrael on mountains, and why Mount Gerizim and Mount Eval in particular?

Rav Shmuel Rabinovitz quotes Rav Shimshon Raphael Hirsch, who notes that these two mountains, situated to the north and south of Shechem, seem very similar. They are situated in the same topographical area, and they are of similar height. They share the same soil, the identical amount of rain and dew, and the same air wafts around both of them.

Despite these similarities, the difference between the mountains could not have been more apparent.

Whereas Mount Gerizim is covered in flowers and green grass, Mount Eval is barren and dry. Due to this difference, Mount Gerizim was

---

1   *Devarim* 11:29.

chosen as the mountain on which to give the *berachos*—the blessings, and Mount Eval was selected for the *klalos*—the curses.

Despite being exposed to identical external factors, the two mountains turned out to be very different. The message being taught here is that externalities have nothing to do with whether a person will be righteous or not. If one is blessed with intellect, wealth, strength, or beauty, it does not guarantee a blessed life. By the same measure, if one is challenged by poverty and weakness, this does not automatically mean that his life will be cursed. In the same way as the external factors did not affect the mountains, so too external factors are not reasons on which we can pin achievement or lack thereof. We are implored by Hashem to choose life and to follow His word. We are the only ones who can make that decision. We must not allow circumstances to become a crutch on which we lean, but we must hear the call of Hashem, no matter the circumstances, and ensure that we are counted among the blessed.[2]

Not That, but If

את הברכה אשר תשמעו אל מצות ה' אלקיכם...והקללה אם לא תשמעו אל מצות ה' אלקיכם.

The blessing, that you will heed the commandments of the Lord your God...and the curse, if you will not heed the commandments of the Lord your God.[3]

The *Kli Yakar* asks why the *pasuk* uses the word אשר in connection with the observance of mitzvos—את הברכה אשר תשמעו אל מצות ה' אלקיכם—and uses the word אם in connection with the non-observance of mitzvos—והקללה אם לא תשמעו אל מצות ה' אלקיכם. Why isn't the Torah consistent? Either use אם or אשר for both.

---

2   *Avnei Derech on Parashas Hashavua* 290.
3   *Devarim* 11:27.

The *Kli Yakar* answers that contained in the change of word is an insight into how we need to relate to every Jew. Our initial assumption needs to be that every Jew wants to do good—to follow the Torah and its laws and to have a relationship with Hashem. Therefore, when discussing Torah observance, it isn't a case of "אם—if" we are going to observe, but rather "אשר—that" you will observe. Our basic assumption is that a Jew wants to keep mitzvos. However, when it comes to transgressing the words of the Torah, then the word אם is the more appropriate of the two words, because it implies that we in no way assume that a Jew will transgress, but rather that he may—"if" you do not listen.

But how can we be sure that this is the case? Perhaps Jews are more inclined to leave Torah than to embrace it. After all, the majority of the Jewish world is not outwardly religious, so maybe this assumption is no longer correct?

The *Kli Yakar* notes that usually, when the Torah uses the word שמיעה, it is followed by some action. For example, in *Parashas Eikev*, it says והיה עקב תשמעון, followed by ושמרתם ועשיתם אותם. Similarly, in the *Shema*, it says, והיה אם שמע תשמעו, followed by ולעבדו בכל לבבכם.

Why in our *parashah* does it say, אשר תשמעו אל מצות ה' אלקיכם, and it is not followed by any action? And in fact, when it comes to non-observance, it says, אם לא תשמעו אל מצות ה' אלקיכם, and it is followed by action, namely וסרתם מן הדרך. So why is there no mention of any actions after the words אשר תשמעו אל מצות ה' אלקיכם?

The *Kli Yakar* answers that when it comes to sin, Hashem usually punishes only if an act was involved. If one thought about sinning but refrained from acting upon that thought, then in most cases there is no punishment. So, the curse will only come about if there is action, and therefore, the *pasuk* says וסרתם מן הדרך after והקללה אם לא תשמעו because only if there is an action will there be a curse.

However, every thought concerning a mitzvah is rewarded, even if it doesn't ultimately lead to an act being performed. The thought itself is worthy of reward.

Therefore, the words of את הברכה אשר תשמעו do not need to be followed by any act, because the reward is not dependent on any action; it comes about through thoughts alone.

This being the case, we can assume that every Jew we meet is connected to Torah and mitzvos, because every Jew has at least thought about performing the mitzvos. It is just that they may not have known that what they term as a good deed, or the decent thing to do, is actually a mitzvah! What happens though is that circumstances prevent them from acting on that thought—but every thought alone is worthy of reward.

So when we meet any Jew, we assume that he is מלא מצוות כרימון because just by thinking positively, a person earns reward. Thus, the word most fitting to describe their Torah observance is אשר as opposed to אם.

שופטים

The Spiritual Power of Mitzvos

שפטים ושוטרים תתן לך בכל שעריך.

You shall set up judges and law enforcement officials for your-self in all your cities.[1]

The word לך in this *pasuk* would seem to be superfluous. If the intention is that we have a duty to appoint judges in our cities, then it would have been sufficient to say שופטים ושוטרים תתן בכל שעריך. As there are no extra words or letters in the Torah, the inclusion of the word לך needs to be justified.

Rabbi Yosef Zvi Halevi Dunner writes that the necessity to appoint judges to rule on points of law and to establish a police force to enforce those laws would not seem at first glance to be uniquely Jewish. Every society that wishes to function in an orderly and civilized manner needs to have regulations and needs to have a way to ensure adherence to those regulations. However, if the function of law is merely to ensure the smooth running of society and avoid a descent into chaos, then those rules and regulations lack any spiritual content and do not impact the personality of one who abides by them.

---

1   *Devarim* 16:18.

The rules and regulations of the Torah, i.e., the mitzvos, are different. When the Torah instructs us to perform a specific task or to refrain from engaging in a particular activity, it is not merely to ensure the continuity of civilized order in society.

The mitzvah has a direct impact on who we are and affects our *neshamah*—the part of us that is spiritual. This is not only true in respect to the mitzvos that are obviously spiritual, such as Shabbos or *tefillah*, but also those that seem to be for the benefit of society, such as the appointment of judges. Every mitzvah that we have been commanded elevates us as individuals and strengthens our relationship with Hashem.

This is the meaning of the inclusion of the word לך in our *pasuk*. The Torah is telling us that the appointment of a judicial system is not merely to ensure the smooth operation of society. The appointment of judges, together with all the other mitzvos, is לך—for your benefit. It elevates and sanctifies who we are by connecting us with our souls and our Creator.[2]

Is My House in Order?

שפטים ושוטרים תתן לך בכל שעריך.

You shall set up judges and law enforcement officials for yourself in all your cities.[3]

Rebbe Yaakov Yosef of Polnah was a disciple of the *Baal Shem Tov* who, together with the Maggid of Mezhritz, took over the leadership of the Chassidic movement after the *Baal Shem Tov* passed away. He also asks why the *pasuk* says שופטים ושטרים תתן לך, and answers that לך teaches us that we must avoid having two standards—one that we apply to ourselves, and a more critical standard that we use with

---

2　*Mikdash Halevi*, p. 585.

3　*Devarim* 16:18.

others. We can't be lenient with ourselves and stringent with others; instead, we need to have the same standard for both.

The same שׁוֹפְטִים וְשֹׁטְרִים—the same exactitude that you display toward other people, תִּתֶּן לְךָ—you also need to develop when dealing with yourself.

Rebbe Simchah Bunim of Peshischa expounded along similar lines.

שׁוֹפְטִים וְשֹׁטְרִים תִּתֶּן לְךָ, he suggests, means that before you start judging other people, לְךָ—judge yourself, as Chazal say, קְשׁוֹט עַצְמְךָ וְאַחַר כָּךְ קְשׁוֹט אֲחֵרִים—ensure that your own house is in order before you proceed to tell others how to run theirs.

Only if someone regularly evaluates his own behavior and sees his own frailties and challenges on one hand, and his strengths and merits on the other, can he fulfill the rest of the *pasuk*: וְשָׁפְטוּ אֶת הָעָם מִשְׁפַּט צֶדֶק.

However, if someone sees mainly the faults and weaknesses of others but turns a blind eye to his own shortcomings, he exhibits a "blindness" that now makes it impossible for him to fulfill וְשָׁפְטוּ אֶת הָעָם מִשְׁפַּט צֶדֶק.

The prerequisite for judging any person is the ability to be impartial and open to both sides of every story. However, if I have a "blind spot", it impinges on my ability to see things clearly, and therefore, my appraisal of the other is automatically flawed.

Our relationships with others and our relationship with the Creator are dependent on שׁוֹפְטִים וְשֹׁטְרִים תִּתֶּן לְךָ בְּכָל שְׁעָרֶיךָ, which all begins with having the same standards for others that we have for ourselves.[4]

---

4   *Otzar Chaim*, p. 94; *Parpera'os LaTorah*, p. 119.

כי תצא

Actively Pursue an Enemy That Needs to Be Captured!

כי תצא למלחמה על איביך ונתנו ה' אלקיך בידך ושבית שביו.

If you go out to war against your enemies, and Hashem, your G-d, will deliver him into your hands, and you take his captives.[1]

Many commentators extend the meaning of the first *pasuk* of the *parashah* to relate not only to a physical battle in which *Klal Yisrael* may engage, but also to a spiritual struggle that every one of us is involved in daily—the struggle against the *yetzer hara*.

This is alluded to by the fact that the word ונתנו is in the singular. If the *pasuk* were referring solely to physical enemies, we would expect it to be in the plural, and therefore, we can say that it is referring to one particular enemy—the *yetzer hara*.

Hence, the words כי תצא למלחמה על איביך mean that when you go out to war against your enemy, namely, the *yetzer hara*, then ונתנו ה' אלקיך בידך, you should be aware that Hashem will always be there to assist you.

There are a few important lessons that can be learned from this *pasuk* that will help us in our battle against the *yetzer hara*.

---

1   *Devarim* 21:10.

Rabbi Shimon Biton suggests two major approaches that are necessary to be successful in our battle against the *yetzer hara*. The first is "כי תצא למלחמה—When you go out to war." In our battle with the *yetzer hara*, we need to go out; we need to be proactive, rather than reactive. We cannot wait until the *yetzer hara* challenges us and then hope to overcome it. Instead, we need to take the fight to it and ensure that we are engaged in battle long before the *yetzer hara* attempts to win us over. We need to have strategies to avoid challenging situations and plan how we will react if such situations arise.

The second approach necessary in our battle is כי תצא למלחמה על איביך—we need to define the *yetzer hara* as our enemy. Too often, we do not even realize that we are in the vice-like grip of the *yetzer hara*, and that the behavior that he is encouraging is harmful or even forbidden. To defeat the *yetzer hara*, we first need to acknowledge and identify him as the enemy.

According to this approach, what do the final words of the *pasuk*— "ושבית שביו—And you should capture a captive"—come to teach us? If ונתנו ה' אלקיך בידך means that Hashem will enable us to defeat the *yetzer hara*, what is there to hold captive? I have beaten the *yetzer hara*, it is no longer, it has ceased to be, so how can I hold it as a captive?

The answer is that while it is true that I may be able to defeat the *yetzer hara* and gain the upper hand in the battle between good and evil, the *yetzer hara* is an experienced adversary and will always pick itself up and challenge us again from a different angle or with a different approach.

In our battle with the *yetzer hara*, we must continuously be on guard, and the aim needs to be not only to defeat it but to hold it captive so that it will not be able to come and attack us ever again.

Defeating it isn't enough if we truly want to be free; we need to capture it as well.[2]

---

2   *Bein Adam LaParashah*, p. 350.

Priorities, Priorities

כי תבנה בית חדש ועשית מעקה לגגך.

When you build a new house, you shall make a guard rail for your roof.[3]

Rabbi Shimshon Raphael Hirsch notes that when discussing a new house, the Torah does not highlight the importance of ensuring that you have the best-quality mezuzos or the need to have two sinks and ovens to assist with the separation of meat and milk. The first thing that the Torah highlights in connection to a new Jewish house is the need to take care of others.

כי תבנה בית חדש—When you build a new house, the first thing you need to take care of is ועשית מעקה לגגך, you need to build a fence on the roof to ensure that others are safe. When creating a new Jewish home, the first priority is to ensure that others feel safe; that others feel welcome and warm within your walls.

This is no less important with regards to one's own family as it is with regards to visitors and guests.

The Gemara tells us that "לעולם אל יטיל אדם אימה יתירה בתוך ביתו"—A person should never introduce extreme fear into his home,"[4] and it then goes on to list some of the terrible things that can happen if the home is ruled by fear as opposed to love and warmth.

Therefore, the fence on the roof not only emphasizes the need for physical safety but comes to represent emotional safety as well, and the wellbeing of others needs to be the primary focus in a Jewish house.

In the same *pasuk*, the Torah tells us that the fence is to be built to avoid a situation of כי יפול הנופל. *Rashi* explains that the use of the definite article with regards to the person who falls teaches us that the person deserved to fall off the roof due to some reason or other. If so, why is there an instruction to build a fence? If the person deserves to

3 *Devarim* 22:8.
4 *Gittin* 6b.

fall, let him fall! *Rashi* answers with reference to the Gemara that says, מגלגלין זכות על ידי זכאי וחובה על ידי חייב—that while someone may deserve punishment, Hashem will use a person in a similar situation to be the agent of that punishment.[5]

Therefore, writes the *Sifsei Chachamim*, you need to build a fence, because if a person should fall off, people will say you have some skeleton in your closest that accounts for you being chosen to be the agent of doom. To avoid such a situation, we have the instruction to build a *maakeh*. Why is this lesson of מגלגלין זכות על ידי זכאי וחובה על ידי חייב being taught to us specifically in the mitzvah of *maakeh*? Perhaps it is a continuation of the idea above. *Maakeh* teaches us that we need to create a safe atmosphere in our homes, one that will make people feel welcome and safe. If we work hard at creating such an atmosphere, then מגלגלין זכות על ידי זכאי—we have an assurance that it won't be in vain. Good people who require such an atmosphere will be drawn to your home. One opportunity to help will be followed by another, life will be affected positively, all as a result of ועשית מעקה לגגך.

The Mishnah in *Avos* says, in the name of Yosi ben Yochanan of Yerushalayim, that "יהי ביתך פתוח לרוחה—Let your house be open wide—ויהיו עניים בני ביתך," which is translated as "treat the poor as members of your household."[6]

One of the advantages of being a "member of the household" is that you can invite your friends to play or for a meal. When the Mishnah says, ויהיו עניים בני ביתך, it means is that the poor should feel so at home and so welcome in your house that they should feel comfortable enough to invite their friends to your house. If you work hard to ensure that others feel safe in your home, then we have a guarantee that it will be turned into a citadel of *chessed*, because מגלגלין זכות על ידי זכאי.

5   *Shabbos* 32.
6   *Avos* 1:5.

כי תבוא

Public vs. Private

יצו ה׳ אתך את הברכה באסמיך ובכל משלח ידך וברכך בארץ אשר ה׳
אלקיך נתן לך.

*Hashem will order the blessing to be with you in your granaries,
and in every one of your endeavors, and He will bless you in the
land that Hashem, your G-d, is giving you.*[1]

The Gemara instructs a person to have a third of his wealth
invested in *karka*—land or property, a third invested in business
activities, and a third at hand in cash.[2]
Rabbeinu Bachya writes that our *pasuk* alludes to this Gemara:

- "יצו ה׳ אתך את הברכה באסמיך—Hashem will order the blessing
  to be with you in your granaries" refers to the third invested in
  business activities.
- "ובכל משלח ידך—and in every one of your endeavors" refers to
  the third ready at hand in cash.
- "וברכך בארץ—He will bless you in the land" refers to the third to
  be placed/invested in land.

---

1   *Devarim* 28:8.
2   *Bava Metzia* 42a.

The question on this explanation of Rabbeinu Bachya is that from that very Gemara, Rabbi Yitzchak learns that "אין הברכה מצויה אלא בדבר הסמוי מן העין—Blessing is only found in that which is hidden from the eye," and the proof he brings is from our *pasuk*! Just as the contents of the storehouse are hidden from the public eye, and the *pasuk* says that they will attract blessing, so too anything that is hidden from the public sight will attract blessing.

According to Rabbeinu Bachya, though, the words יצו ה' אתך את הברכה באסמיך teach us that we need to place a third of our wealth into business, and business is not hidden from the public eye. So how do we reconcile these two opposite teachings from the same *pasuk*?

The *sefer Shemi V'Shem Avosai* suggests that they both come to teach the same thing. Rabbi Yitzchak is highlighting the fact that since *berachah* is only found in things removed from the public eye, any success that may accrue as a result of the third of one's wealth invested in business dealings needs to be treated quietly and with modesty. Once business success becomes open for everyone to see, it is no longer "סמוי מן העין—hidden from eye's view" and not assured of attracting *berachah*.

Material success needs to be appreciated and enjoyed by those who are blessed with it, but for it to be a blessing, that appreciation and enjoyment needs to be in a modest and unobtrusive way—סמוי מן העין.[3]

---

3   *Shenayim Mikra*, p. 383.

My Main Focus Is...

ברוך אתה בבואך וברוך אתה בצאתך.

You shall be blessed when you come, and you shall be blessed when you depart.[4]

Rabbi Moshe Sternbuch quotes the Midrash that says the *pasuk* means:

- "ברוך אתה בבואך—You shall be blessed when you come" to the *beis midrash*.
- "ברוך אתה בצאתך—You shall be blessed when you depart" to go out to work.[5]

First, there is the arrival into the *beis midrash*, and only then is there going out to do business. If one places the *beis midrash* and the learning of the Torah as the primary focus in one's life, then one's business dealings can be viewed as a success. If, however, one reverses the order, and the primary emphasis is on the going out to work, then there is grave danger.

This is why David HaMelech says that ה' ישמר צאתך ובואך מעתה ועד עולם.[6] If the order is first צאתך, i.e., going out to work, and only then בואך, your entry into the *beis midrash*, then ה' ישמרך, we pray that ה' guards, looks after, and protects you in such a challenging environment.

The only way we can safeguard ourselves against the challenges posed in everyday life is to place the *beis midrash* as our primary influence. If we manage to do so, then all our decisions will be made using the Torah as our compass, and we will merit to ברוך אתה בצאתך—see blessing in all our endeavors.

This idea is echoed by the *Meshech Chochmah* in *Parashas Vayelech*, who explains that the reason why the mitzvah of *hakhel*—gathering everyone together to hear the king read from the *Sefer Torah*—occurs at the

---

4   *Devarim* 28:6.
5   *Taam V'Daas*, p. 180.
6   *Tehillim* 121.

end of a *shemittah* year is because after a year of being idle from work, the farmers are keen and eager to return to their usual work routine. Therefore, before they return, they gather together to learn words of Torah to highlight that their emphasis in life is the Torah. Torah comes before their work, it shapes their behavior, and is their real guide in life.[7]

Sharing the Happiness

ולקחת מראשית פרי האדמה אשר תביא מארצך.

And you shall take of the first of all the fruit of the ground, which you will bring from your land.[8]

This *parashah* mentions the mitzvah of *bikkurim*, of taking one's first fruits up to Yerushalayim and handing them over to the Kohen in the Beis Hamikdash in a special ceremony.

This mitzvah only became practical once B'nei Yisrael had conquered and divided up the Land of Israel, a process that took fourteen years.

The Lubavitcher Rebbe asks why it was necessary to wait so long. Why was there a fourteen year delay during which no *bikkurim* were brought?

The Rebbe answers that until each and every Jew had received his portion in Eretz Yisrael, no *bikkurim* could be brought, for how can someone rejoice and thank Hashem for the blessings of his portion knowing that other Jews do not yet have their portion?

Therefore, we had to wait until everyone had received his share of Eretz Yisrael to rejoice with the mitzvah of *bikkurim*.

If this is true regarding physical inheritance, it is certainly also true regarding our spiritual heritage as well. How can I rejoice with the spiritual treasures with which I have been blessed when I know that there is even one Jew who is unaware of the spiritual beauty of leading a proper Jewish life?

---

7   *Maayanah shel Torah*, p. 136.
8   *Devarim* 26:2.

This obligates us, says the Rebbe, to be sensitive to those around us, especially at times when we are experiencing success or joy. Not everyone is in the position to rejoice in his success in the same way as we may be. Not everyone is blessed to experience the beauty of living a true Torah life, and until each and every Jew is in such a position, we cannot rest, we cannot truly rejoice, and we must do whatever we can ensure that everyone is exposed to the beauty of a Torah way of life.

However, the actual mitzvah of *bikkurim* itself would seem to display a gross insensitivity to those less fortunate than ourselves. The Mishnah states that the wealthy people would bring their *bikkurim* to Yerushalayim in baskets covered with gold and silver, while the poor would bring up whatever *bikkurim* they had in plain baskets made from willow branches. They would hand over their *bikkurim* to the Kohen, who would take the fruits and return the baskets covered with gold and silver to the wealthy people who had brought them, but would keep the willow baskets that the poor brought.[9] If we are supposed to be sensitive to the plight of those less well-off then ourselves, why not return their baskets? The reason why we return the gold and silver baskets to the wealthy people is to give them a blessing that in the same way as they brought *bikkurim* this year in baskets covered with gold and silver, so may Hashem bless them that next year they be able to bring *bikkurim* in those same baskets covered with gold and silver, as a sign of the blessings that Hashem has bestowed on them.

This is precisely the reason why we do not return the plain baskets brought by the poor. We do not return them because we wish that they not be stuck bringing their *bikkurim* next year in such baskets. Next year, we hope, they will be blessed to be able to bring *bikkurim* in baskets covered with gold and silver.

Everything we do needs to be calculated to take into account those less fortunate than us, be it physically, financially or spiritually, and to ensure that they can share in our success and happiness.[10]

---

9   *Bikkurim* 3:8.

10   *Le'hachayos es Hayom*, p. 451.

נִצָבִים

Don't Let Go of Me

והיה כי יבאו עליך כל הדברים האלה הברכה והקללה....והשבת אל לבבך
בכל הגוים אשר הדיחך ה׳ אלקך שמה.

*And it will be, when all these things come upon you the blessing
and the curse…that you will consider in your heart, among all
the nations where Hashem your G-d has scattered you."*[1]

The *Alshich* says that there is a big difference between an item
that is thrown and one that is dispersed. When I throw something, it leaves my hand and lands in its place. When I disperse
something or drag it to where it needs to go; I never actually let go of it.

The *Alshich* explains that even in our exile, we see the Hand of
Hashem and His love for us. We are *nidachim*—scattered, and not
nishlachim—thrown. Even in our exile, Hashem never lets go of us, as
Chazal tell us that when we are in *galus*, we need to grieve for the fact
that the *Shechinah* is in exile with us.[2]

The Dubno Maggid says that the idea that the Divine is also in exile
with us is alluded to if we read the *pasuk* in the following way:

---

1   *Devarim* 30:1.
2   *V'Karasa LaShabbos Oneg II*, p. 450.

- **והשבת אל לבבך**—You need to be aware and place this information in your heart.
- **בכל הגוים אשר הדיחך ה׳ אלוקך**—Amongst all the nations to where Hashem your G-d dispersed you,
- **שמה**—He is there, as in **עמו אנכי בצרה**.[3]

Rabbi Yonasan Eibeshitz writes on the verse:

אם יהיה נדחך בקצה השמים משם יקבצך ה׳ אלוקך ומשם יקחך.

If your dispersed will be at the ends of heaven, from there Hashem your G-d will gather you in, and from there He will take you.[4]

When we fulfill the will of Hashem, we draw ourselves closer to heaven, to spirituality, and to Hashem. If we sin, we distance ourselves from heaven, and the more we sin, the greater the distance from heaven, until we reach *katzeh shamayim*—the furthest point from Heaven possible.

However, even if we are so far removed and find ourselves at that furthest point, Hashem will not abandon us, but rather **משם יקבצך ה׳ אלוקך ומשם יקחך**—from there Hashem your G-d will gather you in and from there He will take you, because He has never let go of us and is with us in our exile.[5]

---

3   *Otzar Chaim*, p. 176.
4   *Devarim* 30:4.
5   *Talelei Oros*, p. 192.

I'm Actively Waiting

וְשָׁב ה׳ אֱלֹקֶיךָ אֶת שְׁבוּתְךָ וְרִחֲמֶךָ וְשָׁב וְקִבֶּצְךָ...

Then, Hashem, your G-d, will bring back your exiles, and He will have mercy upon you. He will once again gather you from all the nations, where the Lord, your G-d, had dispersed you.[6]

The *Rambam*, in discussing the obligation to believe in Mashiach, says that someone who does not believe that Mashiach will come and does not wait in anticipation of his arrival, denies the Torah and the authority of Moshe, because the Torah says, "וְשָׁב ה׳ אֱלֹקֶיךָ אֶת שְׁבוּתְךָ וְרִחֲמֶךָ וְשָׁב וְקִבֶּצְךָ וכו׳—Hashem, your G-d, will bring back your exiles, and He will have mercy upon you."[7]

The Brisker Rav asks what the *Rambam* is adding that isn't stated explicitly in the *pasuk*, which clearly says that Hashem will bring us all back. So, obviously, this is part of our belief.

The Brisker Rav answers that the *chiddush* of the *Rambam* is that not only someone who does not believe in the coming of the Mashiach denies Torah, but even if someone does not actively anticipate his arrival—as the *Rambam* says, "אוֹ מִי שֶׁאֵינוֹ מְחַכֶּה לְבִיאָתוֹ—Or someone who does not wait for his arrival"—is guilty of denying Torah. Not only do we have to believe in his arrival, but we also have to anticipate it actively.[8]

To highlight what our attitude should be, Rabbi Nachum Velvel of Kelm quotes the parable of someone who is sick in bed and the doctor is called. A few minutes after the call is placed, there is a knock at the door. Everyone rushes to open it, expecting to see the doctor, but it turns out to be the neighbor asking to borrow some milk. A few minutes pass, and then there is another knock at the door. Again, everyone rushes to open it, expecting to see the doctor, only to be disappointed to see

---

6   *Devarim* 30:3.

7   *Rambam, Mishneh Torah, Melachim* 11:1.

8   *Peninim Mishulchan Gavoha*, p. 231.

the plumber who was ordered three weeks ago. This scenario plays itself out until finally, the doctor arrives, much to the relief of those in attendance.

The sense of anticipation shown by those who open the door expecting to see the doctor who may save the patient's life needs to be the sense of our expectation of the imminent arrival of Mashiach.

The Brisker Rav adds that if someone believes in Mashiach but doesn't live with this heightened expectation of his arrival, it can only mean that he doesn't understand how unwell Am Yisrael is without Mashiach, or he doesn't believe that Mashiach will heal us.

Today, Today, Today!

ראה נתתי לפניך היום את החיים ואת הטוב ואת המות ואת הרע.

Behold, I have set before you today life and good, and death and evil.[9]

Rabbi Yosef Zvi Halevi Dunner asks: Why is it necessary for the *pasuk* to include the word היום—today? It would have been equally understood if the word had been omitted and would have just read "ראה נתתי לפניך את החיים ואת הטוב—Behold, I have set before you life and good." Why the extra word היום?

Rav Dunner notes that we find at least two other places in the Torah where the use of the word היום seems superfluous, and in both places, *Rashi* makes the same comment. The first occasion is in the *pasuk* that reads:

בחודש השלישי לצאת בני ישראל מארץ מצרים ביום הזה באו מדבר סיני.

*In the third month of the children of Yisrael's departure from Egypt, **on this day** they arrived in the desert of Sinai.*[10]

---

9   *Devarim* 30:15.
10   *Shemos* 19:1.

The second occasion is where it says,

והיה אם שמע תשמעו אל מצותי אשר אנכי מצוה אתכם היום לאהבה את
ה׳ אלוקיכם ולעבדו בכל לבבכם ובכל נפשכם.

*And it will be, if you hearken to My commandments that I command you **this day** to love Hashem, your G-d, and to serve Him with all your heart and with all your soul.*[11]

In both cases, *Rashi* explains that the word היום or ביום means that the command that is being mentioned in the *pasuk* should be as fresh to you today as if you had just been commanded to observe it for the first time.

When it comes to mitzvah observance and our relationship with The Almighty, we need to keep things fresh, new, and exciting as if we were keeping the mitzvos for the very first time. מצוה אתכם היום and ביום הזה באו מדבר סיני tell us that every day should feel to us as we have just arrived at Har Sinai and have just received the Torah directly from Hashem. If we could live at this level, our approach to every mitzvah, even those that we have been observing for many years, would be charged and energized.

Using this approach, Rav Dunner suggests that the use of the word היום in our *pasuk* comes to tell us that when it comes to the battle between good and evil, life and death, then ראה נתתי לפניך היום—every day needs to be approached as a new battle. Every day will present new challenges, and even if we were successful in overcoming the difficulties of yesterday, past performance is no guarantee that we will meet the challenges of today, even if those challenges turn out to be the very same ones we conquered yesterday. Every day poses new challenges, but also new opportunities to strengthen our relationship with Hashem and His Torah. We must never become complacent, lazy, or smug. The *yetzer hara* never rests, and we must be vigilant to succeed in overcoming him today as we did yesterday.[12]

---

11   *Devarim* 11:13.
12   *Mikdash Halevi*, p. 648.

וַיֵּלֶךְ

Everything Has a Time and a Place

וַיִּקְרָא מֹשֶׁה לִיהוֹשֻׁעַ וַאֲמֶר אֵלָיו לְעֵינֵי כָל יִשְׂרָאֵל חֲזַק וֶאֱמָץ.

And Moshe called Yehoshua and said to him, in the presence of all Yisrael, "Be strong and courageous!"[1]

The usual way of understanding this *pasuk* is that Moshe Rabbeinu called Yehoshua, and in front of all the B'nei Yisrael instructed him to be strong and courageous.

The *Meshech Chochmah* draws our attention to the *trop*—the cantillation marks, underneath the words לְעֵינֵי כָל יִשְׂרָאֵל חֲזַק וֶאֱמָץ. They are מנח זרקא מנח סגול, which connect the first group of words (לְעֵינֵי כָל יִשְׂרָאֵל) to the next group (חֲזַק וֶאֱמָץ).

In essence, this means that the words should be read in the following way:

"Moshe Rabbeinu called Yehoshua and told him that "in front of the B'nei Yisrael, be strong and courageous."

Yehoshua was an exceptionally humble man. He had been granted the leadership on account of the fact that he prepared and tidied up the

---

1   *Devarim* 31:7.

287

sefarim, tables, and chairs for the *shiurim* delivered by Moshe Rabbeinu. He never moved from the tent and was private and modest.

Moshe Rabbeinu instructs Yehoshua to leave his humility at home in order to be a leader. When standing in front of the Jewish People, Yehoshua had to be strong and courageous—לעיני כל ישראל חזק ואמץ.

There are occasions when the situation demands that we take a leadership role, and at that moment, we are not permitted to shirk our responsibilities and opt for the quieter, more humble position of staying in the shadows. "במקום שאין אנשים, השתדל להיות איש—In a place where there are no leaders, strive to be a leader."[2]

Moshe Rabbeinu informed Yehoshua that his time was now, and therefore, לעיני כל ישראל חזק ואמץ—he needed to be strong and courageous in front of the Jewish People.

A person once approached the Alexander Rebbe and asked him a surprising question. We are taught that everything in this world can be used as part of our *avodas Hashem*—to further our relationship with The Creator. But how can atheism be used as part of one's *avodas Hashem*? The Alexander Rebbe answered that when others approach people for help—be it for tzedakah or to become involved in some worthwhile communal activity—the reply is often "Hashem *ya'azor*." I don't need to help or become involved because I can leave it up to Hashem, Who will take care of you.

At that moment, says the Alexander Rebbe, you have to become an atheist. At that moment, there is no Hashem, and the only person who can help is you![3]

When the need arises, we cannot hide in the shadows and let other people take care of what needs to be done, letting others help with **their** advice or **their** charity. We cannot even hide in the shadows and allow Hashem to take care of it. We need to leave our humility and shyness at home and fulfill Moshe Rabbeinu's charge to Yehoshua—לעיני כל ישראל חזק ואמץ.

---

2   *Avos* 2:6.
3   *Laylah shel Achdus, Haggadah shel Pesach*, p. 43, in the name of Rabbi Shlomo Carlebach.

Happy Birthday!

ויאמר אליהם בן מאה ועשרים שנה אנכי היום.

He said to them, "Today I am 120 years old."[4]

The Talmud explains that this *pasuk* refers to the birthday of Moshe Rabbeinu. He was exactly 120 years old: "ביום זה נולדתי ביום זה אמות—He died on his birthday."[5] What is the relevance of this fact?

The *Menoras Zahav* relates that the famous Reb Zusha of Anipoly would travel from town to town in an attempt to inspire the inhabitants to do *teshuvah*. When he entered the town, he would begin by speaking aloud to himself, listing all the areas in which he needed to do *teshuvah* and enumerating the sins that he transgressed for which he needed forgiveness. On hearing that the saintly Reb Zusha felt the need to do *teshuvah*, the people were inspired to perform their own, and once they had performed *teshuvah*, it was if they had been born anew, with the slate wiped clean and ready to start over again.

The Gemara relates that Rabbi Eliezer states that we should perform *teshuvah* a day before we are going to die.[6] The Gemara asks how a person knows on which day he is going to die, and answers that one should do *teshuvah* today in case he dies tomorrow, and in that way, he will be in a constant state of *teshuvah*.

Therefore, when the *pasuk* at the beginning of the *parashah* says, וילך משה וידבר את כל הדברים האלה לכל ישראל, what was happening was that Moshe Rabbeinu was speaking "to himself" about matters that were pertinent to *Klal Yisrael*, ויאמר אליהם, and he said to them: בן מאה ועשרים שנה אנכי היום—that ביום זה נולדתי ביום זה אמות, ביום זה, to teach everyone that they have to regard each day as potentially their last.

---

4   *Devarim* 31:2.
5   *Rosh Hashanah* 11a.
6   *Shabbos* 153a.

This is not in order to be morbid, but rather to highlight the need for *teshuvah*, and if they perform *teshuvah*, it is as if they are being born pure and free from sin.

If we continuously bear in mind that ביום זה נולדתי, today I was born anew because I corrected my mistakes through *teshuvah*, and why I did so, because ביום זה אמות, because who knows how long I have left?—then we will be in a constant state of *teshuvah*, free from sin in our relationship with Hashem.

Reb Shalom of Komarna notes that this *pasuk* contains two tactics that can be employed to defeat the *yetzer hara*. If the *yetzer hara* tries to tempt a person to sin or have improper and negative thoughts, he should think, "I am a hundred years old, and any moment, I will need to give an accounting in front of Hashem. Why would I be taken in by the machinations of the *yetzer hara*?"

Second, if the *yetzer hara* changes approach and tries to induce apathy as an agent to cause sin, the reply needs to be, "I am a young man of twenty; who has time for apathy?" These two approaches will help us to avoid falling into the traps set for us by the *yetzer hara*.[7]

---

7   *Otzar Chaim*, p. 182.

האזינו

Don't Just Give Me Wings,
Teach Me to Fly

ויבא משה וידבר את כל השירה הזאת באזני העם הוא והושע בן נון.

*And Moshe came and spoke all the words of this song into the
ears of the people he and Hoshea the son of Nun.*[1]

T he instruction to teach this *shirah* to B'nei Yisrael was given to
Moshe Rabbeinu in *Parashas Vayelech*:

ועתה כתבו לכם את השירה הזאת ולמדה את בני ישראל שימה בפיהם.

*And now, write for yourselves this song, and teach it to the
B'nei Yisrael; place it into their mouths.*[2]

It would seem that the instruction was only given to Moshe Rabbeinu.
So why was it that when it came to the actual teaching of the *shirah*,
Yehoshua was also involved? *Rashi* suggests that as this was the last
Shabbos of Moshe Rabbeinu's life, it was one of a "changing of the
guard." Yehoshua began to teach B'nei Yisrael while Moshe Rabbeinu was
still alive so that everyone could see that Moshe Rabbeinu agreed with

---

1   *Devarim* 32:44.
2   Ibid. 31:19.

the appointment of Yehoshua as his successor, and thus the transition would go smoothly.

The *Ibn Ezra* agrees, writing that the involvement of Yehoshua was in order "להגדיל מעלת יהושע לעיני הכל—to ensure that Yehoshua's credentials were established for everyone to see."

Rabbi Shimon Biton explains that the reason why Yehoshua also read and taught from the Torah was to show us that it isn't sufficient just to teach others the material. We have to seek to enable them to be able to explain it to others.[3]

On the day that Moshe Rabbeinu was handing over the mantle of leadership to Yehoshua, his closest student, he involved Yehoshua in teaching Torah to B'nei Yisrael so that we would know for all time that education does not merely mean that we impart knowledge and teach the **theory** of living a Jewish life.

Education means enabling our students, our children, and everyone else with whom we have contact not only to know the material but to be able to apply it as well.

There is a famous quote attributed to Jonas Salk that goes:

"Good parents give their children roots and wings. Roots to know where home is, wings to fly away and exercise what's been taught them."

Perhaps, in light of Rabbi Biton's explanation, we can add that not only do parents need to give their children wings, but they also need to teach them how to fly.

On the day that Moshe Rabbeinu passed the leadership to Yehoshua, he ensured that Yehoshua knew how to fly.

---

3   *Bein Adam LaParashah*, p. 401.

Mussar like Dew, I Only Think of You!

יערף כמטר לקחי, תזל כטל אמרתי.

My lesson will drip like rain; my word will flow like dew.[4]

R abbi Simchah Bunim of Peshischa suggests that *divrei Torah* are compared to rain that falls because just as the benefits of rainfall are not immediately apparent but with time those seeds that were watered by the rain will grow and blossom; those who hear words of Torah are not immediately struck by the positive difference those words make to their lives, but after time will be able to look back and see the spiritual growth that resulted from those words.

As with many things in life, the key to success lies in the ability to be patient. We may not see results immediately, but with constant effort and application, results are guaranteed.

Rashi explains that there is a difference between *matar*—rain, and *tal*—dew. Whereas everyone is always happy to be the recipient of dew on his crops, as it falls at night and doesn't disturb anyone's daily routine (as *Rashi* phrases it, הכל שמחים בו), the advent of rain is often met with resistance, as plans may need to be altered or produce even destroyed as a result of the shower.

Therefore, when giving *mussar* to someone, be it a child or a pupil, one should not do so in an attacking or accusatory way that will only further anger and distance the listener. One must not be like the rain that is not universally welcomed and whose letters (*matar*) spell out "משא, טורח, ריב—burden, toil, and quarrel."

If *mussar* needs to be administered, then it needs to be like טל, soft and gentle, in a way that הכל שמחים בו. This is alluded to in the word טל, which is the first letters of the words טוב לכל.

How can we achieve this? How can we reprimand someone who is guilty of negative behavior in a way that is הכל שמחים בו?

---

4   *Devarim* 32:2.

Rebbe Elimelech of Lizhensk provides the answer. The comparison to rain and dew in this *pasuk* refers to the fact that rain and dew fall to the ground to sustain it without receiving anything in return. Theirs is a selfless act, for the benefit of others, not for themselves.

So too, if our rationale in giving *mussar* is a genuine love for the recipient and a desire to help him achieve his full potential in life, then our words will be like טל and be טוב לכל.

If, however, there is some personal agenda—if we are scolding because we feel hurt, let down and disappointed, and we lose sight of the other person—then our *mussar* is no longer selfless and will be greeted like משא, טורח, ריב.[5]

---

5   *Otzar Chaim*, p. 191.

וזאת הברכה

I Believe in Am Yisrael!

ולכל היד החזקה ולכל המורא הגדול אשר עשה לעיני כל ישראל.

And all the strong hand, and all the great awe, which Moshe performed before the eyes of all Yisrael.[1]

Rashi ends his commentary on the Torah by explaining that the "מורא הגדול—the great awe" that took place "לעיני כל ישראל—before the eyes of all Yisrael" refers to Moshe breaking the *Luchos HaBris* when he descended the mountain and saw the golden calf.

The Lubavitcher Rebbe asks that even though *Rashi* says that Hashem congratulated Moshe on his decision and said, "יישר כחך ששברת—well done for smashing the Tablets," why is this the last thing mentioned in connection with Moshe Rabbeinu? It was hardly his crowning achievement or the moment that best sums up his contribution to Am Yisrael, so why is it the last thing to be mentioned? If anything, it was the greatest tragedy that happened to Moshe. He needed to break Hashem's tablets. What is the message here? The Rebbe explained that the message here is that Moshe was confronted with a dilemma. On one hand, he was holding the two tablets of stone, which were the marriage

---

1   *Devarim* 34:12.

295

contract between the Jewish People and Hashem. This meant that by building the golden calf, the Jews had been unfaithful and deserved to be destroyed. On the other hand, Moshe had a deep love for the Jewish People and couldn't bear to think of their destruction. So what did Moshe do when stuck between the Torah and the Jewish People?

He chose the Jewish People. He broke the Tablets, and in doing so tore up the marriage contract, so now the Jewish People had not been unfaithful, as there had never been a marriage.[2]

No one understood what the Torah meant more than Moshe Rabbeinu. No one had love or appreciation of Torah greater than Moshe Rabbeinu.

He had received it directly from Hashem. And still, Moshe chose the Jewish People over the Torah.

Moshe taught us that learning Torah and performing mitzvos has to bring us to a love of the Jewish People; otherwise, we have diminished its value. A Torah without the Jewish People doesn't make sense, and therefore, with all the pain that is involved, he smashed the *luchos*.

Many years later, Hashem Himself would be faced with the same dilemma. The Jews deserved punishment. They deserved to be destroyed. They no longer deserved to have a Beis Hamikdash. The choice was whether to destroy the Jews or the Temple.

No one understood more than Hashem what the Temple represented. Every sacrifice offered created a "ריח ניחוח—a pleasant odor to Hashem."

No one more than Hashem knew and understood the symbolism of the various vessels that were used and the different sacrifices that were brought. However, when faced with a choice between the Temple and the Jewish People, Hashem Himself reacts in the same way as Moshe, destroying the Temple and exiling the Jews in order to keep them alive.

A Beis Hamikdash without Jews to serve in it is like a Torah without Jews to learn and without Jews to observe. Therefore, Hashem congratulates Moshe Rabbeinu for understanding and teaching the lesson. Every mitzvah in the Torah, including the Beis Hamikdash, has at its root a love for Am Yisrael, for without the Jewish People, there would be no Torah and no Beis Hamikdash.

---

2   Rabbi Y.Y. Jacobson, "The Jacobson brothers discuss it all," April 14.

The First Lesson

תורה צוה לנו משה מורשה קהלת יעקב.

The Torah that Moshe commanded us is a heritage for the congregation of Yaakov.[3]

This is the first *pasuk* that we teach children to say as soon as they start learning. Why? Out of all of the *pesukim* in the Torah, what is the message contained in this *pasuk* that we wish to imprint on our children's minds and hearts?

The *Kesav Sofer* suggests that the lesson lies not in the beginning of the *pasuk*, "תורה צוה לנו משה," i.e., the centrality of Torah in Jewish life, but rather in the end of the *pasuk*, "מורשה קהלת יעקב—a heritage for the house of Yaakov." When did Moshe command us regarding Torah, and when is it a heritage? Only if we are united as "קהלת יעקב—the congregation of Yaakov."

According to the *Kesav Sofer*, the underlying message of the *pasuk* is קהילת יעקב—the unity of the Jewish People as one congregation. It is for this reason that this is chosen as the first *pasuk* we teach our children, because the first and most important lesson to teach is that united we stand, while divided we fall.

- תורה צוה לנו יעקב מורשה—Moshe instructed us with a Torah that is a heritage.
- קהילת יעקב—Because we are united as one people, one nation, and one congregation.[4]

Perhaps that is why the *pasuk* refers to us as קהילת יעקב rather than קהילת ישראל.

What is the difference between the names Yaakov and Yisrael?

The name Yisrael is given to the patriarch Yaakov after he wrestles with the angel, who injures him in his thigh. The *pasuk* gives the reason for the name change as "כי שרית עם אלקים ועם אנשים ותוכל—For you have

---

3   *Devarim* 33:4.
4   *Maayanah shel Torah*, p. 165.

wrestled with G-d and people and have prevailed."[5] We see the name Yisrael represents the struggle that Yaakov had with an angel. It is therefore used to refer to the Jewish People when they are fulfilling the word of Hashem and are at a spiritual peak.[6]

The name Yaakov, by contrast, is derived from the fact that when Yaakov was born, "וידו אחזת בעקב עשו—his hand was holding onto the heel of his brother Eisav."[7]

In this instance, there is no mention of Heavenly figures as there was in connection with the name Yisrael. The name Yaakov is used to describe the Jewish People when they are not at the height of their spiritual achievement. The name Yaakov defines a people who have far to go in reaching perfection. They do not mention Hashem, but instead are engaged in a battle with physicality and are associated with the heel.

Therefore, when Moshe Rabbeinu wishes to impart a lesson in Jewish unity, he uses the name that denotes a people far from spiritual perfection, because unity does not mean that we all must be equally serving Hashem in the best way possible. Unity needs to be found when we are in a state of Yaakov, when many of our number are far from spiritual perfection or religious observance. It is at that point that we need to be unified and love Jews for the sole reason that we are all part of one family. We need to be able to say to each other that "while I may disagree vehemently with the way that you live your life, I love you because we are all part of one people."

תורה צוה לנו משה מורשה קהילת יעקב—Torah is an inheritance when we all live together as one *kehilah*, even if we haven't yet reached the level of Yisrael and are merely קהילת יעקב.

Perhaps that is why this *pasuk* is the first that we teach our children and is found in the last *parashah* of the year. Everything begins and ends with Jewish unity.

---

5   *Bereishis* 32:28.
6   *Ramban, Bereishis* 46:2.
7   *Bereishis* 25:26.

חודש
תשרי

ראש השנה

Calendars and Diaries

Rabbi Benji Levine says that at the beginning of a new year, many people buy either a calendar or a diary. What is the difference between the two?

When one uses a calendar during the year, especially if it is one of those where you tear off a page every day, at the beginning of the year the calendar is full of 365 pages ready to be torn, but at the end of the year, you are left with nothing. Each day, you peeled off one paper until you reached the last day of the year. Once you have peeled off that final day of the year, all that you are left with is the cardboard that held the calendar together.

A diary is exactly the opposite. You may start off with nothing, but by the end of the year, you have a complete reckoning of everything that took place on every day of that year. If a calendar leaves you with a feeling of what might have been, a diary warms you with a sense of what actually was.

Our wish for each other as we start the New Year is that we should not have a year like a calendar, which leaves one empty-handed and pondering about opportunities lost, but rather should be blessed with a year like a diary, where every day is recorded and imprinted on our heart and every day is filled with achievement.

עשרת ימי תשובה

Hashem Loves Us, Even If We Still Have Far to Go

The Mishnah says:

> אמר רבי עקיבא: אשריכם ישראל, לפני מי אתם מטהרין, ומי מטהר אתכם? אביכם שבשמים...מה מקוה מטהר את הטמאים, אף הקדוש ברוך הוא מטהר את ישראל.

Rabbi Akiva says: How fortunate are you Yisrael, before whom do you purify yourselves, and who purifies you? Your Father in Heaven. In the same way as a mikvah purifies the impure, so too Hakadosh Baruch Hu purifies Yisrael.[1]

Rabbi Y.Y. Jacobson quotes the Lubavitcher Rebbe, who asks: What is the meaning of the words, "מה מקוה מטהר **את הטמאים**—In the same way as a *mikvah* purifies **the impure**"? The whole function of a *mikvah* is to purify those who are impure. It is obvious that the *mikvah* is purifying those who are impure. The Mishnah should have just said, "מה מקוה מטהר, אף הקב״ה מטהר את ישראל—In the same way as a *mikvah* purifies," and omit the mention of the impure! Why is it necessary to say מה מקוה מטהר את הטמאים? Who else could it be?

---

1   *Yoma* 8:9.

302

The halachah is that if someone comes into contact with a dead body, he is impure for seven days and needs the water mixed with the ashes of the *parah adumah* to be sprinkled on him on the third and seventh day. After that, the person goes to the *mikvah*, is purified, and returns to normal.

There is another form of impurity, and that is where someone touches a dead weasel or another of the eight types of rodents where the *tumah* is only for one day. In the evening, the person goes to the *mikvah* and is purified. This is known as *tumas sheretz*.

What happens when a person who was *tumas meis*, and therefore needs to wait seven days before going to the *mikvah*, contracts *tumas sheretz* on the second day that only requires a one-day wait?

Is there any point in him going to the *mikvah* and purifying himself from *tumas sheretz* if anyway he needs to wait until the end of seven days to remove the *tumas meis*, or should he wait until the end of seven days and do a "two-for-one *mikvah* dunk"?

The halachah is that even though he will remain impure with the more severe form of impurity, i.e., *tumas meis*, nonetheless, he should take care of the lesser impurity and go to the *mikvah*. He needs to remove whatever impurity he has and then take care of what remains.

That is what Rabbi Akiva is saying: מה מקוה מטהר את הטמאים—just as a *mikvah* purifies those **who will remain** impure, אף הקב"ה מטהר את ישראל, so too Hashem Himself purifies us, even though we have so much more to do.

We stand in front of Hashem and ask for forgiveness for our sins, and we beat our chests and say the *Al Chet*, but we have done so much more against Hashem than we mention and for which we do *teshuvah*. Hashem is entitled to say, "Nice try, but come back when you have repented for everything you have done against me."

But He doesn't. מה מקוה מטהר את הטמאים אף הקב"ה מטהר את ישראל—In the same way as a *mikvah* will purify even though the person remains impure, so too, Hashem will accept our apology, our *teshuvah*, even though there is a very long way to go until we have apologized for everything we've done.

The power of *teshuvah* is such, and Hashem loves us so much, that even though we may still have a long way to go to fix everything that we have damaged, He will accept whatever *teshuvah* we do.

Relationships: Man-and-G-d, Man-and-Man

During the *Aseres Yemei Teshuvah*, we insert unique phrases into the Amidah prayer.

The first is:

זכרנו לחיים מלך חפץ בחיים וכתבנו בספר החיים למענך אלוקים חיים.

Remember us for life, O King Who desires life, and inscribe us in the Book of Life—for your sake, O Living G-d.

Some commentators suggest that the words למענך אלוקים חיים should not be translated as "for your sake, O Living G-d," where the word חיים is a description of G-d, but rather translated as if there were a hyphen between the words למענך and אלוקים, such that the insertion reads: "Remember us for life, O King Who desires life, and inscribe us in the Book of Life **to live a life (חיים) that is purely for Your sake (למענך-אלוקים).**" When read in this way, the word חיים is no longer a description of G-d, but a description of how we should live our lives.

The next insertion reads:

מי כמוך אב הרחמים זוכר יצוריו לחיים ברחמים.

Who is like You, Merciful Father, Who recalls His creatures mercifully for life!

Once again, the word ברחמים is attributed to G-d—"Who recalls His creatures **mercifully** for life."

Perhaps this too need not be the case if we place the hyphen between לחיים and ברחמים. Now the insertion reads: "Who is like You, Merciful Father, Who recalls His creatures **to live mercifully (לחיים-ברחמים).**"

Both additions now become instructions. Both now give the reason for living.

The first is to live a life dedicated to Hashem—לְמַעַנְךָ אֱלֹקִים—which refers to *bein adam la'Makom*, the relationship between man and G-d, and the second is to live with mercy toward others—לְחַיִּים בְּרַחֲמִים—which represents *bein adam l'chaveiro*, the relationship between people.

These insertions into the *Amidah* teach us that during the *Aseres Yemei Teshuvah*, we need to be focused on repairing and improving both our relationship with G-d and with people.

יום כיפור

Teshuvah—Macro and Micro

Rabbi Yosef Tzvi Rimon writes that if we look at the items listed in the *Ashamnu* declaration, we see that some of the things are general, e.g., "אשמנו—We have become guilty," "בגדנו—We have betrayed," "תעינו—We have strayed," and "תעתענו—We have caused others to go astray."

These are all very general declarations without any detail of how we became guilty or whom we have betrayed, etc.

On the other hand, many of the actions listed in the same prayer are very specific:

"גזלנו—We have robbed," "חמסנו—We have extorted," "טפלנו שקר—We have accused falsely," etc.

The *Ashamnu* prayer is teaching us a valuable lesson. Some speak in general terms about *teshuvah* but do not engage in the finer details of what repentance actually entails. On the other hand, some only concentrate on the details of *teshuvah* and miss the larger picture and the broader effects of what *teshuvah* brings to the world.

The lesson of having both approaches in one prayer is that we need to acknowledge that without fixing, repairing and amending the details of our actions, *teshuvah* will be ineffective.

However, if we concentrate exclusively on the practical details, we will remain without any qualitative change of direction. We are merely repairing an old path as opposed to forging a new one. The more general view of *teshuvah* enables us to see our larger picture and to move away from the repetitive negativity of the past.

אשמנו and גזלנו, general and specific, encapsulate the best of both worlds. We accept responsibility for our past actions, we repair them, and now we embark on a brand-new path.

סוכות

Constant Growth

The Gemara tells us that a *sukkah* needs to be built in accordance with the principle of תעשה ולא מן העשוי.[1] This means that when one builds a sukkah, the *schach* needs to be made anew, and one is not permitted to use *schach* that is automatically created. For example, if one built a sukkah next to a vine, and for *schach* he covered the roof of the sukkah with the vine when it was still attached to the ground, and only then cut the vine, the *schach* is invalid. The vine would need to be cut first and only then placed as *schach*. When we place the *schach*, it needs to be fit for its purpose.

HaTzaddik Rabbi Mordechai Shlomo of Boyan states that this law teaches us an important insight into how we are required to serve Hashem. We need to be constantly in a mode of *taaseh*—of action, growth, and movement—and not be *min ha'asui*, i.e., satisfied with what we have already achieved. Spiritual growth is compared to walking the wrong way on a downward escalator; you need to be constantly in motion just to remain where you are.

There is no room for resting on one's laurels when it comes to our relationship with Torah and mitzvos.[2]

---

1   *Sukkah* 11b.
2   *Eileh Hem Moadai*, p, 127.

The Sukkah—Knowledge and New Opportunities

T he *Tur* asks a well-known question: If we need to sit in *sukkos* because that is what we did when we left Egypt, why is the holiday of Sukkos celebrated in Tishrei rather than in Nissan, which is when the B'nei Yisrael first began dwelling in them historically?

The *Chiddushei HaRim* answers that in connection with the mitzvah of *sukkah*, the *pasuk* says:

למען ידעו דורותיכם כי בסוכות הושבתי את בני ישראל בהוציאי אותם מארץ מצרים.

So that your generations shall know that I caused the B'nei Yisrael to dwell in booths when I took them out from the land of Egypt.[3]

To fulfill the mitzvah of sitting in a sukkah, we have to be aware of the reason behind the mitzvah.

It is not sufficient just to sit in a sukkah. We need to have *daas*—knowledge.

The *Chiddushei HaRim* explains that during the year, it is hard for us to have *daas*. After all, during the year we sin, and the Gemara informs us that we only sin as a result of being possessed by a *ruach shtus*—a moment of madness when we abandon all we know to be good and pure and instead sin.[4] Therefore, sin is the opposite of *daas*, and during the year we sin. Thus, during the rest of the year, we are not capable of fulfilling למען ידעו דורותיכם because we do not have *daas*.

However, once we have experienced Yom Kippur and we are cleansed from sin and have removed the *ruach shtus*, we are capable of achieving *daas*, and therefore, Sukkos immediately follows Yom Kippur in the month of Tishrei rather than being placed in Nissan.[5]

---

3   *Vayikra* 23:43.
4   *Sotah* 3a.
5   *Eileh Hem Moadai*, p. 126.

An alternative explanation as to why Sukkos is celebrated in Tishrei and not in Nissan is offered by the Rokeach,[6] who suggests that it all has to do with beginnings. At the beginning of the summer, we celebrate Pesach, and at the beginning of the winter, we celebrate Sukkos. The lesson being taught is that all new beginnings are dedicated to Hashem, Who has given us the ability to break free from any troubles of the past. The winter offers a break from the intense heat of the summer, and the summer provides a renewal from the bleakness of the winter. We thank Hashem for creating a world in which we do not have to be held prisoner by what has happened until now. We can be blessed with new beginnings and create new realities.

As we enter the sukkah, let us be aware that we are free from sin and therefore have *daas* to appreciate the beautiful opportunities that Sukkos and the year to follow offer.

---

6   *Talelei Oros*, p. 51.

About the Author

Rabbi Jeremy Finn grew up in London, where he attended the Hasmonean High School. He later learned in Yeshivas Mercaz HaTorah and was the director of the Gap Program at Ohr Somayach and Aish Hatorah.

He lives in Ramat Bet Shemesh and has been giving weekly *shiurim* on the *parashah* for the past fifteen years.

MOSAICA PRESS
BOOK PUBLISHERS
Elegant, Meaningful & Bold

info@MosaicaPress.com
www.MosaicaPress.com

The Mosaica Press team of
acclaimed editors and designers
is attracting some of the most
compelling thinkers and teachers
in the Jewish community today.
Our books are available around
the world.

HARAV YAACOV HABER
RABBI DORON KORNBLUTH